"Challenging the worldview of sor
advocates for a generous and broa
confronted the hard realities of radical evil, specifically in the form of demonic
oppression and possession. What emerges from this balanced and carefully
argued approach is not only a rich appreciation of the multivalent nature of
human experience, but also a healing balm for all those who suffer *spiritually.*
I highly recommend this book."

—KENNETH J. COLLINS, professor of historical theology and Wesley studies,
Asbury Theological Seminary

"Peter Bellini has presented, for the broader Wesleyan tradition, a thorough
and masterful account of the theological, historical, and practical aspects of a
Christian's obligation and privilege to minister in the spiritual realm through
deliverance. Bellini has recovered neglected aspects of Wesley's theology and
practice, providing a solid basis for the contemporary church, particularly
Wesleyan and Methodist adherents, and her ministry of deliverance through
Christ for the freedom of the abundant life."

—SCOTT KISKER, professor of church history, United Theological Seminary

"While advocacy groups grab the headlines, a quiet revolution is underway
in Christian theology. East and West, Protestant and Catholic, theologians are
working to renew Christianity by retrieving beliefs and practices once central
to Christianity. In this new work, Peter Bellini adds his voice to the chorus in
a daring way, grappling with the reality of demon possession and working to
recover the practice of exorcism. Drawing primarily on John Wesley, Bellini takes
a crucial step toward recovering a form of Christianity that takes evil seriously."

—JASON E. VICKERS, professor of theology and Wesleyan studies, George W. Truett
Theological Seminary

"Sometimes it takes a perceptive observer to point out what many of us
have missed. This Peter Bellini does in his careful and persuasive account of
the deliverance ministry of John Wesley. Not only does this provide a new
perspective on Wesley, but it is an invitation to take as seriously as Wesley
did (and as many non-Western Christians do today) the presence of spiritual
realities in the world."

—HENRY H. KNIGHT III, professor emeritus of Wesleyan studies and evangelism,
Saint Paul School of Theology

"Peter Bellini has done the church and academy a tremendous service by addressing an area of John Wesley's life, ministry, and theology that is grossly neglected. In this very accessible volume, Bellini reminds us that the movement that changed the world was not merely one of abstract theological ideas or ecclesial reform, but a miraculous, supernatural, and powerful movement of God in which entire communities were liberated from the guilt and power of sin."

—MATT AYARS, president, Wesley Biblical Seminary

"Those in the Wesleyan theological tradition should not think of exorcism as practiced only by Pentecostals. It was practiced by Methodists 150 years before there were any Pentecostals. Peter Bellini makes this clear in *Thunderstruck!*, where he highlights John Wesley's own experiences with exorcism. This is not just a historical work. It is a book to encourage the return of exorcism ministries to churches in the Wesleyan tradition today."

—FRANK BILLMAN, mentor in supernatural ministry, United Theological Seminary

"A genuine supernatural worldview is required if Wesleyans are to ever become a spiritually potent people again, rather than a 'dead sect, having the form of religion without the power.' In *Thunderstruck!*, Peter Bellini offers both a vibrant look into our supernatural heritage and prescription for how to participate in the Jesus-initiated work of deliverance today. This work will serve as an invaluable resource to those longing to see God set people free and once again move in power among the people called Methodists."

—MATT REYNOLDS, president and founder, Spirit & Truth

"Early Methodist understandings of supernatural realities and ministry have historically been overlooked in Methodist and Wesleyan studies. In *Thunderstruck!*, Peter Bellini offers an in-depth analysis of John Wesley's understanding of the spiritual conflict he believes is at the heart of so much of the human experience. Bellini proposes that Wesley's practice of engaging the unseen spiritual realm can benefit many Christians today. I recommend *Thunderstruck!* for any Christian, and especially Methodists, who seeks to understand how their part of the Christian tradition has engaged the powers of evil."

—JACK JACKSON, visiting professor of evangelism and world Methodism, United Theological Seminary

"*Thunderstruck!* is an exceptional book that focuses on the theological and practical aspects of Wesley's deliverance. Peter Bellini carefully evaluates Wesley's positions on deliverance with sharp academic discernment. Like John Wesley, he approaches deliverance from the perspective of both rational theology and superrational practice, finding a harmonious balance between the two. It is a rare gem written by a seminary professor based on his pastoral experience of supernatural exorcism."

—ANDREW S. PARK, professor of theology and ethics, United Theological Seminary

"Once again Peter Bellini provides a much-needed resource to the wider Wesleyan movement! *Thunderstruck!* reintroduces Methodists of all types and stripes to a forgotten aspect of John Wesley's vital ministry. This exciting work manages to simultaneously offer the reader first-rate scholarship in Wesley yoked to intensely practical help which every pastor can use. I enthusiastically commend Thunderstruck! to all (both lay and clergy!) who seek the renewal of the church in our day and time!"

—MIKE LOWRY, emeritus bishop-in-residence, United Theological Seminary

"Peter Bellini's in-depth historical analysis reveals Wesley's 'spirit-worldview' and shows how deeply connected Wesley's ministry was to exorcism and deliverance from demonization. The result is another layer of Wesley's holistic understanding of salvation. This is a wonderful historical examination of a neglected feature of Wesley's theology and ministry that is much needed. It is nothing less than a ressourcement of the Wesleyan tradition for all those engaged in ministry today."

—DALE M. COULTER, professor of historical theology, Pentecostal Theological Seminary

"*Thunderstruck!* is the rare book that provides a contribution to both church and academy. Bellini offers a needed contribution to the scholarly study of John Wesley and his underappreciated deliverance ministry in early Methodism. More than this, he offers a call to all who are followers of Jesus Christ to join in the work of releasing the captives and bringing deliverance from bondage to sin and Satan. This book is a gift!"

—KEVIN M. WATSON, director of academic growth and formation, Asbury Theological Seminary

"Deliverance is a neglected area of research and conversation throughout large segments of the Wesleyan tradition. Peter Bellini here provides an invaluable text for understanding John Wesley's thoughts on and practices of deliverance. He also gives us practical resources for the work of deliverance ministry and understanding the gifts of the Spirit more broadly. I highly recommend this important book."

—DAVID F. WATSON, academic dean, United Theological Seminary

Thunderstruck!

Thunderstruck!

The Deliverance Ministry of John Wesley Today

PETER J. BELLINI

WIPF & STOCK · Eugene, Oregon

THUNDERSTRUCK!
The Deliverance Ministry of John Wesley Today

Wipf & Stock
An Imprint of Wipf and Stock Publishers
199 W. 8th Ave., Suite 3
Eugene, OR 97401

www.wipfandstock.com

PAPERBACK ISBN: 978-1-6667-5939-6
HARDCOVER ISBN: 978-1-6667-5940-2
EBOOK ISBN: 978-1-6667-5941-9

04/13/23

Contents

Preface

We do not talk much about demons in the Wesleyan tradition. They are not a part of our daily worldview. We are not accustomed to discerning and identifying their activity in our lives and in the world around us. The reason, perhaps, is that our churches, conferences and boards, seminaries, curricula, and other literature often do not address the supernatural, including the demonic. However, that is not the case outside of the church. Paranormal and occult activity are on the rise.[1] The increase in our culture's interest and participation in the occult is reflected particularly in the entertainment and media industry.[2] Films like *The Exorcism of Emily Rose, The Last Exorcism, The Possession, Deliver Us from Evil, The Exorcism of God*, and a host of other genre-related films have captured the morbid fascination and curiosity of the general public. Although deliverance and exorcism are virtually non-existent ministries in so-called mainline denominational Protestantism, including my own United Methodist Church, the Vatican has recognized the rise of demonization and the increasing demand for more professionally trained exorcists and has developed courses to meet the need.[3] Even professionals in the fields of psychiatry and psychology are coming forward with their encounters with the demonic during therapy and the need for deliverance and exorcism.[4] Why are we Wesleyans out of touch and so far behind in addressing this issue?

I attempt to tackle these and other questions regarding the demonic by beginning with the ministry of John Wesley, the founder of Methodism. This book began as an idea at the intersection of several of my professional interests. I have been in ministry for nearly four decades, serving in various capacities. I began as a campus and prison evangelist.

1. Reid, "Interest in 'The Occult.'"
2. Natale, *Supernatural Entertainments*.
3. "Exorcism"; see also "Catholic Church Recruits," and "Course."
4. For example, see Peck, *Glimpses of the Devil*, and Gallagher, *Demonic Foes*.

Later, I served as a pastor, missionary, and church planter. For the last twelve years, I have been a professor at a denominational seminary, while also serving as a revivalist and conference speaker on the side. While in these various positions, I have always ministered in deliverance and pastoral counseling. I have received clients from within and outside of these ministry assignments. Charismatic interests and practices have greatly informed my research, teaching, and ministry, including the focus on deliverance and healing.

Theological sources, outside of my own, that informed my practice over the years have come from Pentecostal and Charismatic Christianity along with my research in counseling, mental health, and cognitive neuroscience. Over thirty years ago, I had read through much of the written work of John Wesley and have continued to examine his work throughout my tenure in ministry and in academia. However, it was not until around fifteen years ago that I began to read some accounts in Wesley's journals and letters differently than I had read them in the past. The narratives that describe individuals dropping to the ground during Wesley's preaching, struggling with violent manifestations, and finally finding resolution through repentance and prayer caught my attention.

I had heard Pentecostals and Charismatics make comparisons between these incidents and the contemporary phenomenon of being "slain in the Spirit." However, upon closer scrutiny, I realized that they were not the same experience (I unpack this distinction in chapter 5). It struck me that Wesley was engaged in situations where deliverance was actually taking place. In fact, these occurrences that frequently run throughout his journals and letters pressed me to make the conclusion that Wesley functioned in a deliverance ministry. We have no indication that Wesley identified it as such, however, there is little doubt that *de facto* the founder of Methodism was regularly engaging demonic powers in the process of bringing people to Christ—a deliverance ministry.

Rarely, has this conclusion been made by other Wesley scholars, but as a theologian and practitioner of deliverance, I could not help but make the connection. Further examination of Wesley's corpus confirmed my initial hypothesis, and I have since developed this thesis into a more weighted, cogent argument that is offered in this book. Yet, asserting and grounding the thesis that Wesley and early Methodists operated in a viable deliverance ministry was not my only goal. The question why Wesleyans today do not minister in deliverance as Wesley did became a concern of equal significance. Evil and the demonic have not gone out of business. Why are Methodists no longer in the deliverance and exorcism business? And how can we open the store once again? Informing

Wesleyans of John Wesley's deliverance ministry and equipping them for the task today are the primary reasons that compelled me to write *Thunderstruck!*

Rev. Peter J. Bellini, PhD
Professor of Church Renewal and Evangelization in the Heisel Chair
United Theological Seminary
Dayton, Ohio

Abbreviations

AA	Alcoholics Anonymous
ADD	Attention Deficit Disorder
ADHD	Attention Deficit Hyperactivity Disorder
ANE	Ancient Near East
AR-15	ArmaLite Rifle
BC	Bondage Composite
BDSM	Bondage-Discipline, Dominance-Submission
BQ	Bondage Quotient
CRT	Critical Race Theory
DIY	Do-it-yourself
DNA	Deoxyribonucleic acid
DRI	Demonic Resonance Imaging
DSM-5	*The Diagnostic and Statistical Manual of Mental Disorders*, 5th ed.
ER	Emergency room
ESP	Extrasensory perception
EST	(The Forum) Erhard Seminars Training
ESV	English Standard Version Bible
HS	Holy Spirit
LGBT	lesbian, gay, bisexual, and transgender
LSD	lysergic acid diethylamide
MEC	Methodist Episcopal Church
NA	Narcotics Anonymous
NIODA	Non-Interventionist Objective Divine Action

NIV	New International Version Bible
NLT	New Living Translation Bible
NXIVM	personality cult of Keith Ranier
OCA	Orthodox Church in America
OCD	Obsessive Compulsive Disorder
ODD	Oppositional Defiant Disorder
PCR	Pentecostal-Charismatic-Renewalist Christianity
RCC	Roman Catholic Church
SSRI	Selective serotonin reuptake inhibitor
UPS	United Postal Service
WTJ	*Wesleyan Theological Journal*
WWII	World War Two

1

Introduction

"I found more and more undeniable proofs, that the Christian state is a continual warfare; and that we have need every moment to watch and pray lest we enter into temptation."

—Wesley's journal entry for May 17, 1740

ABOUT THE TITLE THUNDERSTRUCK!

"Thunderstruck!"[1] John Wesley (1703–1791), the founder of Methodism, frequently used this specific term in his writing when recounting a peculiar phenomenon in his ministry.[2] When reading his ministry narratives, one cannot

---

1. The circuit riders of the nineteenth century frequently witnessed the same phenomena in frontier American Methodism. It was popularly known as the "Knock-'Em-Down," another colorful phrase to describe this peculiar manifestation of the Spirit. See Xhemajli, *Supernatural*, 151–158.

2. This book assumes that one has basic biographical knowledge of John Wesley and is also familiar somewhat with this theology. John Wesley (1703–1791) was a clergyman in the Church of England and the founder of the Methodist movement where he functioned as a pastor, evangelist, missioner, and theologian. Wesley was raised and trained in the Christian home of an Anglican priest. He was well-learned and trained by his mother Susanna with a classical education. During his time of study at Oxford, he gathered several likeminded young men who were seeking "to flee from the wrath to come" and "holiness without which no one will see the Lord." Called the Holy Club, Bible moths, and Methodists, this committed ascetic evangelical group was methodical in their ways—regular prayer, searching the Scripture, attending the ordinances of God, and works of mercy such as ministering to those in prison. Wesley became an Anglican priest in 1728. Despite

help but be stricken by the word. Thunderstruck was a descriptive image used by Wesley to depict how people, upon hearing his preaching, would suddenly drop to the ground before receiving deliverance from sin.[3] Perhaps for some the word evokes a certain biblical image, as it does for me. "Thunderstruck" brings to mind Luke 10:18–20, when the disciples came back from a kingdom outing of casting out demons and were celebrating their authority over demonic powers. The demons submitted to their command. The disciples were quite impressed and self-assured. Jesus was quick to instruct them that salvation is the main purpose for deliverance and not their newly acquired sense of authority. New names had been written down in glory. Christ made sure to give the disciples a lesson on humility, which is critical for such a ministry.

In verse 18 (paraphrasing), Jesus said, "I watched Satan get kicked out of heaven and crash to the earth as fast as lighting falls from the sky to the ground." Jesus' words seem disjointed from the rest of the context. In my paraphrasing, however, I think his intention was to say, "So you think you are the first ones to have authority over Satan and watch him fall, (lol)?" Christ wanted the disciples to get over the fascination and allure of having (someone else's) power and authority over demons. Yes, knowing that the authority of Christ has been given to us is necessary to cast out demons, but it is even more important to have Christ's humility when doing so, lest we become like the devils that we are casting out.

Perhaps Jesus was alluding to the war in Heaven when Michael, the Archangel, and his angels turned back a cosmic revolt led by Lucifer and one-third of the other angels who chose to rebel against God (Rev 12:7–9). Lucifer was judged and banished to the earth, where he would roam and prowl, here and there, tempting and devouring humanity. He began his mission in the garden.

Later, on the cross, Jesus would defeat and judge the power of both sin and Satan offering deliverance to all. To me, the image of "thunderstruck"

---

these holy endeavors, Wesley still did not experience assurance of his salvation. In attempt to find holiness and assurance through sacrifice, he sailed to Georgia for an unsuccessful mission trip. However, on the journey he met some Moravian Christians who challenged his faith. With the Moravians, especially later those in London and Hernhutt, he learned about salvation and assurance by grace and through faith. On May 24, 1738, at a Moravian meeting at Aldersgate Street, Wesley had his heart strangely warmed and finally received the assurance that Christ died for him, and his sins were forgiven. The Methodist movement exploded soon after, as Wesley joined former Holy Club member George Whitefield preaching in the open air in Bristol and through England. To gather the harvest of new converts, Wesley, following the Moravian pattern, organized societies, classes, bands, and other small groups for discipleship. The Methodist revival spread throughout England, Wales, Ireland, Scotland, Europe, and in the Colonies. For more on the life of John Wesley, see Rack *Reasonable Enthusiast*, and Collins, *John Wesley: Theological Journey*.

3. Chapter 5 will unpack this wonder in detail.

recalls this cosmic backdrop of Christ's eternal victory executed and implemented by early Methodist missions out in the open fields in eighteenth-century England. God's thunder and lightning of judgment struck down the power of sin and Satan, and "many were the slain of the Lord." "Thunderstruck" recalls the deliverance ministry of John Wesley, one that you never thought he had. And one that we need to receive!

WHY SO LITTLE ON WESLEY, METHODISM, AND DELIVERANCE?

Deliverance is in the DNA of Methodism. The reason that God raised up the people called Methodists was to proclaim, "scriptural holiness." "Scriptural holiness" was a term John Wesley used to signify salvation from all sin and perfect love towards God and neighbor. Wesley understood scriptural holiness as the Methodist "grand depositum," meaning the great or large deposit, that God has entrusted to the people called Methodists.[4] The message of scriptural holiness, also known as full salvation, entire sanctification, Christian perfection, perfect love or "love excluding sin" is the unique treasure God has deposited in Methodists to give to the world. Simply put, scriptural holiness is our God-given mission. However, Wesleyans today are often at a loss about the meaning and extent of the phrase. Methodism's "grand depositum" of scriptural holiness actually includes *deliverance* , in both the broad sense of total salvation and in the narrow sense of casting out demons.[5] In fact, Wesley described entire sanctification as "full deliverance."[6] The phrase "love excluding sin" also denotes *deliverance* from all sin. Wesley exclaimed, "By sanctification we are saved from the power and root of sin, and restored to the image of God . . . the heart is cleansed from all sin, and filled with pure love to God and man."[7] Further, God "is able to save you from all the sin that cleaves to all of your words and actions."[8]

Methodists are a people of *deliverance* (from all sin). We can take that designation to its logical conclusion; it is also a deliverance from Satan. If

---

4. Telford, ed. *Letters of John Wesley*, 8:238. "[w]ith regard to full sanctification. This doctrine is the grand depositum which God has lodged with the people called Methodists; and for the sake of propagating this chiefly He appeared to have raised us up."

5. See J. Wesley, "Scripture Way of Salvation," 47. Wesley also called it "perfect love," defined as, "**It is love excluding sin; love filling the heart, taking up the whole capacity of the soul. It is love "rejoicing evermore, praying without ceasing, in everything giving thanks."**

6. J. Wesley, "Scripture Way of Salvation," 167.

7. J. Wesley, "On Working Out Your Own Salvation," 509.

8. J. Wesley, "Repentance of Believers," 166.

we are delivered from all sin, then we can be delivered from the power of Satan and his demons. If Satan is the tempter regarding sin, then deliverance from sin involves deliverance from the tempter or deliverance from Satan. This book is about Wesleyans, and other Christians as well, extending their concept of deliverance (from all sin) to include deliverance from *all* demonic powers. Deliverance from all demonic powers is not outside of our Christian or Wesleyan purview, though it may sound foreign to many. We will see that deliverance from the demonic was a noteworthy dimension of the ministry of Wesley and early Methodists.

Nonetheless, it still seems like an oxymoron: a Wesleyan book on deliverance and exorcism. The undertaking of this particular work is not only needed, but rare. As far as I am aware, not much if any scholarly, pastoral, or lay material has been produced specifically on the deliverance ministry of John Wesley or on deliverance ministry for the people called Methodists. Why is it that in the last one hundred or more years there has been relative silence on this topic? A proper response to the question would probably require another hefty volume. Somehow, we have overlooked, ignored, downplayed, demythologized, or reinterpreted the narratives, references, teaching, and preaching on the subject in Wesley's literary corpus. The disinterest and gross neglect of the topic would be a proper beginning for such a volume, which would require an investigation too vast to be undertaken here.

Hypothetically, I suppose one could take the easy and tired route of reducing early Methodism's thunderstruck phenomena to some socio-psychological explanation. Wesley's detractors and other Enlightenment thinkers did the same. Wesley opposed a closed natural worldview and embraced a spiritual (supernatural) one. In this book, I am taking Wesley at face value. There has been much ink spilled on this debate, including my own. I will not be dealing with that problem directly in this work beyond referencing the issue. Supernaturalism simply offends our modern sensibilities.

In short, the theology and especially the practice of deliverance in Methodism today is sparse for reasons that can perhaps be addressed expeditiously with three questions. Do Methodists today share Wesley's worldview and theological empiricism that can account for the reality of the power of both God and the demonic in our world? Modern science and biblical criticism have been major influences on a mainline Protestant worldview that eschews the "supernatural." My guess is that the tandem of the causal closure of scientific naturalism and the higher criticism of the Bible wiped out the possibility of such a perspective from our seminaries over a century ago. Put another way, we know better than to believe in demons and other fairytales. We have put away childish things!

Further, the stock on sin and evil is down in our day of permissiveness. With a deflationary view of sin and evil, we struggle to see it in society and own it in ourselves. And if we do recognize it, evil is always and exclusively in the other.[9] In any case, our society surely will not fund a spirit-worldview with a whole outdated mythological pantheon of fallen Ancient Near East demigods that rule over a kingdom of darkness and even rent space in our own minds. Sin, evil, Satan, and fallen angels are alive and well on planet Earth? Too much concession and constraint to accept, at least in the West, for a people that are in denial about personal evil and despise the dogma and dictates of organized religion. If there is to be a supernatural order and a spirit-world, then each individual will have to design their own DIY version for their own specific purpose. You know— spiritual but not religious.

Regarding a scriptural spirit-worldview, those who still carry Wesley's torch are some of the more revivalist descendants, such as Holiness, Pentecostal, and Charismatic Christians. While we Methodists were working to become America's denomination in the twentieth century, building a sociopolitical kingdom on earth with the power of our ecclesial machinery, storefront Spirit-filled churches were overthrowing the kingdom of darkness with Pentecostal power from on high. Two different worldviews at work!

Chapter 2 of this book addresses Wesley's worldview. The problem is, in part, a teaching issue. We are no longer *taught* the plausibility and viability of such a worldview that allows for the "supernatural." It's seen as an antiquated oddity like a cave painting or practicing alchemy. There is either no such thing as the demonic, or it exists symbolically as socio-political systems. And for the latter, we do not need the power and authority of the name of Jesus, we just need a dash of liberation theology sprinkled on our own home-baked cultural Marxism to get the job done. And we get that in seminary! It is, in part, a problem with our teaching ministry. What originated with the *professor*, then trickled down to the *pulpit*, and finally to the *pew*. Unlike St. Paul, our people "have been taken advantage of by Satan" and are "unaware of his schemes" (2 Cor 2:11).

Today, Wesleyans are often not *taught* to take the Bible at face value regarding an invisible creation filled with preternatural spirits (Col 1:16). We know better. It offends our scientism. We are not taught to take the demonic seriously, let alone how to minister to persons who are bound by it.

---

9. We live in a time when we claim to despise binaries, and yet we divide incessantly. Bifurcations, in our age, are created to impose and identify the evil. Thus, the evil is found not only in the other, but the other itself is created necessarily out of the demonizing of those who think differently than us. "My" way is the only way. And if you hold to a different position, then you *are* evil. There is hardly any laissez-faire in the conflicts of everyday discourse; not much think and let think.

Consequently, belief in the supernatural for Methodists has gone extinct like the dinosaurs and disco. However, this is not the case in growing two-thirds world Christianity. There, a spirit-worldview is commonly held, and deliverance takes place regularly and normatively, while the church explodes and expands. A spirit-worldview may not be acceptable in the West, but the prevalence and power of the occult, addiction, sexual perversion, radical violence, and overall moral corruption in the West is not diminishing but is on the rise like never before, and Wesleyans, and other Christians feel powerless to confront it. And they are!

The second question for Wesleyans is are we ministering among the people in the streets, fields, and marketplaces as Wesley did? Outside the church's four walls, that is where we encounter real people with real problems. That is where the devil is busy, and the church is absent. That is where we find what we think does not exist. In the shadows of the alleys, fields, offices, and blight of people's souls is the hell on earth that we dismiss and deny, while we ourselves drown in its deceit. "Demons do not exist," we say. "Where?" Well, everywhere and nowhere. All around and nowhere to be found. We see the fruit of evil, but the root remains hidden. And the church lacks any deep spiritual discernment to see in the Spirit.

Ironically, our eyes are blinded by the very one who 'does not exist' (2 Cor 4:4). Doubt or agnosticism about his existence is imperative to his mission. The mission is to steal, kill, and destroy, but, above all, to do so undetected, anonymously. The French poet Baudelaire is credited with saying, "The greatest trick the Devil ever pulled was convincing the world he didn't exist."[10] The "god of this world" has seduced, captivated, and captured its inhabitants through a diversity of deceptions, a plethora of ploys, and an array of targeted traps, knowing that we do not see. We, the church, do not live with the people, nor do we listen and see with our hearts the sounds and sights of suffering. And worse, we do not walk in the light that exposes the darkness. And another day passes.

Wesley did not plan to have a "deliverance ministry." It happened along the way. He also did not plan to have an open-field preaching ministry that would birth a deliverance ministry. It happened along the way. It happened where the people lived and worked. It happens when we are present. George Whitefield was already outdoors preaching to the masses in Bristol and was witnessing a tremendous response from sin-sick souls to the grace-filled preaching of the gospel. The nets were breaking. The harvest was plentiful, but the laborers were few. Whitefield needed help. Wesley obliged. They combined forces. Wesley unleashed an assault on the enemy's camp hurling

10. Baudelaire, "Generous Gambler," 164.

dunamis-filled homiletical missiles targeted at the prison bars of human minds that were being watched over and guarded by the godless garrisons of Satan's soldiers.

Wesley and his Methodists, equipped with the sword of the Lord, full of faith and the Holy Spirit, launched an all-out war on the hordes of hell, bent and intent on plundering the house and overthrowing the "strong man" of sin and death, healing the broken hearted, and setting free the oppressed. The Spirit of the Lord was upon early Methodists with power and authority to preach good news to the poor and minister deliverance to the captives. Are Methodists today walking among the poor with the same power and authority?

That is the third question. Are we walking in the same anointing as Wesley and the early Methodists? Are we walking in the same authority and power that could preach to thousands at a time and witness dozens upon dozens drop as dead under the convicting power of God without anyone laying on hands or without direct prayer for such a manifestation? The manifestations are not the point; the radical salvations are. The fruit of such authority, power, and anointing cannot come from perpetual pastoral prayerlessness; politically correct, arid annual conference-run borderline on heretical programming that invites every spirit but the Holy Spirit; Saturday night specials scanning and scamming sermons from the internet at midnight; weekly gorging on potlucks and bursting from the seams from buckets of chicken baptized in fire and Crisco; late night internet searches down highways to hell looking for forbidden fruit; church decisions devoid of the divine, constipated by committee, and led by the loudest lout or the biggest giver! No, Wesley and early Methodists were not playing church! They were in it all the way!

Early Methodist divine success was not accidental but intentional. It was the fruit of: methodical daily prayer before dawn and throughout the day and night; weekly fasting; daily reading and preaching the Scriptures; weekly partaking of the holy sacrament; a healthy desire to flee from the wrath to come; ruthless self-denial; an earnestness and openness to consistently take part in a discipleship community that holds the soul accountable; participation in acts of mercy with the poor in prison, the hospitals, and in the streets; attending the gathering of the saints for worship; and all the other "means of grace"; and a common vision and heart to see scriptural holiness shake and transform the nations.

There was a steep cost to be a Methodist, and the sacrifice paid off.[11] Today, we have desperately marked down the scriptural Jesus and removed his

---

11. Finke and Stark, *Churching of America*, 156–196.

features that will not sell, for example, his call to sacrificial and holy living. We have sanded down his rough edges, so we can handle him. We have marked down his cost and put him on the discount table in our churches. We have cut the cost and still can't give him away. With our discount Jesus, we Methodists cry out for revival, or at least for more people, from our empty churches but wonder why we do not have enough power to blow our own nose. Today, are the people called Methodists willing to pay the price to be renewed in the doctrine, spirit, and discipline that sparked the original movement?

PURPOSES OF THE BOOK

The primary purpose of this book is to introduce the Wesleyan community and the larger church to John Wesley's ministry of casting out demons, what the church has called deliverance and/or exorcism. The secondary purpose is to stir up the desire and offer direction for Wesleyans and others who feel called today to minister deliverance (clergy or laity). Because deliverance (not only as a practice but also as a concept) may not be clearly defined in the minds of many, it is advantageous for the reader to know upfront the presuppositions and terms used by the author.

The words *deliverance* and *exorcism* need to be defined and clarified. When I speak of both, I am referring to casting out demons from those who are under the influence of Satan (demonized) and even those possessed. The word *demonization*, or *daimonizomai* in the Greek, is a New Testament word that is sometimes wrongly translated as *possession* in relation to the demonic. *Demonization*, I think, is a better translation, implying a process and degrees of demonic influence. Demonization, or being *influenced* by the devil, is not an all or nothing affair, possessed or not possessed. It often happens by degrees. The cases in Scripture, history, current deliverance-exorcism ministries, and my own experience seem to demonstrate degrees of demonization, including but not limited to possession. In my nearly forty years' experience, I found possession—*total* control of human agency by demonic powers—to be quite rare. Most cases are degrees of demonization.[12]

Where there is a degree of demonization, the person needs *deliverance*. Where there is demonic possession, the person needs *exorcism*. Though

12. The Roman Catholic Church also distinguishes between possession and degrees of demonization (oppression). The RCC uses the terms "major exorcism" (possession) and "minor exorcism" (deliverance) or liberation prayer. Only a priest by permission from a bishop and using the Rite of Exorcism can administer major exorcism on behalf of those who are possessed. However, trained priests and laity can administer deliverance prayer for minor exorcism. See the course "Exorcism and Prayer of Liberation," offered by the Sacerdos Institute at the Regina Apostolorum Pontifical Athenaeum.

Scripture gives accounts of deliverance from the demonic, it does not read like a textbook with formal definitions and how-to instructions. Scripture does not dictate a methodology or any sequence of steps for deliverance. The power of narrative lets us peer into Jesus' world and watch him do it, though we can glean much from this. Also, the narrative is primarily about God. Details are not provided because demons are minor characters in the background of the grand theo-drama. Hence, we are not privy to in-depth, extensive explanations concerning the mechanics and machinations of their interactions with the world and individuals. What we know we infer primarily from Scripture and secondarily from the Great Tradition of the faith, Spirit-filled experience, and sanctified reason.

The definitions and distinctions provided are my own but are shared by others in the field as well. Often one will find Protestants, especially Pentecostals and Charismatics, using the term *deliverance,* while Catholics and Orthodox will use the term *exorcism.*[13] For me, both possession and degrees of demonization require the casting out of demon(s), either through exorcism or deliverance. The latter involves demonic influence or attachment in an area(s) connected to ongoing sin committed in one's life. Identifying the sin, repenting, renouncing Satan, and binding and casting out the demon is the overall process of deliverance. Exorcism follows the same pattern, although it is a much more intensive, involved, rigorous process due to the more pronounced nature of control over the subject's agency. In both circumstances pre- and post-work is needed.[14] Deliverance is not a magic bullet.

Though many may not feel that it is *their* job, deliverance is not an optional function of the Church's ministry. Christ and his disciples ministered deliverance, and we are called to do so as well. Together with preaching, teaching, and healing, deliverance was essential to the core ministry of Christ and his disciples (Matt 10:7–9).[15] Christ even teaches us to pray for it daily. Deliverance and exorcism ministry is incorporated in the Lord's Prayer: "Lead us not into temptation but deliver us from evil." We need daily deliverance from temptation and evil. Satan is real, so we pray for victory over temptation and deliverance from all forms of evil. If Christ was tempted, how much more will we be tempted?

The Father also gave us the answer to this prayer. He sent his Son to exercise his authority to deliver people from demonic influence and

13. Under the category of deliverance, some make subdivisions along a continuum of demonization. Typology often varies but frequently uses distinctions such as oppression, obsession, and finally possession.

14. For a thorough handbook on all matters related to deliverance and exorcism, see Bellini, *X-Manual.* For pre and post work in renewing the mind, see Bellini, *Truth Therapy.*

15. See Twelftree, *Name of Jesus,* 209–278.

possession. The Son of God came for this reason: "to destroy the works of the devil" (1 John 3:8). Grounded in Christ's atoning work of the cross, we are enabled "to resist him. Standing firm in the faith . . . " (1 Pet 5:8–9). Wesley and early Methodists, when seeking deliverance from evil, inevitably confronted the demonic as well. Of the cases I reviewed from Wesley's journals and letters, most were instances of degrees of demonization, though there are a couple of possible candidates for possession. In most of the cases, Wesley *indirectly* confronted the evil spirits by interceding to the Lord to set the captive free. He rarely used a *direct* method of confronting the demonic in an unmediated way. With both methods, direct and indirect, the results are the same: victory! This book will examine Wesley's methodology and other methods.

The hope is that Wesleyans and other Christians who have not been exposed to deliverance in theory or practice will gain a better understanding of John Wesley's approach to the subject. There is much to learn. One thing is clear. Wesley and early Methodists were *not* afraid to get their hands and wigs dirty. They jumped into the fray. Love always seems to be messy. Pastor Wesley fervently offered up prayer for the oppressed. Sermons were ardently preached by Wesley the evangelist to the seeker. The clash emerged as the anointed Word collided on the battlefield of ministry with the strongholds of Satan that ruled over casualties of spiritual warfare. As an evangelist and pastor, Wesley encountered the demonic in the field, in homes, and in the marketplace. Like Jesus, he would have found the demonic in places of worship, too, but he was forbidden to preach there. Scripture calls Satan the god of this world who rules in darkness (2 Cor 4:4). Yet, Wesley also viewed the world as his parish. He was not running to hide behind the pulpit. He felt the call to oppose darkness with the light of holiness. The church is the light of the world that shines in the darkness, exposing the demonic.

If we fearlessly confront and minister in the heart of darkness, we too will find the unexpected. Wesley was not looking for demons, but they emerged, nonetheless. It is safest to minister with one's eyes wide open. Evil forces are best met with preparation and instruction. The hope is that the deliverance ministry of Christ and the disciples and that of Wesley and the early Methodists will inspire the reader to do the same. Set the captives free. When alcohol, drugs, sex, tarot readings, healing crystals, astrology, career, new locations, a new career, declaring bankruptcy, a new sports car, a boat, more toys, Tinder, another partner, Zoloft,[16] a nice stock portfolio, exercise, diet, meds, counseling, more followers and likes, other religions, or

16. Though I firmly believe in the power of medical science, psychiatric meds including SSRIs, and quality therapy, like cognitive behavioral therapy, sometimes the problem may need to be addressed also with a spiritual solution.

Christian-Lite no longer work for the weary seeker. When pastoral counseling, referrals to professionals, Sunday sermons, church school lessons, and accountability groups fail. When nothing else works. When nothing else brings victory and peace, we should submit "to be more vile."[17] Perhaps, there is more there than meets the eye. The shattered and enslaved soul may be shackled by forces beyond the help of science, Instagram, self-medication, or lifeless and powerless religion. The person may need deliverance. And you may be called on by God to do it!

OVERVIEW

The book is written for church leaders (academic, clergy and laity) at a level that is moderately academic, methodically practical, and highly exhortative. We will research the written works of Wesley to uncover and analyze his material on deliverance. We will examine the theological import of that material, and how we can think scripturally, logically, and precisely about deliverance. Obviously, basic competence to follow and comprehend the book's level of research in Wesleyan historical theology and systematic theology is required. We will also be exploring Wesley's worldview and his working theory of knowledge. A degree of familiarity with basic philosophical categories and concepts is helpful. In addition, parts of the book are written from a more practical perspective for those who will end up in the trenches, getting their hands dirty and feet wet in deliverance ministry.

Chapter 2 lays the foundations for Wesley's theology and practice of deliverance. Special attention is paid to worldview, both an Enlightenment worldview and Wesley's "spirit-worldview," which comes from his own plain-sense reading of Scripture. Out of Wesley's worldview emerges his own crafted version of spiritual empiricism that provides the epistemological context for his theology of the Spirit, that runs throughout the way of salvation (*via salutis*).[18] Included in this backdrop of an empirical spirit-world is the ongoing war in the invisible, created order between good angels and fallen angels for the soul of humanity. Wesley's worldview and

17. J. Wesley, "Minutes of Several Conversations," 315. Wesley reluctantly accepted God's call through Whitefield to preach in the open air. Wesley considered it almost a sin if a soul was saved outside of church. He finally conceded to this unfamiliar and raw manner of communicating the gospel. He declared, "At four in the afternoon, I submitted to be more vile." So should we!

18. Epistemology is the branch of philosophy that answers questions about knowledge. What is knowledge? What do we know? How do we know? Why do we know? How do we know that we know? How do we justify knowledge? Epistemology attempts to resolve what constitutes a theory of knowledge and why.

his theory of knowledge (spiritual empiricism) set the stage for discerning the strategies of Satan and God's work of salvation.

In chapter 3, the main question is whether Wesley claims a certain gift for his deliverance ministry, or whether it is done by some other means. I unpack this question in the context and categories of the modern Pente-costal-Charismatic movement and the primacy it places on the gifts of the Spirit (the *charismata*) as normative. Wesley clearly believes and operates in the "supernatural," but was he a Charismatic or Pentecostal as we under-stand them today? We need to treat Wesley fairly, not reading into his life's work from a charismatic perspective, or searching for a protopentecostal to substantiate charismatic practices today. Further, we must read Wesley closely to pick up on his particular methodology for deliverance, which is distinct from charismatic methods today. Chapter 3 prepares us to analyze the deliverance ministry of Wesley in chapter 4.

Much of our inquiry and analysis ride on Wesley's borrowing of the *ordi-nary-extraordinary* distinction when evaluating the works of the Holy Spirit. Chapter 4 picks up on the ordinary-extraordinary bifurcation and applies it to Wesley's practical theology of deliverance in terms of *indirect* and *direct* means of deliverance. We will define and differentiate the founder of Methodism's *in-direct ordinary* means of ministering deliverance that sets him apart from the more *direct* means used in modern Pentecostal and Charismatic ministries. In chapter 5 we will tackle actual deliverance phenomenology, often called being "thunderstruck," found in Wesley's *Journals* and *Letters*. What is it, and what is its purpose? Why is deliverance and exorcism such an untidy affair, like the spiritual version of working for Orkin or Roto-Rooter?

Chapter 6 will take a critical look at Wesley's theology and ministry of deliverance and build upon its strengths, seek to fortify its weaknesses, and rectify its errors. Excesses, malpractice, and misunderstanding that often characterize the discourse around demons and exorcism are critiqued and corrected for a balanced approach to Wesleyan deliverance ministry. We begin with an innovative perspective on baptism and its vows of renuncia-tion as a sacramental basis for deliverance ministry. Following, chapter 7 constructs a practical theology and methodology of deliverance that can be implemented in any deliverance ministry. Chapter 8 provides an instrument for ascertaining the need for deliverance (the C1–13 evaluation assessment). Chapter 9 teaches on the gifts of the Spirit and offers a tool for discovering your gifts for ministry. The Appendices provide prayers for deliverance and exorcism and a hymn on spiritual warfare.

2

Foundations for Wesley's Theology and Practice of Deliverance

INTRODUCTION

John Wesley (1703–1791) lived and died in a timespan that virtually covered the entire eighteenth century, a period called the Enlightenment or the Age of Reason. As the title "Age of Reason" indicates, a primacy was placed on the power and scope of enlightened reason over faith to solve the problems of the day, including questions about the universe, our world, and humanity. Sourced by the Scientific Revolution from the previous two centuries, the Enlightenment painted a new emerging picture of the world. The depiction was designed by science, as opposed to faith, and drawn from the palette of reason and senses, and not from the church or Scripture. The *zeitgeist*, or vibe, of the Age of Reason prioritized empirical certainty provided by the scientific method over the 'non-empirical and dubious faith claims' of the church.

The Scientific Revolution had inherited a supernatural or spirit-world-view from the medieval Scholasticism of the church. The Scholastic worldview was a detailed picture of the created order that moved from God, the greatest of all beings, down to lesser spiritual beings like angels, down to the physical universe and humanity, and lower to the creatures of the earth, and so on—a "great chain of being." This picture was primarily informed by Scripture and the Church. It consisted of God, the heavens, and the earth below, or God, invisible creation (the spirit-world, angels, and demons), and visible creation (the physical universe). God rules over heaven and earth, establishing his order of righteousness and goodness over all creation.

The physical universe is governed by God. He is an active agent that rightly orders the world, including everyday institutions and the lives of humanity. Spirit-beings, such as angels and demons, also have agency and interact with our world. Angels are agents of God's will, and demons are agents opposing God's will. This is a brief, rudimentary summary of a Scholastic worldview that was fading as an Enlightenment worldview was emerging. The supernatural world depicting angels, demons, and miracles was obscured by the high-resolution clarity of science with its physical, mechanistic, testable laws of certainty and consistency.

The Thomistic two-tier cosmos of grace and nature, or supernatural and natural realms, had collapsed into a closed system of nature.[1] Natural, physical laws and causality were thought to be sufficient to explain the universe. The historical periods following Scholasticism insisted upon a more certain, tangible, and quantifiable knowledge of reality that could be ratio-empirically verified.[2] Such knowledge was discovered through the telescopic enhancement of human senses, the synthesis of mathematical and empirical descriptions of the universe, the application of Bacon's inductive method, as epitomized in Kepler's orbital laws of planetary motion, and Newton's discovery of three basic mechanical laws.[3]

Nature was collected as data, subdued, handled, and managed into an explainable system of intricate interior causes. The working of the natural world was explained ultimately within itself. Natural laws alone, it was thought, fully explain the universe. Nature's mechanical laws became nature's own sufficient reason, hence nature as "closed." A firm trust was placed in observation and reason. Transcendent categories (e.g., a spirit-world or divine intervention) were no longer necessary, with the exception of a first efficient cause (the God of deism) to wind up the clock of the universe. Naturalism drove supernaturalism out of business.

Christianity, along with nature, was no longer considered a mystery. If the continuous laws of nature could not and need not be broken, then God could not and need not break this natural barrier, at least in the sense that the biblical or medieval worldviews of supernaturalism seemed to require. God created natural laws. Would he violate them? Hence, divine or supernatural action within the natural order was under attack, as seen in cessationism (the ceasing of miracles and supernatural gifts), deism, and a

---

1. Even heaven and earth.

2. We see this in early humanism, the Scientific Revolution, and the Enlightenment; Based on senses and reason.

3. For an insightful analysis on the shift in metaphysics and epistemology that occurred from medieval philosophy to the natural philosophy in the sixteenth and seventeenth centuries, see the classic by Burtt, *Metaphysical Foundations*, 15–20, 28–35.

closed natural universe devoid of "intervention" by God or by other preter-natural beings. An impassable scientific worldview was rapidly becoming the operating lens through which to view the universe for the educated and elite of Wesley's Enlightenment England.

So, how did John Wesley, an Oxford don and high church clergyman, come to embrace the "primitive," "superstitious" practice of casting out demons?[4] What exactly did Wesley believe about the supernatural and par-ticularly the demonic? The concept of *worldview*, how one views the world in a big picture sense, is key to understanding the demonic in general and specifically Wesley's view of the demonic. Either one has room for the su-pernatural in their picture of the world, or they do not. There does not seem to be much middle ground. We will examine the nature of Wesley's world-view that he interpreted from Scripture. I am calling it a "spirit-worldview," simply because it accounts for the category and existence of "spirit," and Wesley used the related term, "spiritual world." We will also look at his theory of knowledge within a spirit-worldview. I am labeling that theory, "spiritual empiricism," the capacity to experience the "spirit-world." Wesley believed that we know God through spiritual experience (spiritual empiri-cism). Wesley realized that once the spiritual eyes and ears are open:

> We have a prospect of the invisible things of God; we see the
> *spiritual world*, which is all round about us, and yet no more
> discerned by our natural faculties than if it had no being; And
> we see the *eternal world*; piercing through the veil which hangs
> between time and eternity . . .[5]

Wesley believed in a spirit-world that we can access with spiritual senses, a spiritual empiricism. Wesley's thoughts echo the Apostle Paul's:

> What no eye has seen,
> what no ear has heard,
> and what no human mind has conceived—
> the things God has prepared for those who love him—
> these are the things God has revealed to us by his Spirit.
> The Spirit searches all things, even the deep things of God. For
> who knows a person's thoughts except their own spirit within
> them? In the same way no one knows the thoughts of God except

---

4. Some critics, such as Robert Southey and John Hampson, would claim that Wesley, by constitution, was "superstitious." Others like Henry Rack, Alexander Knox, and Peter Bellini contend that Wesley was not uncritical, credulous, or an "enthusiast," though open to the supernatural in a reasonable, balanced way. See Rack *Reasonable Enthusiast,* 536–540. Chapter 5 will unpack this wonder in detail.

5. J. Wesley, "Scripture Way of Salvation," 47.

the Spirit of God. What we have received is not the spirit of the world, but the Spirit who is from God, so that we may understand what God has freely given us. This is what we speak, not in words taught us by human wisdom but in words taught by the Spirit, explaining spiritual realities with Spirit-taught words. The person without the Spirit does not accept the things that come from the Spirit of God but considers them foolishness, and cannot understand them because they are discerned only through the Spirit. The person with the Spirit makes judgments about all things, but such a person is not subject to merely human judgments, for, "Who has known the mind of the Lord so as to instruct him?" But we have the mind of Christ (NIV 1 Cor 2:9–16).

With spiritual empiricism, the Holy Spirit plays a significant role in Wesley's theology, particularly in his theology of salvation (soteriology). Salvation is not merely abstract. It is not just adherence to a set of theological propositions. Salvation is the life of God experienced through the work of the Spirit, a religion of the heart. Lycurgus Starkey claims that for Wesley, the Spirit's role in salvation is "the agent or administrator of redemption."[6] It is the "inner revelatory agency of the Holy Spirit" that works in us "the experiential nature of true religion," which is the "experimental knowledge and love of God."[7] The Holy Spirit is the divine agent behind the work of grace in the believer from prevenient to sanctifying, "the whole work of salvation, every good thought, word, and work is altogether by the operation of the Spirit of God."[8] Simply, the Spirit implements and superintends the saving work of Christ in the Christian. The Spirit accomplishes the work of salvation and enlightens us to experience the joy of it as well.

The Holy Spirit is also the divine agent working in and through the church to carry out Christ's mission and ministry in the world. The church is a charismatic body, grace-birthed and grace-filled. The church is baptized in the Spirit to be a witness for Christ in ministry to the world. One of those forgotten ministries is deliverance, casting out demons. A spirit-worldview, spiritual empiricism, and the scriptural command to cast out demons provide the foundation and grounds for the deliverance ministry of John Wesley and the early Methodists.

6. Starkey, *Work*, 26.

7. Starkey, *Work*, 18.

8. J. Wesley, "Appeals to Men of Reason and Religion," 108.

WESLEY'S SCRIPTURAL SPIRIT-WORLDVIEW

From early in his childhood at Epworth, under the tutelage of his mother Susanna, to his days at Oxford, and later as a lifelong learner, John Wesley was unquestionably well-read and well-educated. Although Wesley was a man of *many* books, he hyperbolically claimed that to be a "*homo unius libri*, a man of one book,"[9] the Bible. Of course, this did not mean that he *only* read or needed the Bible, but that the inspired Word of God was his *primary* source for faith and practice. He was stressing the primacy of authority that the church has given to Scripture. In the Methodist 1744 *Minutes*, Wesley chided those preachers who assert to "need no book but the Bible," arguing that such have put themselves "above Paul."[10] In fact, Wesley assigned his preachers to read extensively from the fifty-volume *Christian Library* which he had personally edited. Wesley was a man of many books, though he placed the Bible first and above the rest. The point of Wesley's *homo unis libri* statement was that Scripture was the first and last word on matters of Christian doctrine and practice for the church, including for himself.

The Apostle of Methodism was shaped by Scripture inside and out down to his manner of life and speech, which seemed effortlessly interwoven with the words of sacred Scripture.[11] For Wesley and early Methodists, "the Bible is the whole and sole rule both of Christian faith and practice."[12] Early on, they were not called "Bible-moths" for nothing. Wesley's intention was that Methodist theology and practice would primarily be formed by Scripture, including what we would call "worldview." The term "worldview," of course, is anachronistic, preceding Wesley by over one-hundred years. The notion of "metaphysics," or specifically "great chain of being" would be the closest functional equivalent in Wesley's day for worldview.[13] Wesley even used the term "chain of beings" to describe the invisible and visible order of creation.[14] Worldview is basically a culture's big picture of reality. Worldview is how a particular people group in a given culture understand

9. J. Wesley, "Preface to the Standard Sermons," 3.

10. J. Wesley, "Minutes of Several Conversations," 315.

11. When one reads Wesley's literary works, it seems as if Wesley spoke Bible as a second language or dialect, as his parlance was naturally peppered with scriptural passages and verses. For example, see John Wesley, "Thoughts upon Methodism," 261.

12. J. Wesley, "Thoughts upon Methodism," 258–261.

13. For the world picture or metaphysics that Wesley's world inherited as "the great chain of being," see Tillyard, *Elizabethan World Picture*. The shift from medieval metaphysics to natural philosophy in the sixteenth and seventeenth centuries is charted in the classic by Burtt, *Metaphysical Foundations*.

14. J. Wesley, "Of Evil Angels," 370.

the nature of reality or the big picture of the world. Cultural anthropologist Paul Hiebert's definition of worldview is: "'the foundational cognitive, affective, and evaluative assumptions and frameworks a group of people makes about the nature of reality which they use to order their lives.' It encompasses people's images or maps of the reality of all things that they use for living their lives. It is the cosmos thought to be true, desirable, and moral by a community of people."[15]

As the worldview of the Enlightenment began to shift its perspective from God to humanity, supernatural to natural, faith to reason, and church to nation-state, these shifts impacted how one read, translated, and interpreted the Bible.[16] The Bible was more naturalized, secularized, and humanized to sustain the onslaught of the Age of Reason.[17] For our purposes, the supernatural was often discredited, as we see in *The Jefferson Bible*, which removed those elements but kept and centered on its moral teachings.[18] Deistic interpretations of the Christian faith were naturalistic and reductive, minimizing it to a mere natural religion. Despite these changes, Wesley contended for a plain, yet critical, reading of the biblical texts, including embracing their supernatural worldview.

Wesley, in adopting Scripture as the primary authority for theology and practice, adopted some of the operating worldview held by various cultures in Scripture, including the first century church, specifically its so-called "supernatural" elements.[19] Some of those elements would include the

15. Hiebert, *Transforming Worldviews*, 25–26.

16. Sheehan, *Enlightenment Bible*, 27–53.

17. Sheehan, *Enlightenment Bible*, 27–53.

18. First drafted in 1804 by Thomas Jefferson (1743–1826), third President of the United States.

19. There is an ongoing debate about whether the term "supernatural" should be used when describing divine or preternatural action. "Supernatural" seems to imply 'above' or 'over nature,' meaning outside of the mechanistic laws of physics that govern the natural order. In Wesley's day, the Scottish philosopher David Hume, in his "Of Miracles," strongly opposed miracles defined as a "transgression of a law of nature by a particular volition of the deity or by the interposition of some invisible agent." More recently, non-interventionist responses have been developed for divine action, such as Robert J. Russell's model of Non-Interventionist Objective Divine Action (NIODA). This model of divine agency and action claims that God acts in the world without suspending or breaking his own physical laws that he built into the universe. He works within those laws (i.e., quantum dynamics) to accomplish his purposes. Such a move would allow for God to work within a universe that modern science agrees is causally closed. In this case, "supernatural" would not be an appropriate word to describe God's action in the world. Whether we use the word "supernatural," or similar terms, or not, the notion embraced by Wesley and by this author is that the divine can and does act in the world in unusual or extraordinary ways. This notion also applies to spirit beings, such as angels and demons. For an in-depth overview of the concept of

existence of God, God's agency and action in the world, a created invisible world of angels and demons that interacts with this world, and occurrences of miracles, signs, and wonders. Trusting the veracity and plain sense of Scripture at face value, Wesley adopted its "supernatural" or spirit-world-view. Wesley used the terms "invisible world,"[20] "the spiritual world"[21] "the world of spirits,"[22] among others, thus I derive the term "spirit-worldview." It is a *holistic,* integrative worldview that encompasses and accounts for *all* of reality, visible *and* invisible, matter *and* spirit. A spirit-worldview is a holistic, integrative, and monistic (one reality) worldview with two aspects, visible and invisible (matter and spirit) working together.

For Wesley, only scriptural revelation, not pagan religion or philosophy, gives us a clear view of the invisible world and its spirit-beings.[23] He writes, "Revelation only is able to supply this defect: This only gives us a clear, rational, consistent account of those whom our eyes have not seen, nor our ears heard; of both good and evil angels."[24] As Scripture assumes a spirit-worldview in terms of the elements mentioned, so also does Wesley assume a similar worldview that accounts for the role of the Spirit in his epistemology, anthropology, soteriology, and his theology and practice of deliverance. Consequently, he does not question their reality but goes directly to Scripture as his source to explain the nature of angels and demons, which we will see below.

Logically, Wesley's scriptural spirit-worldview would become the grounds for his deliverance ministry, forming the presupposition of his confrontation with the demonic. On this conclusion, he never hesitated. I contend that belief in some form of a holistic or spirit-worldview is prerequisite for any deliverance and exorcism ministry, as well as ministering in the gifts of the Spirit.[25] It would appear to be a precondition and axiomatic. Although many scholars and learned persons in the Enlightenment would no longer hold to the category of the "supernatural," Wesley, who was also well-educated and current in his understanding and trust of scientific developments of his day, still held on to a holistic or spirit-worldview.

---

the "supernatural" see Xhemajli, *Supernatural,* 3–29. For more on Wesley and the supernatural, see Billman, *Supernatural Thread,* and Jennings, *Supernatural Occurrences.*

20. J. Wesley, "Earnest Appeal to Men of Reason and Religion," 5, 13.

21. J. Wesley, "Earnest Appeal to Men of Reason and Religion," 4.

22. J. Wesley, "Earnest Appeal to Men of Reason and Religion," 5.

23. J. Wesley, "On Good Angels," 362.

24. J. Wesley, "On Good Angels," 362.

25. For further conversation about the importance of worldview in ministry see Bellini, *Unleashed!*; C. Kraft, *Christianity Power*; C. Kraft, *Confronting Powerless Christianity*; M. Kraft, *Understanding Spiritual Power.*

Even the mention of "spirits" for many today brings immediate pause. One does not have to be a 'rocket surgeon' to know that such a belief has been rejected and ridiculed by today's scholars and academics. Yet, Wesley did not scorn science the way a fundamentalist might today. Wesley seemed to embrace a view of religion *and* science.[26] Scientist-theologian Ian Barbour would call this an "integration" model, which respects the integrity of both fields, allows them to have dialogue, and wherever possible, attempts to integrate the work of religion and science.[27] Wesley tended to see religion and science as both/and rather than either/or. During the Enlightenment period, a time of transition from the old worldview to the new, it was not uncommon to still find a learned person holding both worlds in tension, e.g., the renowned polymath Isaac Newton.[28]

For example, we see an integrative or holistic approach to Wesley's theology and practice of salvation (soteriology). In addition to the theological resources of prayer and the cross that offers forgiveness of sin to all who believe, an assortment of resources was prescribed to early Methodists for health and wholeness, such as regular exercise, horseback riding, proper diet and sufficient water intake, electroshock therapy, and the latest medical treatments, along with time-tested, natural folk remedies, among others.[29] Wesley opened free clinics in London and Bristol and pharmaceutical dispensaries in London, Bristol, and Newcastle, and prayed for the sick. He accepted both spiritual and natural resources for wholeness and salvation.

Our focus from Wesley's integrative approach is on the so-called "supernatural" dimension, a spirit-worldview. While well-read in natural philosophy (the sciences of the day), Wesley based his views of divine agency, the existence and work of angels and demons, and miracles, signs, and wonders on his reading of the "plain sense" of Scripture, which we will see throughout this book. Wesley was interested in "plain truth for plain people" and the

26. For a further explanation on John Wesley's integrative worldview and my own work on the interface between religion and science in a spirit-worldview, see Bellini, *Unleashed!*, 64–69.

27. Barbour, *Religion and Science*, 77–103.

28. Hummel, "Faith behind the Famous." Isaac Newton, a generation before Wesley, was a great mathematician, chemist, and physicist who was also interested in theology and alchemy, an odd combination. It was said that he wrote more on theology than science, penning over a million words on the former and a half-million words on alchemy. Newton, in spite of his scientific discoveries, continued to hold the view that God created the universe and was an active agent in history through providence, preserving and governing all things. In light of his scientific research, Newton never doubted God's existence, agency and action, providence, and causal power in the universe. See also Burtt, *Metaphysical Foundations*, 283–302.

29. Bellini, *Unleashed!*, 64–69.

literal sense of Scripture, when possible, interpreting Scripture with Scripture in light of the greater whole that is the basic doctrines of the faith (analogy of faith). And his "stated rule in interpreting Scripture" was to "never to depart from the plain, literal sense, unless it implies an absurdity."[30]

We are familiar with other bold statements by Wesley indicating his commitment to the integrity of Scripture and to its plain sense as a criterion of truth, such as, "if there be any mistakes in the Bible, there may as well be a thousand. If there be one falsehood in that book, it did not come from the God of truth."[31] Whatever we may anachronistically label Wesley in today's terms—an inerrantist, literalist, or an infallibilist—we know that he took Scripture at face value whenever possible.[32] This includes tacitly accepting a worldview that assumed the divine action of God in the world and a created invisible spirit- world that interfaces with our own.[33] The cosmology of Wesley's day precedes Einstein's theories of relativity, quantum mechanics, or any version of the Big Bang theory. But the challenge of deism in the Enlightenment was real, and ideas like divine intervention, miracles, and the supernatural were highly suspect by natural philosophers (scientists) of that time. It seems, in cases where science conflicted with Scripture, Wesley favored Scripture. I guess for Wesley only Scripture could better assist in "fleeing from the wrath to come."

Within his scriptural spirit-worldview, Wesley embraced a particular type of *spiritual empiricism* as his working epistemology or theory of knowledge.[34] Spiritual empiricism allows for the existence and workings of God, angels, and demons in the world, as well as our knowledge of them. The Spirit's work, such as the revelation of Scripture, its illumination to the reader, opening and employing the spiritual senses of the newborn believer, the regenerating and sanctifying work of the spirit in full salvation, and assurance of salvation by the witness of the Spirit are all essential to the Wesleyan "way of salvation." Further, for Wesley and early Methodists, the supernatural knowledge of God was experienced in their evangelistic ministry. They ministered salvation by walking in the power of the Spirit. Their ministry, besides witnessing miraculous conversions, consistently encompassed healing, dreams, visions, prophecy, and other manifestations of the Spirit, including deliverance. A wide array of charismata accompanied the evangelism ministry of early Methodism.

---

30. J. Wesley, "Of the Church," 3, 50.

31. J. Wesley "July 24, 1776," 82.

32. For more on Wesley and Scripture, see Green and Watson, *Wesley, Wesleyans*.

33. J. Wesley, "Scripture Way of Salvation," 47.

34. Many scholars of Wesley identify his working epistemology as a "spiritual empiricism." For their view and mine, see Bellini, *Participation*, 111–128.

WESLEY'S SPIRITUAL EMPIRICISM

To grasp Wesley's familiarity with the spirit-world and dynamics such as deliverance, it is helpful to understand the epistemology implicit in his theology—what I have termed *spiritual empiricism*. Epistemology is the branch of philosophy that asks fundamental questions around knowledge. What is knowledge? How do we arrive at it? How do you know that you know? How can you prove a claim of knowledge? These are the questions asked and tackled by epistemology and are implied in all our thinking, whether we realize it or not. We always do philosophy even when we are "not doing philosophy."

We can therefore ask about Wesley's (functional) implicit theory of knowledge that he utilized to construct theology. What was the instrumental relationship between knowledge and theology? I say "functional" theory of knowledge because Wesley was not intentionally working as a philosopher when he did theology. As Wesley was not a systematic theologian in the technical sense, even more so, he was not a philosopher in any sense nor affiliated with any school of philosophy beyond a certain species of empiricism, which I am calling "spiritual empiricism."[35] He did theology seated at the Anglican three-legged stool (*Scripture, tradition, and reason*) with Scripture as primary. Post-Aldersgate, Wesley would add another source, *experience*, with its appeal to the work of the Spirit. The founder of Methodism's "strangely warmed heart" experience at Aldersgate in 1738 became the

---

35. Epistemologically, Maddox also sees Wesley as an empiricist in the Lockean tradition with a spiritual twist, holding to the idea of spiritual realities being apprehended by spiritual senses. Maddox, *Responsible Grace*, 27. Gunter agrees with the assessment of Wesley as an empiricist but with a "Platonic twist." See Gunter, "Personal and Spiritual Knowledge," 135–138. Although empirical knowledge of the world is senses-based, knowledge of God is not restricted to the same. Gunter, like Maddox, refers to the "spiritual senses." Through the spiritual senses, we gain experiential knowledge of God. Gunter claims that, for Wesley, "the spiritual senses are the gracious work of God through the Holy Spirit." The spiritual sight allowed by Wesley is the Platonic twist that expands the senses past the physical realm, enabling experiential knowledge of God.

Miles would agree. She identifies Wesley's empirical heritage rooted ultimately in Aristotle, but she notes Wesley's understanding of our "spiritual senses" that apprehend the transcendent realm gives him an appearance as a Platonist. See Miles, "Instrumental Role of Reason," 86, 91–3. Wesley's "Aristotelian empiricist way leads to a Platonic destination." Wesley is an empiricist because knowledge comes to the mind via the senses. Ideas are not innate. However, Wesley has a Platonic streak because the nature of the senses is not only physical but also spiritual. These senses encounter a transcendent realm accessing experiential knowledge of God. I would agree that Wesley seems to have elements of both Aristotelian empiricism and Platonic transcendence.

See also Long, *John Wesley's Moral Theology*, 13. Long claims that Wesley "presents us with a 'spiritual sensorium' that uncritically mixes an Augustinian theory of illumination (mediated through Cambridge Platonism) with the sensibility of knowledge plundered from Locke, which Wesley assumed did not conflict with Aristotle."

defining moment and hagiographic symbol of Methodist spiritual empiricism. Following Aldersgate, religious experience became more expected by Wesley and early Methodists. Wesley would further factor the work of the Spirit into the development of his way of salvation (*via salutis*).

Philosophically and theologically, Wesley was an empiricist. Yet despite not being a "professional" philosopher, Wesley was well-read on the subject, both classical and contemporary philosophy. He was versant in Plato and Aristotle and other staple figures and was trained in Aristotelian logic at Oxford.[36] He judiciously engaged the philosophy of his day, including the works of Peter Browne, Bishop Berkeley, John Locke, and David Hume. Wesley's interest in philosophy differed from our modern preoccupation and quest for foundational epistemic certainty, which we inherited from Descartes.[37] Wesley was not looking for incorrigible, immoveable rational grounds on which to build an empirically apprehended and logically derived system of knowledge that could explain everything. Nor was he a post-foundationalist, post-structuralist, anti-realist, or postmodernist that questioned such a rational system of knowledge and its foundationalist grounds. He was not puzzled by the twentieth and twenty-first century philosophical problems of language, "the two dogmas of empiricism," semiotics, deconstruction, and the like.[38] These concerns post-date him. Wesley was interested in (spiritual) knowledge through experience, which is (*spiritual*) *empiricism*.

Wesley's interest in philosophy and further epistemological matters were related to *religious experience* and how we know and experience God. Methodist theologian Thomas Oden quotes Wesley: "Through experience one may 'observe a plain, rational sense of God's revealing himself to us, of the inspiration of the Holy Ghost, and of a believer's feeling in himself the mighty working of the Spirit of Christ.'"[39] Wesley believed that we know

36. Oord, "Types of Wesleyan Philosophy," 154–162. Oord claims that some of the philosophers Wesley read were Aristotle, Augustine, Bacon, Berkeley, Boethius, Robert Boyle, Joseph Butler, Cicero, Samuel Clarke, Descartes, Jonathan Edwards, Erasmus, Hume, Francis Hutcheson, Leibniz, Locke, Malebranche, Cotton Mather, Newton, Pascal, Plato, Thomas Reid, and Voltaire.

37. Descartes' methodological skepticism doubted everything that could be doubted for the sake of finding a certain, immoveable Archimedean point upon which to build his theology and philosophy. He found such a point as one who doubts. *Cogito ergo sum*. He could not doubt his doubting. This monumental move was emblematic of an ongoing epistemological crisis that opened the door to a tidal wave of epistemic uncertainty that led to the erosion of foundationalism and the birth of postmodernism.

38. The Logical Positivists like Bertrand Russell, Ludwig Wittgenstein, Rudolf Carnap, and others, and those who followed, such as J. A. Ayer, J. L. Austin, Gilbert Ryle, Donald Davidson, Noam Chomsky, and others; W. E. V. Quine; Ferdinand de Saussure or Jean Baudrillard; Jacques Derrida.

39. Oden, *John Wesley's Scriptural Christianity*, 84.

God's existence through creation. But further knowledge of God, beyond his mere existence, is by revelation and accessed through spiritual experience. This knowledge can be indirect and limited through our physical senses or direct and extended through our spiritual senses. We can know God *indirectly* through creation via our physical senses.[40] Or we can experience God *directly* through revelation via God's Spirit witnessing to our spiritual senses.

A brief reminder of empiricism recalls that the empiricists' dictum, "there is nothing in the mind which is not in the senses first," became the basis for British empiricism (Locke, Berkeley, Hume). Ideas do not occur first in the mind. Ideas come after the senses perceive the external world and are processed in the mind. With empiricism, reality is not intuited by innate ideas (in the mind first) or received as rational abstractions but experienced first through impressions of the senses and afterwards as perception and cognition.

Regarding innate ideas and natural and spiritual senses, Wesley asserts, "[o]ur ideas are not innate, but must all originally come from our senses, it is certainly necessary that you have senses capable of discerning objects of this kind; Not those only which are called natural senses . . . but spiritual senses exercised to discern good and evil."[41] With "spiritual" empiricism, our knowledge of God comes to us through our awakened "spiritual senses." As we have physical senses (sight, hearing, taste, touch, and smell), so have we inner spiritual senses as well, according to Wesley. There is a parallel. As our five physical senses perceive the natural, empirical world, so also do our inner spiritual senses perceive the invisible, spiritual world.[42]

Wesley assures us that our natural reason cannot transport us "from things natural to spiritual; from the things that are seen to those that are not seen; from visible to the invisible world . . . What a gulf is here? By what art will reason get over the immense chasm?"[43] He continues that God will "give you that faith . . . you shall soar away into the regions of eternity . . . explore even the deep things of God . . . revealing them to you by his Spirit."[44]

---

40. J. Wesley, "Imperfection of Human Knowledge," 339–344. Wesley grants a knowledge of God through creation, but it is extremely limited. "Hence then, for his works, particularly his works of creation we are to learn the knowledge of God. But it is not easy to conceive how little we know even of these." See also J. Wesley, "Farther Appeal to Men of Reason and Religion," 197. "I grant, the existence of the creatures demonstratively shows the existence of their Creator. The whole creation speaks that there is a God. Thus far is clear. But who will show me what that God is."

41. J. Wesley, "Earnest Appeal to Men of Reason and Religion," 13.

42. J. Wesley, "Great Privilege of those Born of God," 225–26.

43. J. Wesley, "Earnest Appeal to Men of Reason and Religion," 14.

44. J. Wesley, "Earnest Appeal to Men of Reason and Religion," 14.

For Wesley, the experience of the divine is encountered through the awakening of our inner spiritual senses, which at first are dead in sin. Wesley, with his empirical bent, was influenced in part by John Locke (1632–1704) and Peter Browne (1665–1735), among others.[45] Wesley's notion of spiritual senses was developed in part from engaging John Locke (*Essay Concerning Human Understanding*) and the philosophical theology of Peter Browne, specifically his *The Procedure, Extent, and Limits of Human*, a critique of Locke.[46] Wesley incorporated religious experience with Browne's theory of analogical knowledge of God and his critical integration of Lockean empiricism. The conclusion is that we perceive the natural world by natural perception, so by analogy or comparison we can perceive the spiritual world (e.g., God) by spiritual senses.[47] Wesley also identified faith as a sixth sense that can perceive and interpret spiritual data.[48] The full quote from Wesley:

> . . . our ideas are not innate, but must originally come from our senses, it is certainly necessary that you have senses capable of discerning objects of this kind: not those only which are called natural senses, which in this respect profit nothing, as being altogether incapable of discerning objects of a spiritual kind; but spiritual senses, exercised to discern spiritual good and evil. It is necessary that you have the hearing ear and the seeing eye, emphatically so called; that you have a new class of senses opened in your soul, not depending on organs of flesh and blood, to be the evidence of "things not seen" as your bodily senses are of visible things; to be the avenues to the invisible world, to discern spiritual objects, and to furnish you with ideas of what the outward "eye hath not seen, neither the ear heard." 1 Cor 2:9.[49]

In "An Earnest Appeal to Men of Reason and Religion," Wesley again equates the spiritual senses with faith. He states that faith is:

> "the demonstrative evidence of things unseen," the supernatural evidence of things invisible not perceivable by the eyes of flesh, or by any of our natural senses or faculties. Faith is the divine

45. The influence or degree of influence of Locke on Wesley is debatable. See Brantley, *Locke, Wesley* for an affirmation of that influence. See Maddox, *Responsible Grace,* for his thoughts on how Wesley's epistemology differs from Locke's.

46. Browne, *Procedure, Extent, and Limits,* 447–468. See also Browne, *Things Divine and Supernatural.* Browne, an Irish bishop and philosopher, was also influenced by Locke. Wesley himself attested to Browne's influence in the writing of his *Compendium of Natural Philosophy.* Wesley also read and was influenced by John Norris.

47. Browne, *Procedure, Extent, and Limits.* 447–468

48. Sell, *Philosophy, History, and Theology,* 148.

49. Waring, *Deism and Natural Religion,* 239.

evidence whereby the spiritual man discerneth God, and the things of God. It is with regard to the spiritual world, what sense is with regard to the natural. It is the spiritual sensation of every soul that is born of God.[50]

Thus for Wesley faith is the "eye of the new-born soul," the "ear of the new-born soul, whereby a sinner 'hears the voice of the Son of God and lives,'" the "palate of the soul; for hereby a believer 'tastes the good word, and the powers of the word to come,'" and "the feeling of the soul . . . "[51] "Spiritual things" are not perceived by "outward senses" nor comprehended by natural reason. One needs "spiritual sight" or "faith" to comprehend spiritual things. Wesley further explains his spiritual empiricism.

> So you cannot reason concerning spiritual things, if you have no spiritual sight; because all your ideas received by your outward senses are of a different kind; yea, far more different from those received by faith or internal sensation, than the idea of colour from sound. These are only different species of one genus, namely sensible ideas received by external sensation; whereas the ideas of faith differ toto genere from those of external sensation. So that it is not conceivable, that external sensation should supply the want of internal senses; or furnish your reason in this respect with matter to work upon.
>
> What then will your reason do here? How will it pass from things natural to spiritual; from the things that are seen to those that are not seen; from the visible to the invisible world? What gulf is here! By what art will reason get over the immense chasm? This cannot be till the Almighty come into your succour, and give you that faith you have hitherto despised.[52]

Both natural and spiritual empiricism are similar in that they are concerned with sense experience. Where they differ, simply, is that natural empiricism experiences the natural world through the natural senses, while spiritual empiricism experiences the spirit-world through spiritual senses.

Let us explore the greater dynamics of grace in relation to spiritual senses. The Holy Spirit ministering conviction awakens one's "inner senses" to the reality of God's work, which is intended to lead ultimately to a regeneration of one's soul. The Spirit takes the regenerated person from being merely a natural man/woman to a man/woman of the Spirt. When one is born of the Spirit, an (ontological) shift takes place from *death* to *life* and

50. J. Wesley, "Earnest Appeal to Men of Reason and Religion," 4.

51. J. Wesley, "Earnest Appeal to Men of Reason and Religion," 4.

52. J. Wesley, "Earnest Appeal to Men of Reason and Religion," 13–14.

from being *in Adam* to *in Christ*. Further a parallel (metaphysical) shift occurs, as one's orientation shifts from the *visible* world to the *invisible* world. Additionally, an (epistemological) shift occurs from our *natural senses* to our *spiritual senses*. Finally, a (soteriological) shift occurs in the justified believer from an inability to perceive God to the ability to perceive the life of God in Christ. Faith, the sixth sense, serves as the faculty of perception for salvation, from beginning to end.

Wesley deemed true knowledge of God as what comes strictly by spiritual experience through spiritual senses. For Wesley, in order for religion to be true, or from the heart, it needs to transcend mere mental assenting to theological propositions or adopting some abstract form of doctrine, important as that may be. Our grace-empowered spiritual senses are enabled to transcend the rational-empirical world of sense and reason or mere abstraction and "see him who is invisible." True religion is Spirit-inspired, heart-felt, and inwardly known by faith. Wesley applied spiritual empiricism to the entire way of salvation (*via salutis*). Prevenient, convincing, justifying, regenerating, assuring, and sanctifying grace are works of the Spirit, perceived and received in the heart of the believer by faith. Spiritual empiricism allows for the individual to *experience* and be *certain* of the fully orbed work of the Spirit in salvation.

Another term we can use for spiritual is "charismatic." Wesley seemed to hold a "charismatic" theory of the knowledge of God and the work of grace. Wesley was an *epistemological charismatic,* identifying the epistemic operations in the *via salutis* as those of the Spirit. Our spiritual senses are awakened by the gift of the Spirit so that we can perceive, receive, and experience the work of grace from prevenient to sanctifying. It was Wesley's insistence on experiencing salvation through the Holy Spirit that was so vehemently opposed by church leaders in his day.

> It nothing helps them to say, "We do not deny the assistance of God's Spirit; but only this inspiration, this receiving the Holy Ghost: and being sensible of it. It is only this feeling of the Spirit, this being moved by the Spirit, or filled with it, which we deny to have any place in sound religion." But, in only denying this, you deny the whole Scriptures; the whole truth, and promise, and testimony of God. Our own excellent Church knows nothing of this devilish distinction; but speaks plainly of "feeling the Spirit of Christ"; of being "moved by the Holy Ghost" and knowing and "feeling there is no other name than that of Jesus," whereby we can receive" life and salvation. She teaches us all to pray for the "inspiration of the Holy Spirit"; yea, that we may be "filled with the Holy Ghost." Nay, and every Presbyter of hers professes

to receive the Holy Ghost by the imposition of hands. Therefore, to deny any of these, is, in effect, to renounce the Church of England, as well as the whole Christian Revelation.[53]

THE WITNESS OF THE SPIRIT

One robust fruit of Wesley's spiritual empiricism is the rich Methodist doctrine of the witness of the Spirit: "The Spirit himself bears witness with our Spirit that we are the children of God," (Rom 8:16).[54] Believers can be assured by the Holy Spirit that they have salvation. Wesley exclaimed, "[t]hat there is in every believer, both the testimony of God's Spirit, and the testimony of their own, that they are a child of God."[55] Christians are assured inwardly, immediately, and directly by the Spirit and outwardly by the fruit of the Spirit produced in their life.[56] Further, their own spirit bears witness with them in their conscience that the love of God has been poured in their hearts.[57] This core Methodist teaching claims the immediate, direct impression of the Holy Spirit upon the human spirit, granting the believer a measure of assurance that she/he is a child of God.[58] Wesley declared, "The testimony of the Spirit is an inward impression on the soul, whereby the Spirit of God directly witnesses to my spirit, that I am a child of God; that Jesus Christ hath loved me, and given himself for me; and that all my sins are blotted out, and I, even I, am reconciled to God.[59]

Because of the bold Methodist doctrine of assurance, Wesley was accused of teaching "perceptible inspiration," and in essence he virtually was.[60] Nature was not a closed system. God sends illumination and is received by the spiritual sense of faith, and the believer can have assurance of it. Our assurance of God's work in us comes from God. For Wesley, the inward witness

---

53. J. Wesley, "Awake, Thou That Sleepest," 34.

54. The inner witness of the Holy Spirit (*testimonium internum Spiritus Sancti*).

55. J. Wesley, "Witness of the Spirit," 113.

56. J. Wesley, "Witness of the Spirit," in *Works of John Wesley*, 133. See also John Wesley, "Witness of the Spirit," 122.

57. J. Wesley, "Witness of our own Spirit," 135–141.

58. J. Wesley, "Witness of the Spirit," 115. See also John Wesley, "Witness of the Spirit," 124–125. "The testimony of the Spirit is an inward impression on the soul, whereby the Spirit of God directly witnesses to my spirit, that I am a child of God; that Jesus Christ hath loved me, and given himself for me; and that all my sins are blotted out, and I, even I, am reconciled to God.

59. J. Wesley, "Witness of the Spirit," 115.

60. J. Wesley, "Letter to Mr. John Smith," 77–78, 84–85.

was the *a priori* certainty in the heart of the Christian of all God's grace-filled work. Wesley asserts: "Since, therefore, the testimony of his Spirit must precede the love of God, and all holiness, of consequence it must precede our consciousness thereof."[61] In other words, "We must be holy of heart, and holy in life, before we can be conscious that we are so; before we can have the testimony of the Spirit that we are inwardly and outwardly holy."[62] Thus, the work of justification or entire sanctification is wrought in our hearts before the Spirit bears witness to it. Once the work is accomplished, then the Spirit bears witness. Following, our own spirit bears witness, as well.[63]

Thus, the epistemological work of the Spirit, which testifies that the work of justification or entire sanctification is completed, is "antecedent" to our consciousness or immediate witness of it. Also, "[t]he testimony of the Spirit of God must, in the very nature of things, be antecedent to the testimony of our own spirit. . ."[64] God does the work, and then we know of it by the witness of the Spirit, and then we receive the testimony of our own spirit. It does not work the other way around that we have the witness, and then God does the work. The function of the Spirit's witness is to provide direct, immediate experience and assurance of God's salvific work in the heart of the Christian. Consequently, "the Methodist doctrine of the Spirit's witness covers the whole ground of the Spirit's work" in salvation.[65]

According to Wesley, the witness also functions as a means to discern and test the work of the Spirit in one's life, as well as the voice of God and the works of darkness.[66] Wesley's epistemological contribution to theology is that the Spirit's work of grace (prevenient to glorifying) precedes our reception and knowledge of it. And the work of the Spirit we receive is followed by the Spirit's witness and then our own. The inward witness of the Spirit is an immediate, direct, conscious impression made on our own spirit by the Holy Spirit. It is not deduced or inferred according to deductive and inductive rationality. Epistemologically it is a non-derivative, non-inferential, self-evident, divine datum, which is self-referencing and self-authenticating, but subject to the question and challenge of rationality of belief.[67]

---

61. J. Wesley, "Witness of the Spirit," 115–116, 127.

62. J. Wesley, "Witness of the Spirit," 115.

63. J. Wesley, "Witness of the Spirit," 127.

64. J. Wesley, "Witness of the Spirit," 127.

65. Pope, *Peculiarities*, quoted in Starkey, *Work*, 63.

66. J. Wesley, "Witness of the Spirit," 121–122.

67. For more discussion on the rationality of belief and the inner witness of the Spirit, see Abraham, "Epistemological Significance."

Wesley argued that the witness of the Spirit, though varying, was not *extraordinary*, or occasional, but mere scriptural Christianity, *ordinary*, and normative.[68] This conclusion is contrasted with his view on the gifts of the Spirit, which he considered extraordinary. Wesley's spiritual empiricism served a soteriological (ordinary) purpose rather than a charismatic-missiological (extraordinary) one. The latter perspective would expand the normative function of the Spirit to the reception and implementation of the gifts in all believers.

Wesley's theology, in a sense, is a theology of the Spirit. From beginning to end, salvation is fueled by the grace and power of the Spirit. Wesley identified the work of the Spirit primarily in his role and operation in salvation. But did Wesley also embrace a charismatic theology of the Spirit—not just for knowledge and salvation but also power and gifting for service in mission—a charismatic grace? We will examine that question in the next chapter.

A SPIRIT-WORLDVIEW, SPIRITUAL EMPIRICISM, AND DELIVERANCE

At this point, we can piece together the context for Wesley's theology and practice of deliverance. A spirit-worldview provides the setting for engaging the demonic. We live in a world that is visible *and* invisible, inhabited by creatures both seen *and* unseen. Spiritual empiricism allows one to perceive the spirit-world and to perceive and receive the salvific work of the Holy Spirit. Wesley extends spirit perception of the spirit-world to perceiving the work of evil spirits as well. Spiritual warfare and deliverance from evil spirits are not a quantum leap for Wesley and early Methodists because of the preconditions of a worldview and an epistemology that account for it.

Wesley held a spirit-worldview, and within that worldview, the invisible things of the Spirit of God are believed and received by faith. A believer, by faith, can experience spiritually the full gamut of God's gracious saving work. Ministry, including deliverance, is also understood in the same light. Contextually, we minister out of a spirit-worldview, and we experience the power of the Holy Spirit to minister in that context. The church is filled and equipped with the power of the Spirit for mission and ministry and is sent out to the world to be a witness (Acts 1:5,8). As intimidating as this may sound to the domesticated Wesleyan, it is gospel truth.

The church is given spiritual power and authority to do the works that Jesus did and greater (John 14:12). Those works are illustrated in the

68. J. Wesley, "Witness of the Spirit," 112.

gospels and continued in the book of Acts. Wesley's comment for Acts 1:5 in his *Notes* indicates that disciples were promised the "extraordinary gifts," which were included in the promised baptism of the Spirit.[69] The ministries and gifts of the Spirit included, among other things, preaching, teaching, witnessing, suffering, healing, working miracles, and casting out demons (Matt 10:7–9; Acts 1:8).[70]

Our interest is in that last ministry, casting out demons or deliverance. Of all the ministries referenced in the Matthew passage, Wesley, in his New Testament *Notes*, expounds on only one: casting out demons.[71] He goes to considerable length to demonstrate to the skeptic the reality of demons and their tormenting work in the unbeliever. Wesley knew that demons are real beings, not symbolic beings, and that they come to wreak real havoc and destruction. Wesley did not explain away, doubt or wrestle, or resort to figurative language to understand the reality and work of Satan. He embraced a scriptural spirit-worldview and a spiritual theory of knowledge that accounted for the existence and operations of invisible, fallen, evil angels. Methodism today would do well to follow Wesley. For the hyperrational Wesleyan, if you are within the bounds of orthodoxy, you already embrace an entire array of suprarational, invisible, unproveable, spiritual realities like God, heaven, hell, and all things made invisible. Each of these is affirmed even in the doctrinal standards of the United Methodist Church.

A spirit-worldview, spiritual empiricism, and the scriptural command to cast out demons provided the foundation and grounds for the deliverance ministry of John Wesley and the early Methodists. Before we explore Wesley's deliverance ministry, let us examine Wesley's notion of demons. What did the founder of Methodism understand about Satan, the demonic, and demonic activity?

DELIVERANCE FROM SIN INVOLVES DELIVERANCE FROM SATAN

Poring over Wesley's corpus for an explicit theological foundation for his deliverance ministry or for casting out demons in particular, readers would be hard-pressed to find anything direct, intentional, or substantial on the subject. Much is *inferred* from his sermons, essays, and tracts that speak to the problem of sin and evil. From those sources, one can find a moderately

69. J. Wesley, *Explanatory Notes*, no pagination given. See comment under Acts 1:5.

70. "Suffering" and "working of miracles" are added in Wesley's *Notes*.

71. J. Wesley, *Explanatory Notes*, no pagination given. See comment under Matthew 10:8.

developed theology of angels and demons, but nothing on "casting out devils." However, Wesley's journal entries and some of his letters give clear,
practical accounts of casting out demons.

Overall, Wesley was not a systematic theologian. He did not set out to
write formal treatises on every subject or locus within theology. Though his
Journals and *Letters* account for deliverance and exorcism in his ministry,
he never purposefully wrote a theological treatise or essay on the subject.
Casting out demons, though a recurring issue, was not a *primary* concern
for him. Nor did he see himself as an exorcist, nor his ministry as primarily
encompassing demonic deliverance. Conclusions about Wesley's deliverance ministry this writer makes based on Wesley's *de facto* practice of deliverance. In that regard, I claim he had a deliverance ministry, though it was
secondary in importance. Most likely, he would humbly view deliverance
in his ministry as the supernatural fruit of answered prayer. In this regard
Wesley's modesty is a stark contrast to the superstar, religious personalities
of today with their salesperson personas, commercial packaging, aggressive
marketing of ministries, and hi-tech presentations.

Although Wesley and early Methodists frequently encountered evil
spirits in their ministry, neither claimed a charism for exorcism, nor did deliverance occupy their *ordinary* attention in matters of salvation. Salvation,
specifically full salvation or holiness, was the *primary* focus of Methodist
mission. Deliverance from *all* sin was the goal. Confronting the demonic
was more of a collateral problem that reared its ugly head when pursuing
repentance and deliverance from sin. However, the problem of deliverance
arose frequently enough that by necessity Wesley demonstrated a working
theology and practice of deliverance.

He believed, though, that deliverance was significant enough to write
about extensively in his *Journals* and *Letters*, as well. Although frequently
overlooked, these documents outline Wesley's *de facto* theology and practice of deliverance. Hence, I make the unique claim that Wesley did function
in an actual deliverance ministry. In the last two centuries, much has been
written in Wesley studies about every facet of his theology and practice, but
few have claimed that deliverance was any integral part of his ministry.[72]
I am making this bold claim to account for the frequent exercise of deliverance in his pastoral ministry. It seems it was a necessary ministry that
Wesley reluctantly had to assume as a part of proclaiming full salvation or

72. Over the last two hundred plus years of scholarly works on John Wesley, only a
few have referenced his dealing with the demonic. However, when references have been
made, the further claim of a regular 'deliverance ministry' is rarely conjoined with it.
In this and other works, I am making that bold claim due to its frequent exercise in his
pastoral ministry as indicated primarily in his journals and letters.

deliverance from all sin. As he pursued his call to spread scriptural holiness, demonic manifestations presented themselves as an obstacle to fulfilling the mission of full salvation. One cannot simply leave those to the ground in torment who had been thunderstruck.

Wesley was peripherally interested and involved in facing the demonic only insofar as he was directly interested in the grace of God setting the human heart free from sin and evil. He was no theologically imbalanced demon-chaser, looking under every rock. His notion of demonic deliverance was tied to the deliverance from temptation, sin, and evil. The demonic, temptation, sin, and (personal and social) evil were all intertwined in a profoundly complicated wickedness.[73] If one were to deal thoroughly with sin, dealing with the demonic would be inevitable. Jesus dealt with sin *and* Satan. Jesus came to deliver people from their sin, and so he confronted Satan in the wilderness and later set the captives free as an itinerant healer and exorcist. Sin and Satan are interconnected.

Wesley held a robust doctrine of original sin and its collateral universal impact on the heart of humanity.[74] Empirically, for Wesley, the proof of general human depravity and complicated wickedness go uncontested.[75] And at the root, he understood Satan standing as the origin of evil, the archetypal Tempter, the god of this world, and the father of all lies.[76] Because demons are instrumental to the whole sin-evil enterprise, early Methodism, a soteriological movement, could not avoid dealing with the demonic. Wesley's theology and practice of deliverance was properly balanced and situated within a larger theology and ministry of full salvation. Wesley was no enthusiast or fanatic!

Yet, unlike many Methodists and mainline Protestants today, Wesley believed in the existence of a real, literal devil, a fallen angel(s) that tempts humanity to evil.[77] And unlike most Methodist writers and preachers over the last century, the Methodist founder penned explicit, detailed homiletical proclamations exposing evil, hell, demons, the devices of Satan, temptation, and spiritual warfare.[78] He realized the imperative to equip early Method-

73. J. Wesley, "On Divine Providence," 313–325. A descript term used by Wesley.

74. His substantial and systematic treatise on "Original Sin" was his most lengthy work. In light of detractors (such as the influential deist John Taylor), Wesley felt the need to lay down the foundation for this debated but necessary truth as a logical premise to proclaiming the need for the new birth.

75. J. Wesley, "On the Deceitfulness of the Human Heart," 335. For example, John Wesley makes it plain in his sermon on the deceitfulness of the human heart.

76. J. Wesley, "Of Evil Angels," 377.

77. J. Wesley, "Of Evil Angels," 372.

78. J. Wesley covered these subjects throughout his literary corpus but perhaps

ists with scriptural teaching on these subjects so that they could overcome temptation and evil. Wesley knew fallen angels truly existed, and more so, that they were an actual threat to salvation and needed to be resisted in the faith. He knew the church was in a cosmic battle against the ancient powers of darkness. He penned in "Of Evil Angels," "[S]atan and all his angels are continually warring against us, and watching over every child of man."[79]

WESLEY'S DEMONOLOGY

Wesley held to the full plain scriptural account that fallen powers of darkness operate insidiously in the world today.[80] So, we need to be vigilant, prepared, and on guard. Satan is no mere trope or literary foil. He did not reduce the existence of demons to quaint relics of the prescientific mind, useful metaphors, psychological adversity ("dealing with one's demons"), or to unjust socio-political structures and systems, as we tend to do with our rational-empirical, scientific worldview. Granted, there can be excesses in claiming the reality of the demonic. Some Christians go to extremes, uncovering a demon under everything. On the other hand, there are Christians who, due to a modern, reductivist worldview, do not believe in the demonic or anything of the "supernatural" order. They would perhaps chuckle at Wesley's "antiquated" belief in demons or angels, seeing it as no different than belief in a flat earth or in leprechauns.

Nonetheless, belief in angels and demons, in some form, was commonplace from the ancient world to Wesley's day, and still is among majority world Pentecostals and Charismatics today. Wesley held what would be considered at the time the historic or orthodox Christian view on angels and demons, as evidenced by his sermons "Of Good Angels" and "Of Evil Angels."[81] Angels as well as demons are invisible, preternatural, created, spirit-beings equipped with superior power and acute rational and volitional faculties compared to other creatures in the "great chain of being." They were organized hierarchically in various orders or classes.[82] Wesley, reflecting a more medieval view (not the neo-Platonic variant) that created beings from highest to lowest were linked on a great chain of being from heaven to earth, places angels at the highest link below God, who is uncreated being.[83]

most explicitly in his sermons.

79. J. Wesley, "Of Evil Angels," 375.

80. J. Wesley, "Of Evil Angels," 371.

81. J. Wesley, "On Good Angels," and, "Of Evil Angels."

82. J. Wesley, "Of Evil Angels," 372.

83. For a historical explanation of the idea see Lovejoy, *Great Chain of Being*.

And within the company of angels, there were hierarchies of order and rank along with various classes with different duties, responsibilities, and jurisdictions assigned to each (Eph 6:12).[84] Wesley contended that evil angels maintained some degree of their original knowledge and power and used each to rule in various domains in both the invisible and visible worlds.[85] Wesley concurs with Scripture that Satan is "the god of this world," and along with the other fallen angels, operates as an authority and power in the world responsible for instigating evil on multiple levels, both personal and socio-political.[86]

Originally, angels were created as "ministering spirits" to serve God in various capacities within the kingdom of God, including warring against the hosts of hell, sending and receiving messages, protecting and ministering righteousness and strength to the people of God.[87] Wesley also noted that angels were initially given freedom, thus the choice to serve their purpose or to rebel. The "elect" angels kept their "first estate," or divinely ordained station, while the others revolted. Wesley speculated that perhaps Lucifer and his cohort fell into pride and envy upon hearing the decree (Ps 2:6–7) "concerning the kingdom of his only begotten Son to be over all creatures."[88]

Further, he acknowledged the traditional account in Scripture of an insurrection, a war in heaven in which one-third of the angels attempted to assert their dominion over God and were driven out of heaven and down to the earth by Michael the Archangel and his hosts.[89] Here, the fallen angels continue their attack on God's purposes by deceiving and tempting humanity with the goal to steal, kill, and destroy.[90]

Although a spirit-worldview persisted even in Wesley's day, a clear shift was taking place among the educated and the elite (not so much among the common folk) towards more of a naturalism that was closed off from supernatural intervention. Preternatural beings like demons, ghosts, witches, phantasms, or angels, were being relegated more and more to superstition. The reality and truth of a thing, such as a planet or a demon, was to be verified by rational, empirical, and scientific explanation, not metaphysics or supernaturalism. Of course, the work of Copernicus, Galileo, Newton, and Kepler, among others, lent itself to a universe that could be explained by the physical mechanistic laws of nature. There was no need for "divine intervention." At best the universe, like a clock, would merely need its maker, a clockmaker, to wind up the machine and let the wheels turn on their own. See Robert Webster, *Methodism and the Miraculous*, 65–70.

84. J. Wesley, "Of Evil Angels," 374.

85. J. Wesley, "Of Evil Angels," 371–72.

86. J. Wesley, "Of Evil Angels," 373–74.

87. J. Wesley, "Of Good Angels," 362–68.

88. J. Wesley, "Of Evil Angels," 372.

89. J. Wesley, "Of Evil Angels," 370, 372.

90. J. Wesley, "Of Evil Angels," 371, 376.

It is paramount to note that although Wesley acknowledged the supernatural knowledge and power of the demonic, he clearly realized that demons were inferior to God and the good angels. In addition, he recognized that believers in Christ have authority and power over evil. The only power Satan and his evil hordes have over us is what is permitted by God and our own will.[91] Jesus soundly defeated the devil at the cross, but God allows humanity to be tempted until the end of the age (John 19:30; Heb 2:14). We are commanded to be armed with God and resist the devil, and he will flee from us (Eph 6:10–18; Jas 4:7).[92] Currently, Satan and his hordes stand judged by God because of the cross, but their sentencing is reserved until the end of time (John 16:11). Then, they will be thrown into the lake of fire, along with Death and Hades (Rev 20:10,14). Related, but only to make a reference, Wesley similarly held a robust, real, literal orthodox view of hell that included eternal conscious torment for fallen angels and unredeemed souls.[93]

THE STRATEGIES AND TACTICS OF DEMONS

Banished out of heaven and relegated to the earth, the demons work as a tight governmental, militaristic unit under the command of Satan, the prince of the power of the air, and are strategically stationed and assigned to specific works of deception and destruction.[94] The powers of darkness are *continually* at war with us, blinding our minds, assaulting our faith, and dampening our love.[95] Wesley specifically unpacks the strategies and ways in which the enemy assails the church. One of his primary tactics is to bombard our hearts and minds with evil thoughts.[96] The war with Satan begins in the mind. Wesley declares that demons, "[w]ell understand the very springs of thought; and know on which of the bodily organs the imagination, the understanding, and every other faculty of the mind more immediately depends. And hereby they know how, by affecting those organs, to affect the operations dependent on them. Add to this that they can inject a thousand thoughts without any of the preceding means."[97] Whether indirectly through the senses to the mind or directly to the mind, the enemy incessantly attacks us.

91. J. Wesley, "Of Evil Angels," 373–74.

92. J. Wesley, "Of Evil Angels," 379–80.

93. J. Wesley, "Of Hell," 381–91.

94. J. Wesley, "Of Evil Angels," 374.

95. J. Wesley, "Of Evil Angels," 375–76.

96. J. Wesley, "Of Evil Angels," 376.

97. J. Wesley, "Wandering Thoughts," 27.

The devious onslaught of his fiery arrows is meant to drive out the fruit of the Spirit in our lives and fill us with doubt, hatred, fear, worry, anxiety, lust, suspicion, animosity, resentment, division, and other evils.[98] The enemy knows that to gain control over our lives and thwart the work of God in us, he must first seduce and capture the mind. The mind is the chief battleground where the war against evil is won or lost. St. Paul recommends the helmet of salvation to cover our heads in battle (Eph 6:17).

Wesley believed that demons are permitted to understand keenly the nature and fine, detailed mechanics of the human mind and its susceptibilities.[99] The Deceiver would aim and fire his wicked darts at those vulnerable places in our minds at strategic, opportune times. Wesley warned that Satan captures our mind by camouflaging his thoughts as our thoughts, making it difficult for us to discern his schemes. We assume his thoughts to be our thoughts.[100] On other occasions, the devil may inject a spontaneous evil thought distinct from our own train of thought, which makes it more evident that the origin of the thought is not our own but from the evil one. Satan utilizes varying devices and tactics to snare us, but we are not ignorant of his schemes because we have the Word and the Spirit of God that give us light to discern and the power to be delivered.[101] Wesley prayed "that we may be delivered from all sin; that both root and branch may be destroyed; that we may be cleansed from all pollution of flesh and spirit; from every evil temper, and word, and work . . . "[102]

The founder of Methodism unveiled that the "grand device of Satan" is to thwart the work of the Spirit in our hearts from start to finish. His assignment is to impede the initial work of salvation, and the "greater work" of entire sanctification.[103] The devil hinders the work of God by causing us to take our eyes off Christ and to look at ourselves and all our sinfulness. At that point, the devil bombs the self-occupied soul with lies from the pit of hell and will even use Scriptures, but with a sinister twist to point them against us.[104] The enemy disqualifies us with a devastating array of doubting and condemning thoughts aimed at our faith and our sense of forgiveness, righteousness, peace, and joy.[105] In this way, he steals our confidence and sti-

---

98. J. Wesley, "Of Evil Angels," 376–77.

99. J. Wesley, "Wandering Thoughts," 27.

100. J. Wesley, "Of Evil Angels," 376.

101. J. Wesley, "Satan's Devices," 32.

102. J. Wesley, "Wandering Thoughts," 27.

103. J. Wesley, "Satan's Devices," 33.

104. J. Wesley, "Satan's Devices," 38.

105. J. Wesley, "Satan's Devices," 34–37.

fles the fruit of the Spirit in our lives. In his sermon "Satan's Devices," Wesley exclaimed that if the devil *cannot* destroy us, he will attempt to *torment* us and even force us to quit pursuing God.[106] With our guard down, Satan establishes a stronghold in our mind and holds us captive in the area(s) of struggle. Thoughts of condemnation, frustration, and self-disqualification soon follow.[107]

Along with our thought-life. Satan also deviously targets our "passions and tempers," as Wesley called them. The evil one works on our emotional life. He tempts us to misdirect and misuse our God-given emotions and desires and direct them toward the "flesh" or our lower physical appetites. The temptation is to put bodily and worldly desires above godly desires, which is idolatry.[108] Or even to flat out directly desire the things that God has forbidden in his Word. By seducing our emotional life, the enemy captures our desire and will, turning us from the love of God and redirecting us toward the works of the flesh (Gal 6). Wesley assures us that as long as we are in this body, regardless of our level of purity or maturity, we will be tempted by the devil. No one is exempt from temptation; even Christ was tempted in every way, though without sin (Heb 4:15).[109]

In his sermon on "Wandering Thoughts," Wesley exclaimed that Satan is not dead and does not sleep.[110] We are called to be vigilant and on guard because Satan and his demons are opportunists, roaming the earth looking to devour whomever they can (1 Pet 5:8).[111] Thus, concerning the spiritual battle, Wesley was emphatic: "I found more and more undeniable proofs, that the Christian state is a continual warfare; and that we have need every moment to watch and pray lest we enter into temptation."[112] When was the last time we heard a Wesleyan preacher or teacher warn us that we will always be engaged in spiritual warfare as part of the Christian life? Anything but that!

SPIRITUAL WARFARE

Wesley recognized that spiritual warfare is not only a reality, but that it can be constant. As Methodists, we have rarely been told this is the case. We

106. J. Wesley, "Satan's Devices," 32.

107. J. Wesley, "Satan's Devices," 35.

108. J. Wesley, "Of Evil Angels," 376–77.

109. J. Wesley, "Wandering Thoughts," 31.

110. J. Wesley, "Wandering Thoughts," 31.

111. J. Wesley, "Of Evil Angels," 375.

112. J. Wesley, "Journal Entry May 17, 1740," 272.

were warned of the evil "-isms" of the day—racism, sexism, classism etc. And they are evil. We have been spurred to awaken and take up our righteous ire against a whole new cadre of -isms and enforce the new social dogma generated by the synods of political correctness. But the correlation was never made between the -isms, or even personal sins, to the demonic.[113] I have been in United Methodism for over three decades as a congregant, an ordained Elder, and a seminary professor, and I cannot recall once the mention of casting out demons or spiritual warfare at charge, district or annual conference, at a worship service or Sunday School class, at conference sponsored programs, or at seminary. The only exceptions have been in churches where I have pastored or at the current seminary where I teach, though I am sure it had to occur somewhere.[114] Why did our leaders forget to warn Methodists that Satan is roaming like a roaring lion seeking to devour us? Why were we not taught how to put on the armor of God and defend ourselves, rather than shipwreck our faith through doctrines of devils and damnable heresies? Is this fanaticism? The founder of Methodism did not think so, and he had an acutely sensitive enthusiasm-detector.

Early Methodists knew what we do not know but need to learn. We are not defenseless or helpless to the onslaught of Satan and his hordes. God has properly fit us for spiritual warfare. Throughout Wesley's writings, he encourages the believers to resist sin and the devil in the power of the Spirit. The Apostle of Methodism charged the church to be equipped with the spiritual weapons that God provides to fight this spiritual war. He listed several of them at the conclusion of his sermon "On Evil Angels." Wesley exhorted Christians to be fortified with God's strength and armor (Eph 6:10–17),[115] the mind of Christ (1 Cor 2:16), awareness and discernment (1 Pet 5:8), holiness (Eph 4:22–24), the indwelling anointing (1 John 2:20), and his Word (Matt 4), to resist the devil (Jas 4:7), and he will flee from us

---

113. Correlations have been made frequently between oppressive evil systems and the demonic in progressive and liberation traditions. The demonic are socio-political systems of evil rather than fallen angels that need to be expelled from individuals, the type of demons that Wesley identified.

114. After I arrived at the seminary where I teach, I held conferences on the Holy Spirit and spiritual warfare. I also offered courses on healing and deliverance. They had never held conferences or courses on such subjects in the past.

115. The armor of God includes the belt of truth, the breastplate of righteousness, the combat boots of peace, the shield of faith, the helmet of salvation, and the sword of the Spirit. The armor consists of God's attributes. Each piece is a property or characteristic of God. We are not armed with *our* truth, righteousness, peace, etc. Instead, God is our truth, righteousness, peace, etc. God is our armor, and each piece represents an attribute of God at work in the believer. In his *Notes* for Ephesians 6:10–17, Wesley describes in great detail the function of each piece of the armor.

(Jas 4:7).[116] Wesley charges us "to attack Satan, as well as secure ourselves, the shield in one hand, and the sword in the other. Whoever fights with the powers of hell will need both."[117] We are guaranteed that he will flee from us (Jas 4:7). We are promised victory!

As noted, Wesley frequently discerned that if Satan cannot destroy you in battle, he will torment you.[118] "If he cannot entice men in sin, he will, so far as permitted, put them in pain," Wesley exclaims.[119] He continues with a litany of seemingly common phenomena that Satan employs to torment humanity, such as "innumerable accidents."[120] He lists: "unaccountable fright or falling of horses," "overturning of carriages," "breaking or dislocating of bones," "the hurt done by the falling or burning of houses," "the hurt done by storms of winds, snow, rain, or hail, by lightning or earthquakes," or, "terrifying dreams," "but to all these, and a thousand more, this subtle spirit can give the appearance of accidents."[121] Satan's assault are both internal (e.g., thoughts, feelings, dreams) and external (e.g., circumstances, accidents, sickness, apparitions, other people). We need to be strong in the mighty power of the Lord and put on the whole armor of God to stand against the devil's strategies and tactics. God is greater than the enemy of our soul and his schemes (1 John 4:4).

MENTAL DISORDERS AND THE DEMONIC

Wesley added to the list of demonic attacks some mental disorders and many "acute and chronic diseases," especially those that arise suddenly "without any discernible cause; as well as those that continue, and perhaps gradually increase, in spite of all the power of medicine."[122] In the case of mental disorders and physical ailments, it is vital to employ the discernment of the Holy Spirit and the best resources of the medical sciences to draw sound conclusions as to the cause(s) of various conditions. Wesley believed in the power of prayer, natural remedies, *and* medical science. For extremists, it is too easy to demonize people or an ailment when dishing out devils. Wesley warned, in Christian life and in ministry, to "First, do no harm." When trying to help, the lines can be blurry, and we can quickly find ourselves doing

116. J. Wesley, "Of Evil Angels," 379–80.

117. J. Wesley, *Notes* for Ephesians 6:17.

118. J. Wesley, "Satan's Devices," 32, and, "Of Evil Angels," 378.

119. J. Wesley, "Of Evil Angels," 378.

120. J. Wesley, "Of Evil Angels," 378.

121. J. Wesley, "Of Evil Angels," 378.

122. J. Wesley, "Of Evil Angels," 378.

damage when we meant to do good. Spiritual malpractice occurs too often in the church.

Proper discernment and treatment are vital. For example, in my work, I make a sharp distinction between mental disorders and demonic "attachments." Relative to the limited scientific and medical advances of his day, Wesley implemented an integrative approach to health, healing, and wholeness, though at times in my estimation he attributes certain phenomena to demons that I would not.[123] A well-informed, interdisciplinary, integrative strategy is imperative in order to avoid excesses and malpractice and to be effective in healing and deliverance.[124] And, of course, we are wise to not minister beyond the grace, competence, and authority given to us (Rom 12:6–8). Refer when needed! In deliverance ministry, balance is a virtue.

DELIVERANCE AND THE WESLEYAN ORDER OF SALVATION

By temperament, Wesley was rarely theologically myopic, obsessive, or overly dogmatic about what he perceived to be non-essentials. So, while he did not focus narrowly in his theological writing on "casting out devils," he did expound upon the broader sense of deliverance (from sin) in which the narrower sense is situated. Casting out demons, for Methodism's founder, is situated within the larger theological context of deliverance as it relates to full salvation. This broader sense of deliverance, as the means to full salvation, is deliverance from sins, sin, death, and the power of Satan.

Deliverance from sins, plural, refers to transgressions, by commission or omission, that have been forgiven. Deliverance from (the) sin refers to liberation from inbred or birth sin that remains in believers after regeneration. Deliverance from death signifies that there is no condemnation in Christ Jesus. We have been set free from the law of sin and death and have been given eternal life (Rom 8:1–2). Finally, deliverance from the power of Satan means that because Christ has defeated the power of Satan, believers have victory over the devil as well (Rom 16:20; Heb 2:14).

Deliverance marks the entire way of salvation (*via salutis*), from justification to entire sanctification to glorification. Let us briefly examine the impact of deliverance on Wesley's order of salvation (*ordo salutis*).[125]

123. See J. Wesley, *Primitive Physick*, and his other works related to healing and wholeness.

124. For an interdisciplinary and integrative approach to healing and deliverance, see Bellini, *Truth Therapy*; *Unleashed*; *Cerulean Soul*; and *X-Manual*.

125. There is an ongoing debate among Wesley scholars about whether he offered a way (*via*) or an order (*ordo*) of salvation (*salutis*). The former expresses a more flexible

In justification, we are delivered from the sins we committed. Deliverance involves freedom from bondage, suffering, guilt, shame, and penalty of our sins, which is death and eternal punishment. In deliverance from our *sins*, Christ brings us into *justification* (forgiven, made right, and adopted as children of God).

For Wesley, all humanity is bound in sin and in need of deliverance. They are asleep, dead in their sin, and unaware of their condemned state. Bondage is the state of the "natural man" until he or she receives the "gift" of the "spirit of fear."[126] He/she begins to awake and realize their bound condition. This person is under the law or in a "legal state."[127] They are awakened out of their heavy slumber by the light and conviction of the law and the right hand of God. The sinner deeply comprehends the utter wickedness of their sin, its guilt and shame, its merit of punishment, and their inability to be set free by their own doing (Rom 7).[128] They cry out, "Who shall deliver me from this body of sin?" and the Spirit reveals the grace of God in Christ.[129] Often at this juncture intercession and assistance are needed in the form of deliverance. Wesley and early Methodists discovered that frequently persons who were bound and in fear, but seeking repentance, would manifest demons that held them in bondage. At this point, they would persevere in prayer and warfare against the devil until the demons were evicted, and the person was delivered from the power of darkness. In chapter 4, we will explore Wesley's deliverance ministry in depth.

Thus, the awakened soul "sees all his iniquities laid on Him, who 'bare them in his own body on the tree;' he beholds the Lamb of God taking away his sins. How clearly now does he discern, that 'God was in Christ, reconciling the world unto himself; making him sin for us, who knew no sin, that we might be made the righteousness of God through him.'"[130] They are made justified by grace through faith (Rom 3:28–30; Eph 2:8).[131] Justification, or being pardoned and made right with God, marks a "relative change," a change in our relation with God.[132] We move from being unrighteous,

---

path of salvation, while the later would indicate a tighter, logical sequence of steps from prevenient to glorifying grace.

126. J. Wesley, "Spirit of Bondage and of Adoption," 98.

127. J. Wesley, "Spirit of Bondage and of Adoption," 99.

128. J. Wesley, "Spirit of Bondage and of Adoption," 102–105.

129. J. Wesley, "Spirit of Bondage and of Adoption," 106.

130. J. Wesley, "Spirit of Bondage and of Adoption," 106.

131. J. Wesley, "Justification by Faith," 60–63. See also, J. Wesley, "Salvation by Faith," 7–16, and J. Wesley, "Righteousness of Faith," 65–76.

132. J. Wesley, "Great Privilege of those Born of God," 224; J. Wesley, "Justification by Faith," 57.

condemned enemies of God to being made righteous, pardoned children of God.[133] Being forgiven, we are delivered from guilt and the condemnation of the devil (Rom 8:1–2).[134] His "legal" hold and accusations against us are broken and made void.[135]

Additionally, deliverance brings us into *regeneration*.[136] Justification and regeneration occur simultaneously with the latter following the former logically, but not in time. We are born again of the Spirit (the new birth) that includes being washed, given new life, and a new nature of righteousness and holiness.[137] More than just a *relational* change, we experience a *real* change.[138] Believers receive more than just an *imputation* of righteousness but also an *impartation* of righteousness.[139] More than salvation from the *penalty* of sin, we are also saved from the *power* of sin.[140] We no longer have to submit to the power of Satan in temptation. We can walk in the Spirit and resist his attacks. Wesley believed living a life above sin is the standard for a regenerated Christian.[141]

Greater still, in entire sanctification, we are also delivered from the bondage and *presence* of *inbred sin*.[142] Believers are liberated from the inner civil war between the flesh and the spirit and are unimpeded and empowered to grow in grace and in holy love. Finally, deliverance also entails liberation from death (Heb 2:14–15). We will, ultimately, be delivered from this body of death (Rom 7:24). We will receive the redemption of our bodies (Rom 8:23). Perishability will put on imperishability, and mortality will

---

133 J. Wesley, "Witness of the Spirit I," 113. "There is in every believer, both the testimony of God's Spirit, and the testimony of his own, that he is a child of God."

134 J. Wesley, "Salvation by Faith," 10; J. Wesley, "Justification by Faith," 57; and J. Wesley, "The First Fruits of the Spirit," 87.

135. J. Wesley, "New Birth," 65–66.

136. J. Wesley, "Salvation by Faith," 10.

137. J. Wesley, "New Birth," 71.

138. J. Wesley, "Scripture Way of Salvation," 45; J. Wesley, "Great Privilege of those Born of God," 224; and J. Wesley, "Sin in Believers," 146.

139. Same as justification defined above. With regeneration (the new birth), the believer experiences an actual, real change in their hearts and lives and not merely an imputed or legal righteousness, in which Christ's righteousness is given or credited to the believer and stands as their own righteousness, while their own sins are forgiven and no longer credited to them. Logically following regeneration comes (initial) sanctification.

140. J. Wesley, "Salvation by Faith," 11, and, J. Wesley, "Great Privilege of those Born of God," 224.

141. J. Wesley, "Sin in Believers," 147, and, J. Wesley, "Marks of the New Birth," 214–15.

142. J. Wesley, "Scripture Way of Salvation," 50. Also, "Repentance of Believers," 158, 168; J. Wesley, "Scripture Way of Salvation," 52–54.

put on immortality (1 Cor 15:53–54).[143] Eschatologically, the resurrection of Christ entails what Wesley calls in his sermon by the same name, "The General Deliverance" (Rom 8:19–22). Not only will the end bring the resurrection of the dead but also a recapitulation or restoration of God's original order and beauty in the rest of creation, a *cosmic deliverance.*

Wesley proclaimed, "'the earnest expectation' wherewith the whole animated creation 'waiteth for' that final 'manifestation of the sons of God;' in which 'they themselves also shall be delivered' (not by annihilation; annihilation is not deliverance) 'from the' present 'bondage of corruption, into' a measure of 'the glorious liberty of the children of God.'"[144] God will "make all things new," "a new heaven and a new earth," and God will tabernacle with his creation (Rev 21:1–5). The entire created order of all things "will be restored, not only to that measure of understanding which they had in paradise, but to a degree of it as much higher than that . . . And whatever affections they had in the garden of God, will be restored with vast increase; being exalted and refined in a manner which we ourselves are not now able to comprehend."[145]

Thus, with Wesley, deliverance is more than just casting out demons, though it includes that practice. It is deliverance of cosmic proportions that includes freedom from sin, guilt, shame, eternal punishment, the power and presence of sin, the condemnation and assaults of the devil, death, and the suffering of the universe itself. In the end, God's deliverance will bring us a new heaven and a new earth. Deliverance marks the entire warp and woof of salvation.

---

143. J. Wesley, "On the Resurrection of the Dead," 476.

144. J. Wesley, "General Deliverance," 251.

145. J. Wesley, "General Deliverance," 249.

3

Wesley, the Almost Charismatic

INTRODUCTION

As we move toward identifying a deliverance ministry in the work of John Wesley, it would be too convenient for some to reread him as either a proto-Pentecostal to one extreme, or to reduce him to a *charisphobic* or a cessationist to another extreme.[1] It would not be the first time Wesley would be remade in someone else's image. Historical projections and revisions, though in political vogue, are to be avoided. Thus, in this chapter, I would like to settle any debate about whether Wesley was cessationist or charismatic. The question is not as inconsequential as resolving a barroom bet. Determining Wesley's position on the issue will be telling when we inquire specifically about the supernatural work of the Spirit tied to deliverance. What was Wesley's understanding of this work in terms of a theology of the charismatic, and how did his theology impact and shape his ministry, including his deliverance ministry? If Wesley had a deliverance ministry, did he have any specific gift (*charism*) of the Spirit for deliverance or healing, or did he minister deliverance in some other manner?

Identifying Wesley's theology and practice of the gifts of the Holy Spirit will inform any prospective claim that the founder of Methodist practiced deliverance and exorcism and by some gifting. The premise is that deliverance and exorcism have historically been understood as charisms of

---

1. This conflation would be convenient for Pentecostal-Charismatic Christians; This caricature would be convenient for conservative Wesleyan Holiness Christians.

45

the church that accompany the preaching and teaching of the Gospel.[2] If Wesley ministered in deliverance and exorcism, did he do so through any specific gift given by the Spirit? Did John Wesley use or claim *any* of the gifts of the Spirit for that matter?

In our day of Pentecostal proliferation, much has been written on the person and work of the Holy Spirit, including the gifts of the Spirit. There has also been a dynamic increase in those praying for, claiming, operating in, and teaching on the *charismata*.[3] Pentecostal-Charismatic Christianity in the last century has exploded throughout the world following the Azusa Street Revival and other similar revivals in India, Chile, Korea, and other parts of the world at the beginning of the twentieth century.[4] Since that time, so-called Spirit-filled denominations, ministries, institutions, ministers, conferences, and teachings have boomed to become the majority expression of Christianity in the world. Supernatural manifestations of the Spirit have become commonplace in Pentecostal, Charismatic, neo-Charismatic, and even non-charismatic churches. Among those manifestations, deliverance and exorcism have been prevalent as well.[5]

The modern Spirit-filled movement, by its widespread propagation and influence, has acutely affected how we understand and minister the gifts of the Spirit. One could say that aspects of evangelicalism and mainline Protestantism have gone through a pentecostalization over the last fifty years. Due to charismatic and so-called third wave movement (neocharismatic) influences, evangelical and mainline institutions have cultivated a greater interest in the Holy Spirit, the gifts of the Spirit, expressive praise and worship music, laying on of hands, prayer for healing, and other practices. I have witnessed this change in my own denomination in each of these areas and others. Praise and worship music, lifting holy hands, taking inventories for discerning gifts of the Spirit, laying hands on a sick parishioner, and praying for healing are no longer thought of as strictly Pentecostal, or as things we Methodists do not do. Many are laying claim to the fruits of Pentecostalism, and others are even claiming the roots of Pentecostalism.[6] Methodists, Pentecostals, Charismatics, and other groups are tracing their

2. Roman Catholic Church, *Catechism*, 463–64. The Roman Catholic Church has always allowed for "major exorcism" throughout history. However, the practice can only be exercised by those who have the office and the gift and are granted permission by their bishop.

3. The gifts of the Holy Spirit.

4. See the classic by Anderson, *Introduction to Pentecostalism*.

5. Jenkins, *New Faces of Christianity*, 98–127.

6. The claim is that one of the theological roots of Pentecostalism is John Wesley and early Methodism. See the classic by Dayton, *Theological Roots of Pentecostalism*, 15–86.

genealogy and adopting John Wesley as their spiritual father. I think it is a valid claim and a good move.

But did John Wesley claim and practice charismatic ministry, including deliverance, as a Charismatic or renewalist Christian would today? The Charismatic movement is one of the fastest growing segments of the global Christian population, ranging anywhere from 25 percent to 30 percent of world Christianity. Many well-versed accounts, such as those from Donald Dayton and Vinson Synan, among others, trace Pentecostalism, at least in part, back to early Methodism and John Wesley.[7] Many Charismatics, including those in my own Methodist tradition (unofficially coined "Methocostals"), often turn to Wesley to moor their spiritual experiences historically and theologically. The evidence has been made plain that there is clearly a *historical* connection between early Methodism and Charismatic movements, but can we also make an *ontological* connection between Charismatic Christianity and the Methodist founder, whose heart was strangely warmed? Imagine if today's Pentecostal and Charismatic movements were able to take a theological DNA test through Ancestry.com. Would the results yield a shared DNA between charismatics and John Wesley, or was Wesley merely a friend of the family? Did John Wesley, the father of Methodism, hold the gifts of the Spirit to be normative to Christian faith and practice as charismatic believers do today? Simply put, was Wesley a "charismatic" Christian?

DEFINING TERMS

First, let us briefly examine the preliminary nomenclature. The term "charismatic" and other cognates and adjacent terms such as "Pentecostal" can be too narrow or too broad in some sense, vague, and problematic, depending on whether they are capitalized. The nomenclature and taxonomies for Pentecostals, Charismatics, and Neo-Charismatics of all stripes are vast and intricate and vary from researcher to researcher. Some scholars use "pentecostal" to encompass all so-called Spirit-filled Christians and institutions, even as it can be used specifically to speak about classical Pentecostalism in North America.[8] While the term "charismatic" can likewise be used in general to describe Christians and institutions that put an emphasis on the person and work of the Spirit, it also can be employed more specifically to

---

7. Of course, there have also been counter and supplemental accounts that trace that lineage through Higher Life, Keswick, and more Reformed lines. I tend to see the full lineage as a both/and rather than an either/or with the greater DNA influence coming from the Wesley-holiness line.

8. Anderson, *Introduction to Pentecostalism*, 6; Yong, *Spirit Poured Out*, 18.

the post-WWII Spirit-filled movement among Catholics and Protestants. A third category is usually reserved for Neo-Pentecostal Charismatics, independents, so-called third-wavers (charismatic evangelicals), and others.

For facility, I will use the broad "PCR" for Pentecostal-Charismatic-Renewalist Christianity.[9] The PCR designation is being used as a broad or general missiological designation referring to the global Christian movement or various expressions, traditions, churches, groups, or individuals that put a primacy on the experience of the person and the work of the Holy Spirit, specifically the charismata, in theology, worship, evangelism, preaching, discipleship, teaching, ministry, and mission. Pentecostal pioneer Smith Wigglesworth, in his classic work *Ever Increasing Faith*, makes an iconic connection between the presence of the Spirit and the charismata: "Wherever the Holy Ghost has right of way, the gifts of the Spirit will be in manifestation; and where these gifts are never in manifestation, I question whether He is present."[10] Wigglesworth's rule of thumb will be my plumbline. Wigglesworth's statement seems consonant with most PCR denominations' and institutions' statements of faith. For example, "Fundamental Truth" number seven in the Assemblies of God doctrinal statement claims the gifts of the Spirit are for all believers. Is Wesley a charismatic in this sense of gift-normativity? And as importantly, can Wesley serve as a model for Wesleyan Holiness Christians seeking more of a charismatic approach to the Holy Spirit?

FOUR GENERAL ASSERTIONS

After review of Wesley's work, it seems that at least four general assertions can be made about Wesley and the *charismata*:

1. Wesley was *not* a cessationist.

2. Wesley applied a holiness hermeneutic when discerning the authenticity of gifts. He distinguished between the extraordinary and the ordinary work of the Spirit.

3. Wesley was *not* a charismatic in theory.

4. However, he *was* a charismatic in practice.

---

9. Coulter and others use the term "neocharismatic" instead of "renewalist." See Coulter, "Defining Pentecostal-Charismatic Christianity."

10. Wigglesworth, *Ever Increasing Faith*, 30.

1. Wesley was not a cessationist.

Deism, Closed Naturalism and Cessationism

In considering Wesley's theology and practice of the charismata, it is no revelation that his eighteenth-century context was averse to any claim of the so-called supernatural or the miraculous. Much of Enlightenment supernaturalist thinking was contested by a tightly closed metaphysical naturalism promoted by the science and deism of the day and a stubborn cessationism left over from the Reformation.[11] Cessationism, as opposed to continuationism, is the view that the miraculous, the supernatural, or the gifts of the Holy Spirit *ceased* either following the first generation of apostles or with the canonization of Scripture.

Closed naturalism is the notion that the universe is fully operable and explained by physical mechanistic laws and in no need of outside causation (i.e., divine). The universe is closed to external influence and operates solely by the laws of physics. Alexander Pope's celebrated lines cannot be forgotten: "Nature and Nature's laws lay hid in night: God said, Let Newton be! and all was light."[12] The universe is a physical system of physical causal closure (closed to outside causation) described by physical laws. The cosmology of Wesley's day was heading swiftly in the direction of closed naturalism.

In the case of deism, which is a type of closed naturalism, there is no divine or supernatural intervention or operation in the universe. God created the universe and literally rested ever since. The universe does not depend any longer on the divine. There was only the need for a *first efficient* cause to create and "wind-up" the physical laws, which will subsequently run on their own. The notions of cessationism and closed naturalism are different in nature, though similar in end results. They both disallow supernaturalism or miracles. Cessationism disallows post-biblical miracles, and closed naturalism denies the existence of miracles in general.

Although cessationsim was not officially adopted by Anglicanism, many Anglican and Puritan Christians of Wesley's day were influenced by a prevailing Calvinist cessationist view that the gifts functioned as evidence (evidentialism) for the veracity of the ministry of Christ and the apostles.[13]

11. Part and parcel of Protestant refutation of Catholicism included refuting their claims of the miraculous and the supernatural, associating it with superstition, gullibility, and fraudulence. Reformers such as John Calvin, Jonathan Edwards, George Whitefield, Charles Hodge, B.B. Warfield, Sinclair Ferguson, and modern Calvinists like John MacArthur have supported the position of Cessationism. See Ruthven, *On the Cessation*.

12. An epitaph intended for Sir Isaac Newton.

13. Some lists claim John Owen, Matthew Henry, George Whitefield, and Jonathan Edwards as cessationists.

The supernatural gave them warrant or credentialing that "authorizes" the message. Following the establishment of the gospel and the church, the gifts *ceased*. It was supposed they were no longer needed once the foundation of the gospel was laid. Some allowed for the miraculous to continue until the end of the Apostolic Age (like Conyers Middleton), while others argued for its continuation until the canonization of Scripture .[14] On the other hand, Wesley vehemently defended "the supernatural" and often rigorously debated the great ecclesial minds of his day, including Conyers Middleton, William Warburton, Bishop of Gloucester, Bishop Joseph Butler, and others, on this issue.

Despite an antagonistic climate, the founder of Methodism thoroughly defended the authenticity of biblical miracles and the occurrence of post-biblical miracles in his lengthy letter to the polemical Middleton. Middleton, in opposition, explained away post-biblical miracles by attacking the credibility of the church fathers in his treatise *A Free Inquiry into the Miraculous Powers*. Wesley's basic position, in line with Anglican tradition, was that miracles still occurred in post-biblical and post-apostolic ages, but in less frequency after the first two or three centuries. In his sermon, "The More Excellent Way," Wesley asserted that "'the love of many,' almost of all Christians, so called, was 'waxed cold,'" following the alleged conversion of Constantine.

> It does not appear that these extraordinary gifts of the Holy Ghost were common in the church for more than two or three centuries. We seldom hear of them after that fatal period when the Emperor Constantine called himself a Christian, and from a vain imagination of promoting the Christian cause thereby heaped riches, and power, and honor, upon the Christians in general; but in particular upon the Christian clergy. From this time, they almost totally ceased; very few instances of the kind were found. The cause of this was not (as has been vulgarly supposed,) "because there was no more occasion for them," because all the world was become Christian. This is a miserable mistake; not a twentieth part of it was then nominally Christian. The real cause was, "the love of many," almost of all Christians, so called, was "waxed cold." The Christians had no more of the Spirit of Christ than the other Heathens. The Son of Man, when he came to examine his Church, could hardly "find faith upon earth." This was the real cause why the extraordinary gifts of the Holy Ghost were no longer to be found in the Christian Church—because the Christians were turned Heathens again, and had only a dead form left.[15]

---

14. Middleton, *Free Inquiry*.

15. J. Wesley, "More Excellent Way," 26–27.

Wesley's commitment to the authority of Scripture, the testimony of the Church Fathers, and his own church tradition prevented him from denying the existence of miracles in the early church. Further, his predilection for the confirming power of experiential religion precluded him from denying the real, empirical work of the Spirit, even the miraculous in his own life and ministry. In a clever defense against accusations made by the Bishop of Gloucester regarding cessation, Wesley fired back, "I presume you will allow there is one kind of miracles (loosely speaking) which are not ceased . . . lying wonders, diabolical miracles, wrought by the powers of evil spirits . . . And why should you think that the God of Truth is less active than him."[16] In other words, one may believe divine miracles have ceased and yet attribute early Methodist miracles to the devil, as if Satan is more active than God.

Just as influential as the Middleton variety of cessationism was John Toland's variety of deism and the skepticism of David Hume with his treatise "Of Miracles."[17] Deism and closed naturalism were not touting cessationism, but instead claimed miracles simply were not metaphysically possible and thus not justifiable. By definition, miracles are a *violation* of nature. In stark contrast, when Wesley spoke of the charismata or the supernatural, it was often in defense against the prevailing cessationist and deist views of his day, which were greatly debated amongst his contemporaries.[18] Wesley moved away from both the prevailing closed naturalism and cessationism of his time, demonstrating in his writings and ministry that he affirmed the supernatural and the gifts of the Spirit even in his own day. However, Wesley steered clear of enthusiasm and carefully balanced revelation with reason in his analysis of the supernatural:

> First, I acknowledge that I have seen with my eyes, and heard
> with my ears, several things, which, to the best of my judgment,
> cannot be accounted for by the ordinary course of natural causes,
> and which I therefore believe to be ascribed to the extraordinary
> interposition of God. If any man choose to style these miracles, I
> reclaim not. I have diligently inquired into the facts . . . I cannot

16. J. Wesley, "Letter to the Bishop of Gloucester," 160.

17. Toland was a deist who held that there is nothing supernatural in Christianity, but that the revelation of Christianity can be explained through reason. See his 1696 work *Christianity Not Mysterious.* Lord Herbert of Cherbury and Anthony Collins were further English influences in Enlightenment deism; See Hume, *Enquiry Concerning Human Understanding, Section X.* Hume, along with Voltaire, argued that a miracle is a violation of the laws of nature, which are unalterable. A belief in miracles, for Hume, is an unjustifiable belief that cannot be verified.

18. Burns, *Great Debate on Miracles,* 9–130.

account for either of these in a natural way. Therefore, I believe they were both supernatural.[19]

Simply put, Wesley was not a cessationist.

2. Wesley distinguished between the extraordinary and the ordinary.

In our first point we concluded that Wesley was not a cessationist. He believed in the supernatural, even in his own day. Let us further inquire whether he *personally* experienced the miraculous. And if so, how frequently and by what means? In reading Wesley's writings on the miraculous or the gifts of the Spirit, one notices that he consistently makes a division between the *ordinary* and the *extraordinary* work of the Holy Spirit, a division with antecedence in numerous sources, including the Puritan John Owen and Jonathan Edwards in Wesley's day.[20] In his sermon "Scriptural Christianity," Wesley identifies the *extraordinary* gifts as the "gift of healing, of working other miracles, of prophecy, of discerning spirits, the speaking with divers kinds of tongues, and the interpretation of tongues." Wesley adds that not everyone had these gifts, "perhaps one in a thousand." However, the gift of the Holy Spirit was "for a more excellent purpose": the cultivation of the "ordinary fruits," which are "essential to all Christians in all ages." The father of Methodism again clarifies, "Indeed I do not mean, that Christians now receive the Holy Ghost in order to work miracles; but they do doubtless now 'receive,' yea, are 'filled with the Holy Ghost,' in order to be filled with the fruits of the blessed Spirit."[21]

The Bifurcation of the Ordinary and Extraordinary

Thus, Wesley employed a conventional and convenient *ordinary-extraordinary* distinction regarding the work of the Spirit. For Wesley, the work of the Spirit in salvation was *ordinary*, meaning common, regular, and available to all at all times, while the miraculous gifts of the Spirit were not necessary for salvation and hence were *extraordinary* and not given to all. Wesley himself would claim no gift for himself, though in my estimation he operated in many. In a letter to a Rev. Mr. Downes, Rector of St. Michaels, Wood-street, he retorts, "I utterly disclaim the 'extraordinary gifts of the Spirit' than those

---

19. J. Wesley, "Letter to the Bishop of Gloucester," 155.

20. Owen, *Pneumatologia*, 11, 754; For example, see Edwards, "Love More Excellent Than Extraordinary Gifts of the Spirit," 8:157.

21. J. Wesley, "Farther Appeal to Men of Reason and Religion," 107.

that are common to all real Christians."[22] Later in the letter he elaborated on what *is* "common to all real Christians," "gospel-obedience and holiness of life," meaning, "all outward as well as inward holiness."[23]

We see the same logic in Wesley's "Farther Appeal to Men of Religion and Reason": "Neither do I confound the extraordinary with the ordinary operations of the Spirit. And as to your last inquiry, 'What is the best proof of our being led by the Spirit?' I have no exception to that just and scriptural answer which you yourself have given,—'A thorough change and renovation of mind and heart, and the leading a new and holy life.'" The true mark of the Spirit is holiness. Again, in "Letter to a Roman Catholic," he spells out the ordinary work of the office of the Holy Spirit. Wesley gives a shorthand for the order of salvation (*ordo salutis*), yet encapsulates it in holiness:

> I believe the infinite and eternal Spirit of God, equal with the Father and the Son, to be only perfectly holy in himself, but the immediate cause of all holiness in us; enlightening our understandings, rectifying our wills and affections, renewing our natures, uniting our persons to Christ, assuring us of the adoption of sons, leading us in our actions; purifying and sanctifying our souls and bodies, to a full and eternal enjoyment of God.[24]

Again, in his sermon "Scriptural Christianity," Wesley exclaimed that at Pentecost, "all were filled with the Holy Spirit." But were *all* given gifts of the Spirit?[25] No! Wesley countered "that even in the infancy of the Church, God divided them with a sparing hand."[26] How sparing, we ask? Wesley claimed, "Perhaps one in a thousand."[27] Then why did the church receive the Holy Spirit at Pentecost if it was not for the gifts? Wesley directly responds, "for a more excellent purpose than this, that . . . It was to give them (what none can deny to be essential to all Christians in all ages) . . . "[28] Then he lists the following *ordinary fruit*, setting them above the gifts of the Spirit: "the mind which was in Christ, those holy fruit of the Spirit . . . [love, joy, peace . . .] to enable them to crucify the flesh . . . and to walk as Christ also walked . . . "[29]

Wesley lists some of the *extraordinary* gifts of the Holy Spirit again in *The More Excellent Way* (1787): "healing the sick, prophesying, in the proper sense

22. J. Wesley, "Letter to Mr. Downes," 98.
23. J. Wesley, "Letter to Mr. Downes," 102.
24. J. Wesley, "Letter to a Roman Catholic," 82.
25. J. Wesley, "Scriptural Christianity," 37.
26. J. Wesley, "Scriptural Christianity," 38.
27. J. Wesley, "Scriptural Christianity," 38.
28. J. Wesley, "Scriptural Christianity," 38.
29. J. Wesley, "Scriptural Christianity," 38.

of the word, that is, foretelling things to come; speaking with strange tongues, and the miraculous interpretation of tongues," only to then speak of the *ordinary* gifts which would make us more "useful in our generation."[30] Wesley contended that ordinary gifts, such as "convincing speech" and the "gift of persuasion" should be coveted rather than a "demonstration of the Spirit and power."[31]

For the father of Methodism, the ordinary work of the Spirit (soteriological) was normative and preferable to the extraordinary work (the charismatic). Wesley defined and discerned a true movement of the Spirit not by demonstrations of power but by the fruit of holiness. Embedded in Wesley's bifurcation is what I am calling a "holiness hermeneutic," which is his method of interpreting and discerning whether a belief or a practice stems from the ordinary (normative) and essential (salvific) work of the Spirit. In this way, Wesley bifurcates and prioritizes certain ordinary works of the Spirit over extraordinary ones. A holiness hermeneutic is what prevents him from making gifts normative, as fruit is normative, and ultimately discounts him as a modern day charismatic. The *ordinary fruit* was available to all believers, and the *extraordinary* work, though available, was given on occasion to some but should not be hastily claimed or primarily pursued.[32] Anything more was enthusiasm.

This bifurcation appears to be an operative hermeneutical framework for Wesley when approaching the charismata and the question of their normativity. Free Methodist theologian Howard Snyder has also identified this bifurcation made by Wesley, claiming that Wesley made an unbiblical distinction, for example, when he divided the list of gifts in 1 Corinthians 12 between extraordinary or ordinary.[33] Wesley makes this bifurcation when commenting on certain "charismatic-related" passages in his *Explanatory Notes upon the New Testament*. Although Bengel's *Gnomon* was his source in this work, Snyder notes that Wesley "employs the ordinary/extraordinary distinction, in contrast to Bengel."[34] Under Acts 1:5, Wesley claims that all true believers will be baptized with the Holy Ghost, but adds that the "extraordinary gifts of the Holy Ghost also are here promised."[35] Wesley comments on Acts 8:15, the Samaritan Pentecost, that they might receive the Holy Ghost "in his miraculous gifts, or his sanctifying graces? Probably

---

30. J. Wesley, "Earnest Appeal to Men or Reason and Religion," 26.

31. J. Wesley, "More Excellent Way," 27.

32. J. Wesley, "More Excellent Way," 27.

33. Snyder, "Church as Holy," 14, 58.

34. Snyder, "Church as Holy," 28. See his notes.

35. J. Wesley, *Explanatory Notes upon the New Testament*, 393.

in both."[36] For Wesley, miraculous is another word for extraordinary in identifying the gifts, and "sanctifying graces" is a reference to one of the ordinary works of the Holy Spirit.

Again, in his *Notes* on 1 Cor 12:9, Wesley qualifies the gift of faith as an *extraordinary* trust as opposed to *common* saving faith. 1 Thess 1:5 declares that the word came with "power," the "Holy Spirit," and "with much assurance." Wesley adds that with the Holy Spirit, "neither are the extraordinary operations of the Holy Ghost ever wholly withheld."[37] Wesley is making a distinction in part between the *ordinary* accompaniment of the word with conviction and the *extraordinary* accompaniment with miraculous gifts. Also, in 1 Pet 4:10, "as everyone hath received a gift" is debated by Wesley to mean either *ordinary* or *extraordinary*, "although the latter seems primarily intended."[38] Throughout his *Notes*, Wesley makes similar distinctions with many other charismatic-related passages.

For Wesley, the use of the *ordinary-extraordinary* bifurcation substantiated the imperative of a holiness hermeneutic. However, Wesley's intent in bifurcating the work of the Spirit and prioritizing the Spirit's work was hardly to prohibit the display of the charismata among Methodists, which were frequently manifested. Prioritizing the Spirit's work served apologetic, soteriological, and pastoral purposes, as Wesley built a movement that raised disciples to be holy and responded to detractors who claimed he was an enthusiast. The holiness hermeneutic also provided a clear guideline for those, like Thomas Maxfield and George Bell, who did operate normatively, and then some, in the gifts of the Spirit.

I affirm the need for Wesley's holiness hermeneutic to prioritize holiness over gifting and to employ it as a method for discerning the spirits, especially during times of revival and awakening. However, I believe he could have asserted the holiness hermeneutic without making the unnecessary *ordinary-extraordinary* division of labor. Ultimately, I concur with Snyder, regardless of Wesley's pastoral intentions; his division of the work of the Spirit into ordinary and extraordinary categories is unscriptural. The fruit take precedent over the gifts, indeed. However, Wesley overplays the priority of holiness to the exclusion of charismatic normativity, which is unscriptural and unnecessary. This exclusion continues to this day in the Wesleyan Holiness movement where many have become cessationist, while

36. J. Wesley, *Explanatory Notes upon the New Testament*, 425.

37. J. Wesley, *Explanatory Notes upon the New Testament*, 754.

38. J. Wesley, *Explanatory Notes upon the New Testament*, 884.

others forbid speaking in tongues, prophecy, the miraculous, casting out demons, and other supernatural manifestations.[39]

Ultimately the ordinary-extraordinary bifurcation of the work of the Spirit is unscriptural and unnecessary.

3. "In theory," Wesley was not a charismatic.

Although Wesley and the early Methodists experienced a profusion of manifestations of the Spirit, Wesley never claimed to be endowed with apostolic or extraordinary (supernatural) gifts.[40] John Whitehead, in his early *Life of the Rev. John Wesley* (1739), quotes the scholarly Bishop Joseph Butler's critical remark to Wesley, "Sir, the pretending to extraordinary revelations and gifts of the Holy Ghost is a horrid thing, a very horrid thing." Wesley replied, "I pretend to no extraordinary revelations, or gifts of the Holy Ghost: none but what every Christian may receive, and ought to expect and pray for," referencing the ordinary work of salvation.[41] In a tract he wrote called "The Office and Operations of the Holy Spirit," the Bishop of Gloucester accused Wesley of claiming apostolic and miraculous gifts and being a false prophet and a fanatic—weighty accusations in the Enlightenment, the age of reason.[42] Wesley responded, "I do not pretend to any extraordinary measures of the Spirit.

39. Following the Azusa Street Revival, there was a radical break between Wesleyan Holiness and Pentecostal Christians over the doctrine of the Baptism with the Holy Spirit. The former group believed it was entire sanctification, while Pentecostals claimed it was for power with speaking in tongues as the initial evidence of the experience. Ever since, the two groups have had a fierce rivalry with Wesleyan Holiness institutions, not only forbidding speaking in other tongues and other operations of the Spirit like casting out devils, but also codifying such restrictions in their official denominational "manuals" and "disciplines." Recently, such strictures have loosened a bit in mainline Wesleyan Holiness denominations. However, more traditional groups like those institutions affiliated with the conservative Wesleyan Holiness movement, e.g., The Interchurch Holiness Convention, God's Bible School, Wesleyan Holiness Association of Churches, and others strictly forbid the practice of speaking in tongues.

40. Wesley and the early Methodists experienced supernatural visions, dreams, trances, angelic visitations, the prophetic, healing, and deliverance. They even witnessed divine judgment on those who opposed the movement, as some were stricken ill and even with death. However, Wesley never attributed his own supernatural manifestations to any particular gifts of the Holy Spirit. For more on the supernatural manifestations in Wesley and the early Methodist movement, see Xhemajli, *Supernatural*, 30–61; Jennings, *Supernatural Occurrences*; and Billman, *Supernatural Thread*.

41. Whitehead, *Life of John Wesley*, 2:120.

42. J. Wesley, "Letter to the Lord Bishop of Gloucester," 119.

I pretend to no other measure of it than may be claimed by every Christian minister,"[43] and later, "I claim no *extraordinary gift* at all."[44]

When confronted by the Bishop with the fact that Wesley claimed to pray for the sick and God healed them, Wesley did not deny the accounts but attributes being used in this work to the "providence of God," who "now hears and answers prayer, even beyond the ordinary course of nature."[45] Here, Wesley does not respond with false humility but with his consistent retort given throughout his ministry when so accused. Throughout the letter, Wesley affirms the supernatural work of the Spirit but deflects any claim to possessing an extraordinary gift of the Spirit. Wesley would not give his detractors further fodder for accusation. The healings were merely God's answer to prayer or the providence of God.

Although in my estimation, Wesley experienced the manifestation of the gifts, he did not believe or teach that the gifts of the Spirit were normative to the Christian life, but extraordinary and occasional. Simply, the Spirit's ordinary and primary work is salvific leading to sanctification and growth in grace, and for Wesley, this could occur without miraculous gifts given to the believer.[46]

His letter to Gloucester is revealing. Wesley claimed no extraordinary gifts for himself. Yet he acknowledged witnessing the supernatural on many occasions, even a "sudden deliverance of [one] John Hayden."[47] He could not attribute these events to natural cause. He surmised they were extraordinary, not the working of miracles through a person, but directly from God. He attributed the supernatural "to the extraordinary interposition of God."[48] In reference to supernatural events Wesley witnessed, as well as the deliverance of John Hayden, and one account of Wesley's own instant healing, Wesley testified:

> First, I acknowledge that I have seen with my eyes, and heard with my ears, several things, which to the best of my judgment, cannot be accounted for by the ordinary course of natural causes, and which, I therefore believe, ought to be ascribed to the "extraordinary interposition of God" . . . I cannot account

43. J. Wesley, "Letter to the Lord Bishop of Gloucester," 118.

44. J. Wesley, "Letter to the Lord Bishop of Gloucester," 125.

45. J. Wesley, "Letter to the Lord Bishop of Gloucester," 124.

46. J. Wesley, "Letter to the Lord Bishop of Gloucester," 148, 165. Wesley's ultimate response at the end of the letter to the Bishop of Gloucester that asked what the operations of the Holy Spirit were. Wesley pointed to the work of salvation as the work of the Holy Spirit and summed up those operations with sanctification listed first.

47. J. Wesley, "Letter to the Lord Bishop of Gloucester," 155.

48. J. Wesley, "Letter to the Lord Bishop of Gloucester," 155.

for either of these in a natural way. Therefore I believe they were both supernatural.[49]

In caring for the flock, pastor Wesley was also safeguarding against charismatic excesses like those he witnessed in the tongue-speaking French Huguenot prophets and in his own preachers, Thomas Maxfield and George Bell, self-proclaimed prophets and faith healers who spoke in tongues and flippantly predicted that the world would end on February 28, 1763.[50] Although Wesley's unbiblical bifurcation is not to be affirmed, its related holiness hermeneutic is profitable, especially as he applied it to problems in ministry. When understanding Wesley's use of this bifurcation of the work of the Holy Spirit, we need to not only interpret it in its soteriological and apologetic context, but also its pastoral context.

Father Wesley created an intentional, well-organized, systematic structure and regimen of accountability to facilitate a widespread revival that would spread over multiple continents and foster growth in grace among the faithful. He knew excesses would arise and the imperative to safeguard the flock. Wesley observed as in the case with Maxfield and Bell, and others like the French Prophets, that a push for the normative function of extraordinary gifts could be dangerous, leading to claims of impeccable perfectionism, antinomianism, and schism, as Maxfield separated from Wesley to start his own work.

As we have noted, clearly Wesley is not prohibiting the use of the gifts or claiming that they have ceased, though he sees their distribution as limited. He is exercising pastoral oversight and discernment by evaluating the fruit of the ministry. His conclusion was incisive and prophetic not just for his time but even for our day. It is scriptural to claim that both gifts and fruit should be normative in the life of the believer. However, the fruit of the Spirit manifested in one's life and ministry must be placed above gifts and offices of the Spirit, provided the environment from which they arise. Hence, this reinforces the importance of a holiness hermeneutic.

49. J. Wesley, "Letter to the Lord Bishop of Gloucester," 155.
50. See Newport and Lloyd, "George Bell."

Ultimately, Wesley claimed no extraordinary gift.

4. Wesley was a practicing charismatic.

Visions and Trances

Although Wesley and early Methodists did not teach or seek supernatural manifestations, they occurred rampantly, nonetheless. Dreams, visions, healing, and deliverance were quite common among the people called Methodists. On one occasion Wesley traveled to Everton and interviewed three persons who had claimed to experience trances and visions.[51] Upon interviewing them, Wesley discovered that they were all in agreement about when the trances occurred and the nature of the trances. When they "were in the fullest of the love of God" their senses and strength were taken away in an instance, and they felt transported to another world.[52] One afternoon, Wesley heard women singing hymns downstairs, and one Alice Miller fell into a trance.[53] They called on Wesley, who immediately came "to test the spirits." Seeing the young woman seated on a stool against the wall with her eyes open, Wesley feinted a blow toward her face. Her eyes did not move. Wesley writes:

> Her face showed an unspeakable mixture of reverence and love, while silent tears stole down her cheeks. Her lips were a little open, and sometimes moved, but not enough to cause any sound. I do not know whether I saw an human face look so beautiful . . . I observed her countenance change into the form of fear, pity, and distress; then she burst into a flood of tears, and cried out, "Dear Lord; they will be damned! They will all be damned! . . . Dear Lord, they will go to hell . . . Cry aloud! Spare not!" . . . "about seven her senses returned. I asked, "Where have you been?"—"I have been with my Saviour." "In heaven, or on earth?"—"I cannot tell; but I was in glory." "Why then did you cry?"—"Not for myself, but for the world; for I saw they were on the brink of hell" "Whom did you desire to give the glory to God?"—"Ministers that cry aloud to the world: else they will be proud; and then God will leave them, and they will lose their own souls.[54]

Wesley later describes a terrible vision of hell that a man, who was overthrown by sin and despair, received prior to his conversion:

51. During the Everton Revival. See J. Wesley, "Journal Entry for August 4, 1759," 509.

52. J. Wesley, "Journal Entry for August 4, 1759," 509.

53. J. Wesley, "Journal Entry for August 4, 1759," 509.

54. J. Wesley, "Journal Entry for August 4, 1759," 509.

When he found power to speak, he cried out, "I thought I had
led a good life; I thought I was not so bad as others; but I am the
vilest creature upon earth; I am dropping into hell! Now, now;
this very moment!" He then saw hell open to receive him, and
Satan ready to cast him in; but it was not long before he saw the
Lord Jesus, and knew he had accepted him. He then cried aloud
in an unspeakable rapture, "I have got Christ! I have got Christ!"
For two hours he was in the visions of God; then the joy, though
not the peace abated.[55]

The Methodist leader claims to have known several people who were
changed through visions and dreams of Christ on the cross or Christ seated
in glory.[56] Wesley did not judge the validity and origin based on the outward display of emotion, although it was present, but "from the whole tenor
of the life; till then many ways wicked, from that time holy and just, and
good."[57] He did not contend that visions or manifestations should be relied
upon for guidance. They needed to be tested "by the law and the testimony"
and the fruit produced.

Healing

Although Wesley never claimed to have the gifts of healing, he did see many
healed through what he attributed to the prayer of faith. Wesley believed God
was able to heal, and it was his providential will to heal. Wesley recalled several instances in a letter to the Bishop of Gloucester when God healed the sick
through his prayers.[58] Once when Wesley had a headache and his horse was
lame, he prayed for both and saw instant recoveries. Wesley went to visit a Mr.
Lunell, who had a violent fever. At the very moment he saw Wesley's presence,
he was revived and gradually recovered. Wesley prayed for one woman who
had been unable to talk for a long time. As soon as Wesley and others began
to pray, she was immediately healed and able to speak. A Mr. Meyrick was also
rendered "speechless and senseless." He received his healing while they were
still praying. Wesley prayed for many who had what he called "spotted fever,
which had been extremely mortal."[59] Every person prayed for was healed.

Healings occurred throughout early Methodism, especially through
the ministries of Thomas Maxfield and George Bell. Wesley witnessed that

55. J. Wesley, "Journal Entry for August 4, 1759," 504.

56. J. Wesley, "Letter to the Bishop of Gloucester," 142.

57. J. Wesley, "Letter to the Bishop of Gloucester," 142.

58. J. Wesley, "Letter to the Bishop of Gloucester," 123–24.

59. J. Wesley, "Letter to the Bishop of Gloucester," 124.

Bell had claimed many gifts of the Spirit, including discernment of spirits and prophecy (even predicting the end of the world).[60] In my estimation, both Maxfield and Bell closely resemble modern charismatics today. They frequently experienced manifestations of the Spirit and exhibited the gifts of the Spirit as normative. Often Maxfield and Bell would operate in the gifts and allow others under their leadership to do so.[61] Wesley often discerned that the fruit accompanying these revelations was "tinctured with enthusiasm"[62] and not of God and would prevent them.[63] Specifically, he was referring to "screaming when praying," a "heated imagination," "credulity," prophesying directly from God, end-time prophesying, impetuosity, "pride," and stirring up division against Wesley, among other misdeeds.[64]

Although extremely patient and yielding with both men, Wesley was pressed to the point of discouraging Maxfield and Bell from permitting these manifestations and even forbidding them to minister due to excesses.[65] On one occasion, when Wesley and others confronted Bell with his errors, they found that "they could make no impression upon him at all."[66] Bell was "as unmoved as a rock."[67] Both Maxfield and Bell frequently resisted Wesley's or anyone's correction.[68]

Wesley had his qualms about Bell, but he was present to investigate one alleged healing of hard lumps in a young woman's breasts. She had experienced the painful lumps for four years, when one began to discharge. She was admitted to St. George's Hospital and treated, but the situation became worse. The woman then attended a prayer meeting where Bell prayed for her. In a moment, both breasts were healed. The next day the woman

60. J. Wesley, "Journal Entries from November 22–26, December 4–26, 1762, and April 11, 1763," 122–24, 131–32.

61. J. Wesley, "Journal Entries from November 22–26, December 4–26, 1762, and April 9–15, 1763," 122–26; 131–32.

62. J. Wesley, "Journal Entries from November 22–26, December 4–26, 1762, and April 9–15, 1763," 123.

63. J. Wesley, "Journal Entries from November 22–26, December 4–26, 1762, and April 9–15, 1763," 123.

64. J. Wesley, "Journal Entries from November 22–26, December 4–26, 1762, and April 9–15, 1763," 122–32.

65. J. Wesley, "Journal Entries from November 22–26, December 4–26, 1762, and April 9–15, 1763," 122–32.

66. J. Wesley, "Journal Entries from November 22–26, December 4–26, 1762, and April 9–15, 1763," 125.

67. J. Wesley, "Journal Entries from November 22–26, December 4–26, 1762, and April 9–15, 1763," 125.

68. J. Wesley, "Journal Entries from November 22–26, December 4–26, 1762, and April 9–15, 1763," 126–27.

felt a little pain, but after she prayed, it went away. Wesley confirmed that both breasts were completely made whole in a moment.[69] Wesley writes of one of the most acute healings that he experienced in his own life.[70] He was in bed for nearly three days with a "disorder." He was seized with a cough that rendered him unable to speak in the presence of around two hundred people. At that point, he began to cry out to the Lord for an increase of faith. In that very instant, it was observed by all that Wesley had been delivered from the pain and sickness.[71]

In one instance recorded in his journal for December 15, 1742, Wesley prayed for a Mr. Meyrick, who was on his deathbed without a pulse. The attending physician claimed he could do no more for the man and announced that he would not make it through the night. Wesley and those assisting prayed until they began to see several responses; first his eyes opened, then his speech returned, and finally his strength. Wesley documents that Mr. Meyrick was restored to "perfect health."[72] It seems that this was a raising from the dead or something quite close. Wesley did not recollect other extreme cases such as this but did record numerous other healings by the hand of God as a result of prayer. In most cases, Wesley notes that these were accomplished "for the glory of God," to say, the healings were by God and for God.

Wesley on Deliverance

We will be examining more extensively the deliverance ministry of John Wesley and early Methodism in the next chapter. It is sufficient to say at this point that as the founder of Methodism bifurcated the work of the Spirit between ordinary and extraordinary work in terms of the gifts of the Spirit, he also bifurcates the work of deliverance. Through his teaching and preaching ministry, Wesley is introduced to deliverance ministry. He discovered that under the conviction of his preaching, people who were demonized would begin to manifest the evil spirits that were holding them in bondage. It was as if God, through the preaching of his Word, was exposing, judging, and even loosening the evil spirits that had been covertly residing in their hosts.

As the Word ministered conviction and people began to repent and turn to God, the demonic strongholds would begin to come down. Chains would snap. People were being freed, and battered demons were losing

---

69. J. Wesley, "Journal Entries from November 22–26, December 4–26, 1762, and April 9–15, 1763," 76–77.

70. J. Wesley, "Letter to the Bishop of Gloucester," 156.

71. J. Wesley, "Letter to the Bishop of Gloucester," 156.

72. J. Wesley, "Journal Entry for December 15, 1742," 406.

their grip and emerging to the surface. Saints then would gather around the bound and pray until the demons fully evacuated, and the person would find peace with God. Pastor Wesley and early Methodists encountered this scenario recurrently on the preaching field, in people's homes, at prayer and small group meetings, and at worship services. Though Wesley observed these manifestations and witnessed people be delivered through the Word and prayer, Wesley never claimed an extraordinary gift of exorcism or healing. He acknowledged and functioned through the ordinary means of prayer and faith in God.

CONCLUSION: AN ALMOST CHARISMATIC

So, what are the results of our DNA test? Is Wesley a charismatic? Did he hold to the belief and practice that the gifts of the Spirit are normative in the life of the believer or at least for himself? As much as I would like to view Wesley as a charismatic, Wesley did not seem to espouse or teach the notion that supernatural manifestations of the Spirit are normative for the believer, which characterizes PCR Christians. Yet, in practice, the *charismata* clearly operated through Wesley and the early Methodists in a regular or normative manner. That said, Wesley can be considered a charismatic on one of two counts, making him half a charismatic, or playing on Wesley's "an almost Christian," "an almost charismatic."

The issue for Wesley was not a matter of belief and practice of the supernatural. He clearly believed it and saw it work in his ministry. The question was the mode of delivery of the supernatural: gifts versus answered prayer. Would the supernatural occur primarily through the gifts of the spirit or by answered prayer? Wesley claimed and ministered the latter. Charismatics today would claim both but put a primacy on the gifts of the Spirit. This distinction alone prevents categorizing the father of Methodism as a modern day charismatic. He differed with charismatics on the normative means of delivery of the supernatural. Wesley held a more restrictive view of the gifts. He believed that they were still active but was convinced that their distribution was more restrained and selective.

Even though he acknowledged a continuationist position throughout his writings, at least in one place he was skeptical of their continuation or restoration.[73] He pens, "Whether these gifts of the Holy Ghost were designed to remain in the Church throughout all ages, and whether or no they will be restored at the nearer approach of the 'restitution of all things' are questions

---

73. Continuationism, contrasted with cessationism, contends that the supernatural gifts of the Spirit did not cease or pass away, but continue until the end of time.

which are not needful to decide . . . even in the infancy of the Church, God divided them with a sparing hand."[74] Following, Wesley elaborated on how sparing: "Perhaps not one in a thousand."[75]

On the other hand, Charismatics—with their view of Pentecost and the fulfillment of Joel's prophecy in Acts 2—hold a view that the latter-rain outpouring of the Spirit will democratize the Spirit's manifestations. God will abundantly pour out his Spirit on *all* flesh and give gifts to *everyone*, young and old, male and female, Jew and Gentile, slave and free. Everyone will be given a gift.[76] It will be an outpouring, not a drizzle.

Thus, we observe a stark distinction between Wesley and modern-day Charismatics in the breadth of distribution of the gifts of the Spirit: sparse versus abundant distribution. For Wesley, the Lord allocated gifts with only a "sparing hand." Where Wesley was reluctant to attribute spiritual giftedness, Pentecostals and Charismatics identify gifts in abundance, and even to a fault at times. But on the other hand, we note a sharp contrast between Wesley's safeguarding holiness hermeneutic used to test the spirits and the excesses found in *certain* quarters of the Charismatic movement that permits prosperity peddling, self-conferred, manufactured ministry titles, demonizing theological education, hollow diploma mill doctoral degrees, off-target end time prophecies, unbiblical manifestations like animal noises, and detecting a demon under every rock. The safeguards within early Methodism, including the holiness hermeneutic and small group accountability, wisely anticipated potential problems that immature believers may face regarding the gifts of the Spirit. Such problems would increase in direct proportion to the increase of spiritual manifestations, as can be observed across PCR history.[77]

The Apostle of Methodism was also reticent to claim any supernatural gifting in an age that questioned claims of divine intervention and fanaticism. He was leery of being labeled an enthusiast (an extremist), which was anathema for the time.[78] He observed such enthusiasm in Maxfield and Bell and abhorred it. More so he struggled with their unwillingness to be

74. J. Wesley, "Scriptural Christianity," 38.

75. J. Wesley, "Scriptural Christianity," 38.

76. Acts 2 and 1 Corinthians 12:7, "A spiritual gift is given to each of us so we can help each other." (NLT).

77. Unfortunately, PCR history is replete with ministers who operated powerfully in the gifts of the Holy Spirit but were mixed up in immorality, adultery, alcoholism, homosexuality, fraud, racism, false doctrine, false prophecy, or other sin, e.g., B.H. Irwin, Charles Parham, William Branham, A. A. Allen, Leroy Jenkins, Lonnie Frisbee, and Paul Cain, among others.

78. Webster, *Methodism and the Miraculous*, 72–73.

corrected. Their belief that they were gifted and anointed by God obscured any earnest self-examination. Pride had blinded them to their excesses. Maxfield and Bell at times embodied the best and worst of Charismatic Christianity. On one hand, as good Charismatics, they believed in the normative allocation and operation of the gifts of the Spirit for ministry. On the other hand, they failed to test the spirits and evaluate their manifestations based on Wesley's holiness hermeneutic. Their ministry embodied an irreconcilable tension of spiritual gifts and hyped-up carnality.

Unlike Maxfield and Bell, Wesley had a more modest view of the dissemination of gifts. He was therefore reluctant to claim them. Wesley underestimated God's willingness to disperse broadly his gifts among clergy and laity, so that everyone would be equipped with a gift(s). However, Wesley was a spiritual empiricist. He could accurately discern a work of the Spirit. In my estimation, if Wesley were alive post-Azusa Street Revival, he would have perceived the hand of God in the tidal wave of twentieth century Pentecostalism and would have accepted charismatic normativity, though still as secondary to holiness. A post-Azusa Wesley would have observed the profusion of gifts and miracles just as he viewed the abundance of conversions in his day and would have expected the same for himself and his ministry. Hence, he is not a charismatic in *today's* sense of the word, because he was born in a different time. But I consider him a *prepentecostal*, an antecedent, or a forebearer of what was to come. Calling him a flatout charismatic is anachronistic. But he was an eighteenth-century version of a charismatic, whatever that term may be: perhaps a (reasonable) "enthusiast."[79]

As scholars such as Donald Dayton, have evidently pointed out, Wesley (early Methodism) is a major root of American Pentecostalism.[80] The entire pneumatic dimension of early Methodism, its spiritual empiricism, the work of the Spirit throughout the *via salutis*, and its charismatic revivalism, is unmistakably a nascent or embryonic form that merged with later forms and evolved into the modern PCR movement.[81] Many, but not all, of the characteristics of early Methodism present an inchoate PCR Christianity. There are too many common traits and phenotypes to deny the family resemblance. The "charismatic" gene is carried out throughout the family line.

---

79. Rack, *Reasonable Enthusiast*, 536–40.

80. Dayton, *Theological Roots of Pentecostalism*, 15–86.

81. Dayton, *Theological Roots of Pentecostalism*, 15–86. The other four roots that ground (American) Pentecostalism are the nineteenth century American Holiness movement, the nineteenth century divine healing movement, the rise of Pentecostal language for Spirit baptism, and the rise of premillennialism.

LEARNING FROM A BALANCED WESLEY

The four inferences we have drawn from Wesley concerning the gifts of the Spirit further serve as correctives for a proper balance for Wesleyans of all stripes, who often neglect the miraculous power of God, and for today's PCR movement, which often lacks a robust doctrine of sanctification and sound theology for its supernatural experiences. Simply put, *all* the work of the Spirit should be *normative* in our lives, including the gifts and fruit of the Spirit. The Spirit gives gifts to and produces fruit in *every* true believer (1 Cor 12:7). No Christian should ever settle for anything less than the promises of God in Scripture. However, PCR Christians would do well to take heed of the Wesleyan corrective of a holiness hermeneutic in their theology and practice of the *charismata*. Biblically, fruit takes priority over gifts and should be the seedbed from which the gifts spring forth. Between the two chapters on the *charismata*, 1 Corinthians 12 and 14, is situated chapter 13, the more excellent way to minister the gifts, the way of love. We are to pursue earnestly the gifts as good charismatics but do so in love as those who prioritize God's holy love above seeking power.

On the other hand, Wesleyan Christians would do well to *not* make an unscriptural division of extraordinary and ordinary gifts, which results in denying their normative use in Scripture. Wesleyan Christians may be "underachieving" as a result and could use a charismatic upgrade to their faith.[82] 1 Corinthians 12:31 exhorts us to covet the gifts, as PCR believers indeed model well for us. How many times have people gone unchanged, unhealed, bound up, and defeated because some Wesleyan Christians eschew the miracle-working power of God and fail to minister in the gifts with the authority that Christ has given us to set the captives free?[83] We have educated, professional clergy who can exegete texts, argue for JEPD and Q, preach a hermeneutically and liturgically correct homily, explain the *filioque,* host a class for new members, and refer those with addictions,

82. Not meant to sound Pelagian but related to not walking in the miraculous power of God as we should be.

83. The Azusa Street revival and the ensuing Pentecostal movement in North America began primarily with holiness Christians. Pentecostalism, early on, drew heavily from the ranks of the Holiness movement, creating a divide between the two movements that in many ways has lasted until this day. Both movements claim a baptism of the Spirit. The Holiness movement contends the baptism of the Spirit is for entire sanctification, while Pentecostals claim it is a baptism of power with speaking in tongues as the initial evidence. Holiness denominations have officially opposed the initial evidence position since its incipience. Some Holiness denominations forbid the speaking in tongues in general, though among some these strictures have loosened a bit, i.e., the Wesleyan Church has recently acknowledged the gift but not as initial evidence nor is it for everyone.

mental disorders, and other challenges to the proper professionals for treatment and care, but *cannot* discern and cast out demons, heal the sick and impaired, operate in the gifts and power of the Spirit to set someone free and lead them to Christ, or prophesy to an ecclesial grave of dry bones.[84]

There is a power outage in our Wesleyan communities, mainline and holiness. We minister in much toil and self-effort, as if we were living in pre-electricity days. Flip the switch of faith and power up! Wesleyans could use more Holy Spirit dynamite (*dunamis*) in their ministry. The Holiness church needs a fresh baptism of the Holy Spirit and fire for the work that is before us. No more fireproof, asbestos-filled Christians who resist the Holy Spirit.

Yes, we need the fire but not to burn the church down—strange fire. We need the fire in the fireplace, so that it does not burn the house, or its inhabitants, but instead constructively heats up the house. We need balance, gifts, and fruit. The gifts are judged by the fruit from which they spring and the fruit that they bear. Ultimately, fruit and not gifts are a reflection of true spiritual growth, health, and maturity. Christ emphasized that a tree is judged and known by the fruit, particularly love. Our calling and gifting from God are irrevocable and not a sign of our salvation (Rom 11:29). Let us not be fooled. It is possible to operate in the gifts of the Spirit, while not walking in the fruit of the Spirit, like the Corinthian church. From Saul to Solomon to Judas, people who had fallen from a state of grace could still operate in the gifts of the Spirit.

Theoretically, one could display supernatural signs and wonders throughout their ministry, and yet it could still be possible to hear the final condemning words from Christ: "I never knew you." Simply, the fruit and not the gifts are the scriptural way in which the tree is judged to be good or evil. However, that does not mean the gifts are to be denied or relegated to the apostolic age or to charismatic superstars. The prophecy of Joel in Acts 2 declares that the power of the Spirit for service is poured out on *all* people. Today, Christians should walk in the same anointing, power, and authority that Christ and the apostles did because the same Holy Spirit and promises are given to us unto the end of the age. We should not quench the Spirit by forbidding speaking in tongues or despising prophecy, as Paul exhorts, or any other gift (1 Cor 14:9; 1 Thess 5:20–21). But in love, we should eagerly seek the gifts of the Spirit for the edifying of the Body of Christ and the work of the ministry.

84. Theories from source criticism on the origins of the Pentateuch and the synoptic gospels; *filioque* is Latin for "and through the Son" and was added by the West to the third article of the Nicene Creed on the Holy Spirit. Their objective was to disprove claims of subordinating the Son, though it some regard it also created further division between the church in the East.

4

Wesley on Ordinary and Extraordinary Means of Deliverance

ORDINARY AND EXTRAORDINARY BIFURCATION OF THE WORK OF THE SPIRIT

Although a significant segment of mainline Methodists today does not practice deliverance, encounter demons in their ministry, or even believe that demons exist (literally), the same cannot be said for Methodism's founder, John Wesley. Wesley not only acknowledged the existence of demons but often encountered them in his ministry. He did not profess to be an exorcist or claim special gifts for such a ministry. However, through ordinary Christian practices, such as preaching the Word, repentance, faith, prayer, and worshiping God, Wesley and early Methodists ministered deliverance to those in captivity.

As noted in the previous chapter, Wesley consistently made a distinction between the ordinary (soteriological) and extraordinary (charismatic) work of the Spirit with precedence given to the former. He prioritized fruit over gifts, holiness over power, and also utilized the fruit of holiness as an interpretive guide to ascertain the origin (divine or otherwise) and purpose of so-called extraordinary gifts. Wesley frequently bifurcated the work of the Spirit on the basis of what I call a "holiness hermeneutic." Wesley's ordinary-extraordinary distinction and related holiness hermeneutic allowed him to test, acknowledge, and permit the miraculous without normalizing it. Holiness was an ordinary work. Gifts were extraordinary and were given to serve the higher call of holiness. If the supernatural gift aligned with the Word and the greater service of scriptural holiness, then Wesley affirmed its divine origin.

Wesley's holiness hermeneutic prioritized and made normative the salvific work of the Spirit over the manifestation of the gifts of the Spirit. In this regard, he differs from modern charismatics who see both the work of salvation *and* the gifts as normative. This ordinary-extraordinary distinction will be key to understanding Wesley's method of deliverance. We recognized that although the ordinary-extraordinary distinction of the Spirit's work is unscriptural, it is vital that we prioritize fruit over gifts (holiness hermeneutic) in our discernment and practice of ministry.

WESLEY AND THE PARANORMAL AT EPWORTH

Regarding the existence of the devil, paranormal historian Owen Davies claims that Wesley adhered to "the old elite, theological conceptions of diabolism."[1] Simply put, Wesley held a scriptural view of the demonic that is confirmed throughout Christian tradition."[2] Satan and the hosts of hell, once angels in God's service, fell from grace and were cast down to earth. These fallen angels constitute a hierarchy of demonic powers that rule the kingdom of darkness. Neither the Bible nor I will attempt to *prove* in the Cartesian sense that demons exist. The Bible assumes it.[3] And I have seen too much in ministry that cannot be explained naturally or explained away. Although we would like to dismiss them, demons are neither myth nor metaphor but truly exist, and their mission is to tempt, deceive, and destroy the souls of women and men. We are called to watch, pray, and put on the whole armor of God so that we can resist Satan's attacks.

In terms of demonology, Wesley's view would not have been considered a product of Enlightenment rationalism, which would have dismissed the existence and operation of preternatural spirits. From early exposure to the paranormal, including "Old Jeffrey," the house ghost at Epworth, sister Anne Wesley's levitation experience, to later encounters with the demonic in ministry, Wesley acknowledged the existence of demons and the havoc

1. Webster, *Methodism and the Miraculous,* 72; Davies, "Methodism," 82, 264.

2. J. Wesley, "Of Evil Angels," 379–80.

3. The weight of an appeal to Scripture varies from Christian to Christian. Positions on the authority of Scripture range from inerrant, infallible, sufficient, divinely inspired, human inspired, partially inspired, errant, etc. I believe recognition of an invisible creation with angels and demons is a scriptural issue and a worldview issue. The supernatural will not register in certain worldviews, like a modern scientific one. Certain worldviews account for the supernatural with their own internal justification for such a belief.

they wreak on the human soul.[4] Old Jeffrey, so named by younger sister Emily, was the Wesley "family poltergeist" haunting the parsonage at Epworth for several decades.[5] The family members would regularly hear ghastly noises, clamoring, groans, voices, and unfastening of door locks coming from inside the parsonage.[6] Where else would one expect an evil spirit but in the parsonage of an Anglican minister?

Wesley's younger sister Anne wrote to him describing an incident when the bed, with their sister Nancy sitting on it, levitated, while Anne and her other four sisters and a girlfriend were playing cards. The girls identified the phenomenon as Old Jeffrey. Following, Anne maintained that the bed with Nancy upon it was lifted up again unaided several times even at a "considerable height."[7] Needless to say, they were all terrified. Some family members experienced physical assaults committed by unseen assailants.[8] Yes, typical kids' imagination, we cannot take it seriously, right? I have seen too often entry level witchcraft begin with children dabbling and experimenting with Ouija boards and levitation.[9] Susanna Wesley, hardly one given to enthusiastic imagination, wrote that Old Jeffrey could often be heard protesting more emphatically when prayers were lifted up for King William III. As expected, John tested the veracity of the claims and found them to be valid.[10] Later, Wesley would publish some of these accounts in his *Arminian Magazine*.[11] Early Methodist theologian Adam Clarke published them as well.[12] To some, these testimonies may

4. Webster, *Methodism and the Miraculous*, 70, 93.

5. Webster, *Methodism and the Miraculous*, 70, 93.

6. Webster, *Methodism and the Miraculous*, 70, 93.

7. Webster, *Methodism and the Miraculous*, 71.

8. Webster, *Methodism and the Miraculous*, 71.

9. In my experience in deliverance ministry, this has often been the case. Children, often girls, hear different old wives' tales and urban legends about magic, ghosts, talking to the dead, levitating, hypnosis, telekinesis, prayers to characters like Mary Worth, hexes, spells, and Ouija boards, and begin harmlessly to test them to see if they really work. Our culture also supplies their curiosity with a seemingly innocent array of books and movies centered around magic, the paranormal, the occult, and witchcraft. Children innocently experiment when parents are unaware. Demons are indifferent. They play for keeps. Often these events and encounters can easily become entry level demonization and witchcraft. Scripture clearly prohibits the practice of such: Exod 22:18; Lev 19:26,31; 20:6,27; Deut 18:10–14; 1 Chr 10:13; 1 Sam 15:23; 22:23; 2 Chr 33:6; Isa 8:19–22; 19:1–4; 47:8–14; Mic 5:10–12; Acts 8:9–13; 19:17–20; Gal 5:19–21; and Rev 18:23; 21:8; among others.

10. Webster, *Methodism and the Miraculous*, 71.

11. Webster, *Methodism and the Miraculous*, 93.

12. Webster, *Methodism and the Miraculous*, 93.

seem unbelievable, but these learned Methodists hardly considered the accounts to be fanciful or superstitious.

Later, Wesley would face more demonic encounters and have much to say about them. He crafted sermons on the topic, penned his encounters in his journals and letters, and combated the demonic in his ministry. He believed his view on the subject was grounded in Scripture and confirmed empirically by the reliable eye-witness testimonies of his day, including his own. Wesley's *Journals* and *Letters* are saturated with dozens of demonic encounters in his evangelistic and pastoral ministry (e.g., Oct. 25–28, 1739; Jan. 11, 1741; Jan. 13, 1743; June 5, 1753, and May 25, 27, 1768 among many others). This aspect of early Methodist lore is often ignored, demythologized, or reduced to an antiquated peculiarity held over from medieval demonology by scholars of Wesley and ministers of mainline Methodism.

WESLEY RESPONDS TO A CHARGE OF EXORCISM

Let us begin our inquiry into Wesley's deliverance ministry by getting straight to the question of whether Wesley claimed a gift of deliverance or exorcism. In a letter to the Bishop of Gloucester, Wesley defended himself against multiple accusations leveled by the Bishop. Of the many charges, one was that Wesley employed "exorcisms in form, according to the Roman fashion."[13] Wesley was being accused of practicing exorcism, as a Roman Catholic priest would. Wesley succinctly recalls the account:

> The short of the case is this: Two young women were tormented of the devil in an uncommon manner. Several serious persons desired my brother and me to pray with them. We, with many others did; and they were delivered. But where, meantime, were the "exorcisms in form, according to the Roman fashion?" I never used them: I never saw them: I know nothing about them.

Here, Wesley does not directly deny having a charism for exorcism. It seems his denial is using exorcism either of the Roman rite or any other form. However, the implication is that he is not claiming to perform an exorcism. But as he responds elsewhere in the letter, the Lord answered his prayer in an extraordinary or supernatural way and delivered the individual. He attributes the deliverance to prayer and the hand of God. This remains his position throughout the letter, responding to a host of charges. The thrust of his retort against the Bishop's accusations is that he claims *no* extraordinary gift but merely minsters in the ordinary operations of the Spirit. However, on

---

13. J. Wesley, "Letter to the Lord Bishop of Gloucester," 124.

occasion as God sees fit, the Lord answers prayer "beyond the ordinary course of nature" or the providence of God brings it to pass.[14] This modest posture is taken by Wesley throughout his ministry, claiming to possess no miraculous gift of the Spirit, including for deliverance. Yet, that does not hinder him from driving out demons in his evangelistic and pastoral ministry.

ORDINARY AND EXTRAORDINARY MEANS OF DELIVERANCE

Wesley not only believed demons exist and encountered them as well, but he also practiced deliverance in his ministry through what he would call "ordinary means." The father of Methodism employed the same ordinary-extraordinary distinction regarding the work of the Spirit to the practice of deliverance and exorcism. Wesley lists "casting out devils" as one of the chief *extraordinary* or spiritual gifts.[15] Casting out demons by "extraordinary means" involved the *gift* of faith. Wesley separated *ordinary*, saving faith from the gift of *extraordinary* faith that works miracles.[16] In his comment on Matthew 12:20, Wesley called this mountain-moving faith "a supernatural persuasion given a man, that God will work thus by him at that hour."[17] Consequently, by extraordinary faith, demons may be expelled directly. Although he did not lay claim to this gift, Wesley was convinced that ministers could also expel demons by *ordinary* means, such as *hearing the Word, repentance, prayer*, and *worship*. Wesley would employ these ordinary means in his deliverance ministry. In his sermon *A Caution Against Bigotry*, Wesley identified two of the *ordinary* means by which all ministers of Christ may cast out devils, *hearing the Word* and *repentance*:

> By the power of God attending his word, he brings these sinners
> to repentance; an entire inward as well as outward change from
> evil to all good. And this is, in a sound sense, to cast out devils
> out of the souls wherein they had hitherto dwelt.[18]

Striking demonic manifestations would accompany Wesley's deliverance ministry. Frequently, people under conviction were "thunderstruck" and dropped to the ground in spiritual combat by the power of the Spirit. "Thunderstruck" refers to God's 'thunder and lightning' judging sin and

14. J. Wesley, "Letter to the Lord Bishop of Gloucester," 124.

15. J. Wesley, "Letter to the Rev. Dr. Conyers Middleton," 16.

16. J. Wesley, *Notes on the New Testament* , Matt 7:22.

17. J. Wesley, *Notes on the New Testament,* Matt 12:20.

18. J. Wesley, "Caution Against Bigotry," 483.

Satan. These encounters were attended by all sorts of peculiar demonic manifestations, such as howling, groaning, roaring, convulsing, speaking in strange voices, and other eerie expressions. However, the result in most cases was repentance, deliverance, and peace with God.

In an April 17, 1739, journal entry, Wesley was preaching from Acts chapter 4, when he asked the Lord to "confirm" his Word. At that very moment, an individual cried out in "the agonies of death."[19] Wesley and the others present continued fervently in prayer. Two others then joined in, "roaring for the disquietness of their heart."[20] Not long after, all three found rest. The latter two broke out in praise, and the former was "overwhelmed with joy and love, knowing that God had healed his backslidings."[21]

While Wesley was preaching at Newgate, several people:

> dropped on every side as thunderstruck. One of them cried aloud. We besought God in her behalf, and he turned her heaviness into joy. A second being in the same agony, we called upon God for her also; and he spoke peace into her soul. In the evening I was again pressed in spirit to declare, that "Christ gave himself a ransom for all." And almost before we called upon him to set to his seal, he answered. One was so wounded by the sword of the Spirit, that you would have imagined she could not live a moment. But immediately his abundant kindness was showed, and she sang of his righteousness.[22]

Thunderstruck! Wesley perceived that the Spirit of God, human will, and demonic powers were all active and engaged during these conflicts. He understood these occurrences as primarily a work of the Holy Spirit, battling against the enemy to claim the person's soul. Through the preached word, the sword of the Spirit exposes and penetrates the shackled heart. The blow to the stronghold of darkness causes the persons to fall to the ground, or as Wesley frequently described it, they were, "thunderstruck," which is quite a graphic description for an even-tempered man not prone to hyperbole. The battered enemy refuses to release the soul from its clutches. After much convulsing (demonic) and supplicating, the individual finds repentance and relief. Wesley identified these struggles as the "chief times at which Satan is cast out."[23] *With that clear, succinct statement, he acknowledges what is occurring is actually deliverance.* Wesley also

19. J. Wesley, "Journal Entry for April 17, 1739," 187.

20. J. Wesley, "Journal Entry for April 17, 1739," 187.

21. J. Wesley, "Journal Entry for April 17, 1739," 187.

22. J. Wesley, "Journal Entry for April 17, 1739," 188–89.

23. J. Wesley, "Journal Entry for July 19, 1759," 502.

often used an image of the sword of the Spirit 'wounding and healing' the sinner. One was "struck through, as with a sword, and fell trembling to the ground."[24] As Wesley would preach, "God was present, both to wound and to heal."[25] Wound sin and Satan! Heal the soul! The imagery is graphic and violent but appropriate for a battle account.

In his letter to the Bishop of Gloucester, Wesley quotes the Bishop, who is quoting Wesley recounting an instance of a "mass deliverance" during Wesley's preaching. 'Mass deliverance' was a phenomenon that frequently occurred during Wesley's field preaching.[26]

> those who had lately cried out aloud during the preaching. I found this had come upon every one of them in a moment, without any previous notice. In that moment they dropped down, lost all their strength, and were seized with a violent pain. Some said they felt as if a sword were running through them; others, as if their whole body was tearing to pieces. These symptoms I can no more impute to any natural cause, than to the Spirit of God. I make no doubt it was Satan tearing them as they were coming to Christ.[27]

Wesley speaks directly: "Those outward symptoms which I had met with before, bodily agitations in particular, I did not ascribe to the Spirit of God, but to the natural union of soul and body. And those symptoms which I now ascribe to the devil, I never ascribed to any other cause."[28]

Wesley's commentary on the violent dynamics of being thunderstruck suggests that the Spirit of God works conviction through the preached word.[29] The sword of the Spirit pierces the heart and strikes the devil. The person attempts to turn to Christ in repentance. The devil violently digs his clutches into the heart of the person, desperately attempting to maintain his stronghold. Since the body is connected to the soul, in Wesley's view, there are collateral effects in the body. The person shrieks in pain, cries out, loses balance, and drops to the ground while shuddering, until eventually they are delivered.

24. J. Wesley, "Journal Entry for July 30, 1739," 213.

25. J. Wesley, "Journal Entry for April 16, 1773," 490.

26. These were frequent during field preaching. Instead of a one-on-one ministry situation, many would receive deliverance at the same and different times throughout his preaching.

27. J. Wesley, "Letter to the Lord Bishop of Gloucester," 143–44.

28. J. Wesley, "Letter to the Lord Bishop of Gloucester," 144.

29. The circuit riders frequently witnessed the same phenomena in frontier American Methodism in the nineteenth century. It was popularly known as the "Knock-'Em-Down," another colorful phrase to describe this peculiar manifestation of the Spirit. see Xhemajli, *Supernatural*, 151–58.

While Wesley witnessed deliverance through *preaching* and *repentance*, he also witnessed deliverance through other ordinary means of grace, such as *prayer* and *worship*. In a journal entry for October 1, 1763, Wesley records a powerful four-and-a-half-hour deliverance session that ended with a woman being set free through corporate prayer and singing.[30] For years, the woman was haunted by a demon that tormented and tempted her to kill her father and herself. She unsuccessfully attempted to commit suicide on several occasions. She would often throw raging, violent fits until her brother had her fitted for a "strait waistcoat" that meticulously bound her limbs together and to her bed. Nonetheless, with uncanny strength, she often broke free effortlessly with a mere twisting of her limbs. Her doctor concluded that her condition was "partly natural, partly diabolical."[31]

One day Wesley came to visit her. He interviewed the woman. She claimed to be possessed of the devil and did not want prayer. Wesley prayed anyway. She convulsed and began to scream in agony, swearing, cursing, and blaspheming God.[32] Wesley did not stop praying until the convulsion and screaming ceased. Two days later, he followed up. Although more lucid and able to pray, the woman still insisted that the devil was going to kill her. Wesley exhorted her to have faith and continued to intercede.

Later, Wesley led a group from 10:30 in the evening until 3:00 in the morning to pray for her deliverance. She was once again restrained and strapped to the bed. She began to roar, convulse, and "bark like a dog." Wesley painstakingly described her demonic manifestations. Her face was grossly distorted. Her mouth stretched from one side of her face to the other, and her eyes were crossed and bulging out of the sockets. Her convulsing throat and body were swollen as if she would burst.[33] The intercession went on into the morning. Several individuals left, unable to sustain the exhausting battle. Along with the straps of the waistcoat, four men sought to hold the woman down with all their strength (reminiscent of the Gadarene man).

The more that they prayed, the more violent she became. Suddenly, she had a vision of the tormenting demon and began to cry out to God. Then, the group felt led to worship and sing. The Spirit fell mightily. She continued to cry out for deliverance and the power to believe. Immediately, she became quiet.[34] Wesley invited her to sing a hymn with the words,

30. J. Wesley, "Journal Entry for October 1, 1763," 148–51.

31. J. Wesley, "Journal Entry for October 1, 1763," 148–49.

32. J. Wesley, "Journal Entry for October 1, 1763," 149.

33. J. Wesley, "Journal Entry for October 1, 1763," 150.

34. J. Wesley, "Journal Entry for October 1, 1763," 151.

"O Sun of Righteousness, arise
With healing in the wing;
To my diseased, my fainting soul
Life and salvation bring."

At 2:30 a.m., the demon said he would kill the woman, but "instead of a tormentor, he sent a comforter. Jesus appeared to her soul and rebuked the enemy . . . and she mightily rejoiced in the God of her salvation," Wesley exclaimed![35] She was fully delivered, set free, and saved through the power of intercession and song.

A BRIEF ANALYSIS OF WESLEY'S 'ORDINARY' METHODS

Even though Wesley employed no extraordinary gift but used what he termed ordinary means for deliverance, the woman was set free. To this supernatural work of God, Wesley would normally respond in this manner: "I believe God now hears and answers prayer, even beyond the ordinary course of nature."[36] Wesley simply believed that through prayer God would perform supernatural or extraordinary works. So, Wesley accessed the supernatural not by gift but by prayer. In deliverance, Wesley sought the move of God through ordinary means (prayer) rather than exercising a gift of faith, discerning of spirits, or a gift of healing. His method stemmed from his ordinary-extraordinary distinction and his reticence to claim the later. Nonetheless, the Apostle of Methodism believed and witnessed the supernatural work of God!

With nearly four decades of deliverance ministry, I resonate with the demonic encounter Wesley describes. Although it may seem exaggerated and dramatic to those unfamiliar with such confrontations, this was actually a normal deliverance session. All the usual manifestations of a prolonged deliverance session were present: bodily contortions, preternatural strength, screaming, speaking with another's voice, animal sounds, swelling and bloating of the body and throat, visions of the demonic, demonic threats to kill, self-mutilation, and violent manifestations increasing with prayer.

To combat the demonic attack in this and in other sessions, Wesley employed common means of grace, such as the Word of God, repentance, prayer, and worship. These elements are key to any successful deliverance session. I have used these same ordinary means in my ministry and have

---

35. J. Wesley, "Journal Entry for October 1, 1763," 151.

36. J. Wesley, "Letter to the Lord Bishop of Gloucester," 124.

found them to be scriptural, essential, and effective in deliverance. Like Wesley, I consider these *ordinary* means available to any believer, making deliverance ministry a *normative Christian practice*. Further, I also qualify these means as *indirect*. They are *indirect* because the minister is not *directly* addressing the devil during the deliverance process, such as, "*I* cast you out, spirit of fear, in the name of Jesus." Rather, Wesley's methods were indirect (Jude 9).

He indirectly faced the devil by directly supplicating God or preaching his Word. Wesley did not confront the devil directly, using the name of Jesus to face demons directly. However, Scripture is clear in Luke 10:18–20 and in a host of other passages that we have been given authority and power to cast out demons *directly* using the name of Jesus. In fact, we have been equipped with an arsenal of weapons, such as the cross, the blood, the armor of God, and the virtue of humility. Some believers are also given extraordinary means (gifts), such as gifts of faith, healing, or discerning of spirits for deliverance. Know that we can *indirectly or directly* face and overcome the demonic, through so-called *ordinary* or *extraordinary* means, just as Christ and his disciples did (Matt 10:8; Luke 10:18–20).

We are *all* called to set the prisoners free. We are *all* called to minister deliverance when the need arises. Each of us has been given authority to cast out demons in Jesus' name: "And those who believe shall use my authority to cast out demons" (Mk. 16:17). Do you believe it? Will you use the authority in Jesus' name given to you to put Satan under your feet and even drive out evil spirits from those who are oppressed? Or are you still living in unbelief and fear? Or perhaps you think the duty belongs to someone else? Those who have ears, hear the call of the Spirit to empower you to bind the strong man of the house and liberate the captives.

5

Thunderstruck! God's Judgment and Demonic Manifestations

As with Christ and his disciples, deliverance was an essential component to Wesley's evangelistic and pastoral ministry. John Wesley and many early Methodists had fruitful deliverance ministries that effectively drove demons out of oppressed souls. The founder of Methodism was convinced that ministers could, without any special gift, expel demons by *ordinary* means, such as *hearing the Word, repentance, prayer*, and *worship*. Wesley would employ these ordinary means of grace in his deliverance ministry. In the previous chapter, we examined Wesley's so-called ordinary means of deliverance and the various demonic manifestations he faced. In this chapter, we will identify and analyze that peculiar manifestation of deliverance that occurred in Wesley's ministry, "being thunderstruck" or "falling out in the Spirit."

DELIVERANCE, THUNDERSTRUCK, AND BEING 'SLAIN IN THE SPIRIT'

Frequently accompanying Wesley's ministry of deliverance was a phenomenon that today is often called being "slain in the Spirit," which Wesley called being "thunderstruck," simply, a power encounter. For example, while Wesley was preaching at Newgate, several persons:

> dropped on every side as thunderstruck. One of them cried aloud. We besought God in her behalf, and he turned her heaviness into joy. A second being in the same agony, we called upon God for her also; and he spoke peace into her soul. In the

evening I was again pressed in spirit to declare, that "Christ gave himself a ransom for all." And almost before we called upon him to set to his seal, he answered. One was so wounded by the sword of the Spirit, that you would have imagined she could not live a moment. But immediately his abundant kindness was showed, and she sang of his righteousness.[1]

Analyzing the description of "thunderstruck" in these narratives and witnessing many slain in the Spirit, I have come to the conclusion that they are *not* exactly the same phenomenon. I propose making a distinction between the two terms, "thunderstruck" and "slain in the Spirit," based on the *state* of those being "thunderstruck" and their *contexts*.[2] Though there are similarities, both are of the Spirit, and both result in dropping to the ground, phenomenologically, they are clearly distinct. I speak as someone who has been on the giving and receiving end of being "slain in the Spirit" and having witnessed many "thunderstruck" in my ministry as well.

Being "thunderstruck" in Wesley's day seemed to be related to an *unbeliever's* or a *backslidden* believer's repentance and deliverance from the demonic. I am highlighting that the recipient was bound in sin, which is what I discovered in Wesley's narratives. Being "slain in the Spirit" in today's church is often connected to a *believer* in the context of worship. I highlight that the recipient is a believer. My simple analysis of the *slain* phenomenon is that the mind is "short-circuited" by the powerful, euphoric presence of God, and they "fall out" under the anesthesia of the Spirit. In that sedate state, God often speaks intimately to the person's heart, ministers healing, and/or performs a deeper gentle work of the Spirit. This is the testimony of thousands. The event is usually quite peaceful and characterized by quietness and stillness. This is not the case with being thunderstruck.

The two phenomena are distinct. "Thunderstruck" is related to deliverance from sin and the demonic and is often unsettling and forceful. The person reacts almost involuntarily with convulsions, screaming, and quaking. Conversely, "slain in the Spirit" is related to worship, which can open the door to healing and receiving other gifts such as words, visions, or prophecy. Rather than a disquieting experience, being "slain," ironically, is actually a peaceful experience. I believe both types occurred in Wesley's day and today, though most of what Wesley documents is the "thunderstruck" type.

1. J. Wesley, "Journal Entry for April 17, 1739," 188–89.

2. Many in my estimation erroneously conflate the two experiences and contend that they are the same thing. They would identify being "thunderstruck" as being "slain in the Spirit." For an example see Xhemajli, *Supernatural*, 48.

We notice "thunderstruck" phenomena throughout Wesley's *Journals* and *Letters* and the journals of other early Methodists. Is this phenomenon biblical? In certain places in the Old and New Testaments, though debatable, there seems to be something loosely related to being either thunderstruck or slain in the Spirit (see 1 Kgs 8:11, 2 Chr 5:14, Ezek 1:28, Luke 8:28, John 18:6, Rev 1:17). In Scripture and in revival history, there are accounts of both unbelievers and believers "falling as dead" under God's power.[3] Sometimes the "slaying" is related to the overwhelming presence of the glory of God. This was the case when the priests in Solomon's day could not enter the temple or would fall prostrate to the ground because of the majesty and heaviness of God's holy presence. In this sense, being slain in the Spirit is connected to a believer's worship of an awesome and holy God.

On the other hand, the presence of God has a different effect on an unbeliever or one bound. For example, the Gadarene demoniac fell to the ground at Jesus' presence (Luke 8:28), and the demon(s) spoke out in fear regarding the day of judgment and identified themselves by name. In John 18:6, we see the officers of the Temple thrown back at the power of Jesus' word, when they came to arrest him. I would categorize these occurrences as being "thunderstruck" since the recipients are in an unregenerated or sinful state and encounter the power of God as judgment against evil. Similarly, in Wesley's time, it seems that the "thunderstruck" phenomenon occurred more in unbelievers or those bound in sin and was related to the conviction of sin with its internal struggle against the stronghold of darkness.

As we know, Wesley understood that the *ordinary* and *indirect* means of casting out demons by the preached Word of God could bring one to repentance. He did not confront demons directly using the name of Jesus. Nonetheless, Wesley's method of using the ordinary means got the job done. Here are some more notable examples of being "thunderstruck":

> Some said, they felt as if a sword was running through them; others, that they thought a great weight lay upon them, as if it would squeeze them into the earth. Some said, they were quite choked, so that they could not breathe; that their hearts swelled ready to burst: Others that it was as if their heart, as if their inside, as if their whole body, was tearing all to pieces. I can make no doubt, but it was Satan tearing them, as they were coming to Christ.[4]

3. Wesley's contemporaries George Whitefield and Jonathan Edwards witnessed the phenomenon, as did Charles Finney, Peter Cartwright, and others later in the Second Great Awakening and the Cane Ridge Revival of 1801.

4. J. Wesley, "Journal Entry for March 12, 1743," 415.

And now the arrows of God flew abroad. The inexpressible groans, the lamenting, praying, roaring, were so loud, almost without intermission, that we who stood without could scarce help thinking all in the church were cut to the heart.[5]

One sunk down, and another, and another. Some cried aloud in agony of prayer. One young man, and one young woman were brought with difficulty . . . and continued there in violent agonies, both of body and soul . . . the bodily convulsions of young man were amazing: the heavings of his breast were beyond description; I suppose, equal to the throes of a woman in travail. We called upon God to relieve his soul and body: And both were perfectly healed.[6]

In other instances, Wesley and others used the phrase "fell down as dead" to describe the phenomenon. Wesley writes, "While I was speaking, one before me dropped down as dead, and presently a second and a third"[7] And again:

That evening six were wounded and fell to the ground, crying aloud for mercy. One of them, hearing the cry, rushed through the crowd to see what was the matter. He was no sooner got to the place than he dropped down himself, and cried as loud as any. The other three pressing on, one after another, were struck just in the same manner. And indeed all of them were in such agonies that many feared they were struck with death. But all the ten were fully delivered before the meeting concluded.[8]

On some occasions, when persons were persecuting, mocking or opposing God or early Methodist preachers, they were stricken but did not fall down *as* dead. They just fell down dead or sick. Wesley interpreted it as God's hand of judgment![9]

I preached at Darlaston, late a den of lions, But the fiercest of them God has called away, by a train of "surprising strokes." But not by me, I was not there.[10]

---

5. J. Wesley, "Journal Entry for July 22, 1759," 506.

6. J. Wesley, "Journal Entry for August 28, 1759," 511–12.

7. J. Wesley, "Journal Entry for July 22, 1759," 506. Presumably from John Walsh.

8. J. Wesley, "Journal Entry for June 4, 1772," 471.

9. J. Wesley, "Letter to the Lord Bishop of Gloucester," 124–25.

10. J. Wesley, "Letter to the Lord Bishop of Gloucester," 124.

I preached at R, late a place of furious riot and persecution; but quiet and calm, since the bitter Rector is gone to give an account of himself to God.[11]

Hence we rode to T-n, where the Minister was slowly recovering from a violent fit of the palsy, with which he was struck immediately after he had been preaching a virulent sermon against the Methodists.[12]

One of the chief of those who came to make the disturbance on the First instance hanged himself.[13]

Mr. C spoke so much in favor of the rioters that they were all discharged. A few days after, walking over the same field, he dropped down, and spoke no more.[14]

Mr. S, while he was speaking to the society against my brother and me, was struck mad.[15]

I was informed of an awful providence. A poor wretch, who was here last week, cursing and blaspheming God, and labouring with all his might to hinder the Word of God, has afterwards boasted, he would come again on Sunday, and no man should stop his mouth then. But on Friday God laid his hand on him, and on Sunday he was buried.[16]

At Wapping, Wesley had prepared to preach on Romans 3:19 but could not open his mouth. He sought God for immediate direction. He was unsure what to preach. Wesley opened the Bible to Hebrews 10:19 and began to read and apply the passage:

While I was earnestly inviting all sinners to enter into the holiest by this new and living way, many of those that heard began to call upon God with strong cries and tears. Some sunk down, and there remained no strength in them; others exceedingly trembled and quaked: Some were torn with a kind of convulsive motion in every part of their bodies, and that so violently, that

11. J. Wesley, "Letter to the Lord Bishop of Gloucester," 124.
12. J. Wesley, "Letter to the Lord Bishop of Gloucester," 124–25.
13. J. Wesley, "Letter to the Lord Bishop of Gloucester," 125.
14. J. Wesley, "Letter to the Lord Bishop of Gloucester," 125.
15. J. Wesley, "Letter to the Lord Bishop of Gloucester," 134.
16. J. Wesley, "Letter to the Lord Bishop of Gloucester," 135.

> often four or five persons could not hold one of them . . . one
> woman greatly offended . . . also dropped down in as violent an
> agony as the rest . . . Twenty -six of those who had been affected
> . . . were in a moment filled with peace and joy.[17]

Wesley goes on to describe the experience of others that did not experience deliverance:

> But a few gave a more intelligible account of the piercing sense
> they then had of their sins., both inward and outward, which
> were set in array against them round about; of the dread they
> were in of the wrath of God, and the punishment they had de-
> served, into which they seemed to be just falling, without any
> way to escape. One of the told me, "I was as if I was just falling
> down from the highest place I had ever seen. I thought the devil
> was pushing me off, and that God had forsaken me." Another
> said, "I felt the very fire of hell already kindled in my breast;
> and all my body was in as much pain, as if I had been in a fiery
> furnace."[18]

In most of these cases cited, persons are smitten with the Word of God
and led into repentance by God's Spirit. Along the way, they experience
tumultuous and even violent manifestations before they ultimately find deliverance and peace with God. One cannot help but ask if all these intense
phenomena are necessary, and if so, for what purpose?

WHAT IS THE PURPOSE OF BEING THUNDERSTRUCK?

What do all these manifestations mean? Wesley often determined the purpose of these manifestations by their *outcome*. A holiness hermeneutic is
employed to discern the origin and purpose of these experiences. Wesley
believed these "thunderstruck" encounters had a divine purpose. Regardless of the unsettling nature of the manifestations, if the result of hearing
the Word of God was repentance, prayer, deliverance, and salvation, then
Wesley determined that it was a work of God. Wesley interpreted this thunderstruck phenomenon as a complex, multifaceted battle that involves the
inward work of God on the human will, as well as demons thrashing the
soul, and the soul struggling to be loosed from the devil, who is ripping at
both the soul and body.[19] These thunderstruck power encounters are similar

17. J. Wesley, "Letter to the Lord Bishop of Gloucester," and *Wesley's Journals*, 3: 204.

18. J. Wesley, "Letter to the Lord Bishop of Gloucester," 136–37.

19. J. Wesley, "Letter to the Lord Bishop of Gloucester," 142–44, and, John Wesley,

to the experience of the boy in the gospels who the demon tried to throw into the fire. The demon would slam him to the ground, throw him into convulsions, and would maul and batter his body before Jesus delivered him (the prayer and fasting type) (Mt. 17:14–18; Mk. 9:14–29; Luke 9:37–43).

It appears that God's Spirit would penetrate the human heart through the preached Word. The person would respond by attempting to draw near to Christ in their quest for repentance. The enemy would "tear," or strike, at them as they came closer to Christ, trying to thwart their advance.[20] After this long bout of accompanying "convulsions," "roaring," and much "agony," the penitent person would find deliverance, salvation, and peace. Wesley seemed to understand that an interior war for the soul was taking place between God's Word in the human heart and the enemy's tormenting stronghold of sin, with the body often suffering as a casualty, collateral effects of a spiritual clash.

In trying to make sense of this complicated phenomenon, Wesley explained, "if the mind be affected to such a degree, the body must be affected by the laws of the vital union. The mind I believe was, in many of those cases, affected by the Spirit of God, in others by the devil, and in some by both; and, in consequence of this, the body was affected also."[21] In his letter to Dr. Rutherforth, Wesley concisely states; "I speak of them as outward symptoms which have often accompanied the inward work of God."[22] In another words, being thunderstruck seems to be the collateral effect of God's power colliding with the kingdom of darkness and felt by the penitent sinner in both body and soul, a power encounter. Falling to the ground is not the goal but a side effect of the deliverance encounter. Meanwhile, Satan is not only attempting to hold on to the individual but is battering them along the way. Simply, to be thunderstruck is when God's thunder and lightning judge sin and Satan. One may wonder why someone must go through this 'abuse.' Why perform deliverance? Well, a person doesn't have to give their sin and demons up. They can permit them to abuse them quietly and stealthily their whole life. There is no easy way out! Satan comes to steal, kill, and destroy! If 'thunderstriking' was the way Christ ministered deliverance to the child, then there was no better way for it to be done.

Some deliverances transpire effortlessly without problems. Others can be complicated and drawn out, like long surgeries. In this sense, I would compare spiritual deliverance to delivering a child (as an observer,

---

"Letter to Reverend Dr. Rutherforth," 357–58.

20. J. Wesley, "Letter to the Lord Bishop of Gloucester," 144.

21. J. Wesley, "Letter to the Lord Bishop of Gloucester," 142.

22. J. Wesley, "Letter to Reverend Dr. Rutherforth," 357.

obviously). Pushing, heavy breathing, roaring, convulsions, and pain can accompany childbirth, and at times can accompany the new birth as well. Being thunderstruck and similar manifestations are merely new birth pains. Thus, to be thunderstruck, in itself, is not the goal to be sought by the minister or the seeker. Deliverance and redemption are the goals. But at times, there are other collateral effects, like thunder, lightning, and quaking, that manifest when hell is shaken, and a new creation is birthed!

Christ made it clear to the disciples that peripheral effects of deliverance, such as demonic manifestations, giftings, demonstrations of authority and power, or triumphant feelings of elation following the battle are not grounds for boasting or celebration. The pastoral goal is to deliver a soul from death to life.

INDIRECT AND DIRECT MEANS OF DELIVERANCE

In the previous chapter, I distinguished between John Wesley's *ordinary and extraordinary* means of deliverance. He identified *ordinary* means, such as the Word of God, prayer, repentance, faith, and worship, in contrast to the extraordinary, or charismatic, means. Another distinction occurs between *indirect* and *direct* means. Wesley's *ordinary* means were *indirect*, meaning that he usually did not directly address the devil and cast out demons with a first-person formula or command, using the name of Jesus, such as, "I cast you out, spirit of rage, in the name of Jesus!"[23] Instead, Wesley's ordinary means *indirectly* addressed the demonic by directly addressing God through prayer, faith, or worship.

I believe that Wesley's *ordinary* and *indirect* means are vital components of a deliverance ministry. I have found them effective as Wesley did. However, I would add that there are also ordinary *direct* means, such as using authority in the name of Jesus. And there are *extraordinary-direct* means, such as utilizing the gifts of healing or discerning of spirits. Wesley did not employ the *ordinary-direct* means of authority in the name of Jesus. Nor did he claim an *extraordinary* gift for deliverance, such as faith, which Wesley considered a gift that could be used for exorcism. There is more than one way to fillet a fish!

23. Jude 9, "The Lord rebukes you [Satan]!"

THE ORDINARY-DIRECT AND EXTRAORDINARY-DIRECT MEANS

Let us review. We have examined Wesley's methodology for the Spirit's gifting and deliverance. We have judged that his ordinary-extraordinary bifurcation of the gifts of the Spirit is unscriptural. But is it unscriptural as applied to deliverance? We have established that casting out demons is a work that is expected, available, and common to *all* believers. Christ has given authority to all members of his church to cast out demons, both through indirect and direct means. So, is deliverance ever extraordinary?

Gifting, in general, we resolved in chapter 4, is not extraordinary but ordinary. Gifts are given to everyone. Gifts as a whole are ordinary, and their use should be normative in the body of Christ. But *specific* gifts may be extraordinary. Not everyone has *every* gift (1 Cor 12:29–30). Not everyone has the gifts that are used for deliverance, such as faith, discerning of spirits, and healing. So, in this sense gifting for deliverance is extraordinary, but not the practice of deliverance in general, which is ordinary through indirect or direct means. Thus, in terms of *specific* gifts, Wesley's ordinary-extraordinary distinction is scriptural but not for gifting in general. Gifts are normative. Gifts are for everyone. They are not extraordinary. *Particular* gifts, though, are selective as the Spirit chooses (1 Cor 12:11). Everyone has gifts (ordinary); not everyone has *all* the gifts (extraordinary).

I will present the full scope of approaches available for believers today, touching on the methodologies that Wesley normally *did not* use, such as the *ordinary-direct* method and the *extraordinary-direct* method. I am continuing to use the only valid version of Wesley's ordinary-extraordinary distinction (deliverance) for our conversation. In my own everyday speech on deliverance, I would not use Wesley's language (ordinary-extraordinary). I focus on the universal mandate and equipping of all believers to cast out demons in the name of Jesus. Some may have more tools or gifts to assist in that task than others, but the name of Jesus with or without other gifts will get the job done.

The *ordinary-direct* method is one that directly confronts the devil and is available to all believers. This method for casting out demons was established by Christ and the disciples in the Scriptures and is for all believers. In Luke 10:18–20, Jesus gives his disciples "authority to trample on snakes and scorpions and to overcome all the power of the enemy." In that same passage, he promises them "nothing will harm you," because the demons must submit to Christ's followers who wield the authority of his name. Therefore, Jesus commissioned his disciples to confront demonic powers directly and to expel them using his authority (Matt 10:1,8).

In Mark 16:17, Jesus said, " . . . those who believe; In my name you shall cast out devils." At the beginning of the verse, Mark identifies who "you" refers to, the "believer." In Matthew 10:1,8, again, the disciples are authorized to "drive out devils" with the authority that Christ delegated to them. Simply, Jesus directly cast out demons by his own authority, and the disciples directly cast out demons by the authority given to them in the name of Jesus.[24] And all who believe have been granted that same authority, as witnessed by the disciples, by the saints throughout the Christian tradition, and by deliverance ministries today. We can directly confront the powers of darkness. There is a need for a comprehensive and contemporary scriptural strategy that utilizes *both* means, direct and indirect. Though the end is more important than the means with deliverance. Ultimately, deliverance is a subset of healing, which is a subset of sanctification, which is the core of salvation. The end goal is salvation (Luke 10:19–20).[25]

A DELIVERANCE STORY OF HOPE

At the time of writing this book, I was preaching at a church where one of my seminary students was the pastor.[26] Following the service, we were in his office. He received a phone call. The woman had called several times that week. She was hearing demonic voices and was being tormented by ghastly images that would not go away. He invited her to come to the office. My student and his associate did not have much experience at the time in deliverance. I thought it would be a good learning opportunity for them. I said I would guide them through the deliverance session if they would be willing. They were.

The young lady came in, and I asked her to share her story. What a story! She claimed that her mother was a witch who had dedicated her to Satan at birth. Both of her sisters were witches who had put curses on her throughout her life. As a child she had been sexually abused by an uncle and other family members for years. She fell into depression at an early age. As a teen, she began to use hard drugs to cope, including methamphetamines and fentanyl. She was sexually promiscuous. She got pregnant and had an abortion that was detrimental to her emotional and mental wellbeing. She became suicidal.

24. Twelftree, *Name of Jesus*, 209–78.

25. J. Wesley, "Scripture Way of Salvation," 43.

26. Intentionally, I will not share much in this volume from my personal experience of deliverance. This book is dedicated to the deliverance ministry of John Wesley. For more incidents, see Bellini, *X-Manual*.

She had a live-in boyfriend who would prostitute her so she could support her drug habit. Once when she had passed out, he carved several Satanic symbols into her chest with a knife. These were his markings of ownership, he claimed. He would also beat her regularly. She ended up having several more children. As she was abused, so she would abuse her children until Children's Services took them away from her, which, for her, was the last straw. She began to cry out and ask God for help. She did not want to lose her children. She believed God could save her and her children. I did not ask about her contact with any church, or previous religious beliefs, but she seemed to be convinced that her life was over, and only God could help. She had lived at least a dozen lifetimes in hell at only twenty-four years old.

At the conclusion of her story, I discerned she was ready for deliverance. We shared the good news of Jesus Christ with her. She was broken and desperate, a good place to be for Jesus. This was an ER situation. I coached her on what a deliverance session looks like, and she agreed to it. Before I could tell my student to go and lay hands on her, I heard the Spirit whisper to me to bind the spirit of violence because she will strike him if he tries to pray for her. I bound the spirit of violence, but I could tell it was only restrained. My student approached to lay hands on the woman, and she started to growl like a rabid wolf and show her teeth. I told the devil to be silent, and she struggled to stop. However, she began to manifest in other ways. Her eyes rolled back. Her head and neck twitched. She started rocking back and forth, moaning and groaning unintelligibly. I told my student to look her in the eyes and bind the devil in Jesus' name. He did so, and the war began. She started to speak with a man's voice and began growling and cursing again. After a half hour of direct confrontation with the devil and some stuck points and resistance, we prayed through. She experienced deliverance.

You could tell she was free because her countenance was totally changed. She was full of light and joy. Tears streamed down her face. When she came in, she looked full of desperation and anxiety and was shrouded in darkness. She said she felt a huge weight lift from her. I led her through a systematic repentance of each sin that the Spirit brought to her mind. She received Christ's forgiveness and gave her life to Jesus. I heard the Spirit say that she is open to be filled with the Spirit and to be baptized in his power, so she could go back into her troubled world and live a victorious life. She was open to receiving more.

Full of faith and the Holy Spirit, we prayed for her. Soon she was speaking in other tongues and praising God uncontrollably. Wow! When was the last time you saw that in a Methodist church? She who is forgiven much, loves much! Of course, we knew she would need extensive follow up and comprehensive assistance and care: therapy, social work, detox, legal assistance, and so on. This was just the beginning of a long and rough journey, but the church was willing to help and walk alongside. We were elated and filled with the joy of the Lord. This is what deliverance is all about—a party in Heaven that shakes the entire cosmos when one soul is delivered and brought into the kingdom.

I GIVE YOU POWER AND AUTHORITY!

How did all of that happen? The name of Jesus! There is power in his name. Sure, it was a process for the woman to get to that point, but the breaking point was when we confronted Satan directly in the name of Jesus. Incorporating the *direct* means of deliverance means using the name of Christ to confront evil spirits. Do we feel awkward or fearful confronting Satan in Jesus' name? Is using the name of Jesus in this way odd to us? Are we uncomfortable using his name? Jesus has given us his name for other Christian practices, such as prayer. We pray to the Father "in the name of Jesus." Utilizing his name is not unfamiliar. We baptize in the name of the Father, the Son, and the Holy Spirit. We use the Lord's name liturgically on a regular basis. We recall that renouncing Satan is even part of our baptismal rite. It is sacramental. Walking in the sacramental life involves walking out our baptismal vows, including renouncing Satan and resisting evil, in the name of Jesus. Deliverance in a sense reinforces and renews our baptism.

Furthermore, we are also given the name of Jesus to cast out demons *directly*: "In my name you will drive out demons" (Mk. 16:17). Of course, it is Jesus who casts out the demons, not our name or authority. But since Christ gave *us* authority to cast out demons, we can use the authority of his name as a power of attorney, if you will, to act on behalf of Christ and deliver the oppressed. The mediatorial work of Christ instrumented through the sacraments is represented in the elements but declared as a speech-act when we declare, "I baptize you in the name of. . .," "Or I renounce you, Satan, in the name of Jesus." There is power in the name of Jesus! And it has been given to us as a gift to live out the Christian life in Christ and to defeat Satan!

Wesley usually did not use the name of Jesus to confront the devil directly as part of his *ordinary* arsenal, though there is questionably some evidence that he may have done so on rare occasions. However, Scripture is clear that we can confront demons and are commanded to do so. Because of the authority given to us in the name of Jesus, demons will submit to us, and we can drive them out. Many do not use the *ordinary-direct* method because they do not know or believe the authority that is given to them.

Every believer, simply by exercising faith in God's promise (Luke 10:19), can implement the name and authority of Jesus to cast out demons and heal the oppressed. In this sense, the normative practice of deliverance through faith in the name of Christ is given to *all believers*; no special gift is necessary. Note that there are other *ordinary-direct* ways that can accompany the use of Jesus' name, such as the use of the blood of Christ, the armor of God, the keys of the kingdom, and even the virtue of humility (Jas 4:6–10).

Another method is the *extraordinary-direct means* of deliverance, which is through the gifts of the Spirit (1 Cor 12:7).[27] The Spirit often couples one or more gifts with the ordinary-direct means of the name of Jesus, the Word of God, prayer, repentance, and/or worship to equip the saints with a holy arsenal to storm the gates of hell. In my deliverance ministry, the Holy Spirit often manifests discerning of spirits and gifts of healing, among others. He combines these gifts with the use of the name of Jesus to accomplish the work of deliverance. The discerning of spirits helps me to know the type of spirit(s) that has bound the person, so that I can address them directly and cast them out. The Spirit also uses the gifts of healing to release and restore broken souls from the power of the devil. For example, in Luke 6:18, 8:2, and Acts 10:38, Jesus *healed* those who were *oppressed* by the devil. Consonant with the eastern Christian tradition and early Methodism, these passages suggest that deliverance is a type of healing. Demonized souls are sin-sick souls. In the ministry of Christ, deliverance ministry went hand-in-hand with his healing ministry. It should be so for us today as well.

Both indirect and direct approaches are valid. And both ordinary and extraordinary means are valid. I am encouraging *all* believers to use *every* means available to be equipped for deliverance ministry. Methodism's evangelistic and pastoral ministry was frequently confronted by the demonic, and it responded well. One of the intentions of this book is to inspire Wesleyans and all believers alike, in this evil day, to reclaim their scriptural authority and power in Christ (ordinary and extraordinary) and the deliverance ministry of the church, which has been so often neglected or abused in the church today. The occult, addiction, sexual perversion, radical violence, racism, and other evils are on the rise. The church needs to be properly equipped to face this present darkness.

Matthew 10:8 and Luke 10:18–20 make it clear that *all* Christ's disciples have been given the authority to continue Christ's ministry of liberation. In Wesley's day deliverance was a vital component to Methodism's overall ministry of healing and salvation, and it should be today for the people called Methodists as well. It is high time to stop making excuses and

---

27. There is a gifts inventory in chapter 9 of this book.

walk in it! Souls are at stake! So many are bound in sin and addiction and need to be set free, while others have been battered by abuse and trauma and need healing. We have been given all the gifts and resources of the Spirit needed to do the same works as Christ and even greater, if you can believe that (John 14:12).

6

An Analysis of Wesley's Deliverance Ministry

A CRITIQUE OF WESLEY'S DELIVERANCE MINISTRY

Yes to a Spirit-Worldview, Spiritual Empiricism, and a Theology of the Spirit

In the next two chapters, we will be critically constructing a Wesleyan framework for deliverance. Wesley has much to offer us, but we need to examine his theology and practice critically through the lens of Scripture. We cannot merely echo *en toto* his theology of deliverance without analyzing it first. I try to be a faithful player for Team Wesley, but surprisingly, I have learned that Wesley does not *always* get everything right. Just most of the time! Consequently, in the spirit of Wesley, Wesleyans should evaluate their teaching according to Scripture. In Scripture, Paul instructed the churches to "follow me as I follow Christ." We follow Wesley *as* Wesley follows Christ and the Holy Spirit. Not only is Wesley not above error, but also, he is not above his own time. He is a product of it, as are we of our time. The Spirit has revealed much in the last two hundred years following Wesley about the gifts of the Spirit and deliverance. In addition to using Scripture in our critique, I will also be incorporating a high view of the charismatic work of the Spirit, a Wesleyan Charismatic theology of deliverance. Wesley with a charismatic update and upgrade!

It is imperative that a Wesleyan theology and practice of deliverance embrace Wesley's views on a spirit-worldview, spiritual empiricism, and a robust theology of the Spirit as foundational. Our adoption of such a foundation is not because it's Wesley's, but because it resonates with Scripture. Christ and his disciples assumed such a worldview, which is evident in the way they carried out deliverance. The reality of a spirit-worldview, fallen spirit-beings, and the need to engage them in the power of the Spirit is presupposed and apparent in Scripture.

We would also do well to uphold Wesley's holiness hermeneutic when discerning the root (origin) and fruit of manifestations and gifts and when pursuing and operating in the gifts as well. The prioritization of holiness before power, fruit before gifts and character before charisma is a very needed directive for a balance that is often absent in the PCR world today. In many circles, the pursuit of gifts and power has become an end in itself. The temptation can be too much to bear for immature believers who are pressed early in their walk in such circles with receiving the baptism of the Spirit and the gifts that follow. Such overwhelming power can be volatile and dangerous in inexperienced and irresponsible hands, like giving an AR-15 rifle to a child. I value the older Holiness-Pentecostal order that placed receiving entire sanctification *before* receiving the baptism or filling of the Spirit. The Lord wants to sanctify us to fit or prepare us for the Master's use (2 Tim 2:21).

Of course, we want all what the Spirit has for us, but we need to teach that the Spirit is also *Holy,* the Holy Spirit. He is the Spirit who is holy and who makes us holy, the Spirit of holiness, the sanctifying Spirit.[1] We cannot forget his primary work in the church and place all other operations of the Spirit in proper perspective. The Lord wants to do a sanctifying work *in* us before he does a powerful work *through* us. Thus, we affirm Wesley's emphasis on holiness.

No to an Unscriptural Ordinary-Extraordinary Divide

While we affirm Wesley's careful use of a holiness hermeneutic to prioritize the Spirit's sanctifying work over his charismatic work, it is not necessary to bifurcate or split the Spirit's work into ordinary or extraordinary categories, which is unscriptural. I prefer to understand the work of the Spirit as *salvific (sanctifying)* grace and *charismatic* grace; both are for everyone. The early Methodist and Holiness movements cried, "Full Salvation for all." The Charismatic movement cried, "The power and gifts of the Spirit are for all."

1. Holiness and sanctification are biblical and theological words simply meaning to be more like God, and more specifically, to be more like Jesus Christ.

It's a both/and. Any language that divides the general work of the Spirit into ordinary-extraordinary or anything similar along the lines of frequency, breadth, or (un)commonalty of occurrence is not found in the New Testament. Gifting of the Spirit is not extraordinary but common and given to all. Charismatic grace as well as sanctifying grace is for everyone. Only specific gifts are not ordinary or common to all. For example, not everyone is a prophet. Not everyone works miracles (extraordinary).

We identify the gifts of the Holy Spirit from the various scriptural lists (Isa 11, Rom 12, 1 Cor 12, Eph 4, and 1 Pet 4) and narratives (Gospels and Acts). The gifts, though miraculous, are not irregular or extraordinary. Perhaps they are irregular to the everyday, natural order of things, but not to the life of the believer. The supernatural manifestations and workings of the Spirit are regular and normative to the ministry of Christ, the disciples, and to subsequent generations as Acts 2:38 promises. The Spirit of Pentecost that descends as tongues of fire upon all people regardless of age, sex, race, or socio-economic status will empower and equip them to be witnesses of the risen Christ.

Witnessing is defined by what is subsequently revealed in the Gospels and in the Book of Acts. The disciples preached the gospel with signs and wonders following them as promised (Matt 10:8; Mark 16:17; Luke 10:9; John 13:12; Acts 2:43; 5:12; 6:8). The Word of God was proclaimed through both verbal and non-verbal acts, the non-verbal acts being miraculous signs and wonders. The gifts were meant to be as common and normative as the preaching and teaching of the Word of God because they work together.

Preaching and the sign-gifts mutually bear witness to the truth in Christ and cannot be separated. Paul alludes to their connection in Romans 15:19: "by the power of signs and wonders, through the power of the Spirit of God. So from Jerusalem all the way around to Illyricum, I have fully proclaimed the gospel of Christ." The gospel was *fully proclaimed* when it was proclaimed not only by word but also *by the power of signs and wonders*. The implication seems to be that if there are no signs and wonders, then the gospel would not have been *fully* proclaimed. Something would have been missing. Paul declared to the Corinthians that he would not preach with mere human words when he arrived, but that he would also *demonstrate* the power of the Spirit, for the kingdom of God consists not of words but of the *power of God* (1 Cor 2:4–5; 4:20). Preaching the gospel involves demonstrating or illustrating the power of God through miraculous signs and wonders.

The writer of Hebrews similarly declares "So what makes us think we can escape if we ignore this great salvation that was first announced by the Lord Jesus himself and then delivered to us by those who heard him speak? And God confirmed the message by giving signs and wonders and various miracles and gifts of the Holy Spirit whenever he chose" (NLT Heb 2:3–4). The preaching of the gospel of Jesus Christ included signs, wonders, miracles, and gifts of the Spirit. Their function was to confirm the preaching. Other translations say "testified" (NIV) or "witnessed" (ESV). The meaning is the same. The miraculous was an integral dimension of the gospel witness. The Spirit is poured out on the entire church so that we can be witnesses, including testifying through the gifts that God has given us, and *everyone*, not just *some*, is given a gift(s) (1 Cor 12:7). Wesley's understanding of gift distribution appears more cautious and restrictive than what Scripture depicts as corporate. Regarding deliverance, all can cast out demons in Jesus' name, but only some may have added gifts for the task.

Yes to Both Indirect and Direct Means

We observed in the last chapter that Wesley's methodology for casting out demons was *indirect*. He normally did not *directly* address demons when casting them out. His usual method was to intercede for God's intervention to drive out the devil. The *indirect* means would have been the *ordinary* means for Wesley. He did not seem to operate out of the scriptural injunction that God has given *us* authority to put Satan under our feet (Luke 10:19–20). The *direct* means by way of faith or a gift, was the *extraordinary* means. Both indirect and direct means are available to the church when ministering deliverance. I have employed both. In the end, it is Christ through his name who is expelling the demons, not you or me. We have merely been given a power of attorney of sorts when we have been given his name and authority to cast out demons. We are acting on his behalf because he has given us his name to do so. We have no authority but Christ's authority, which he gives us in his name.

   This authority from Christ also comes with an admonition that we are not to fear the devil or anything that he threatens to do (Luke 10:19–20). When I train ministers for deliverance, so many fear that the enemy can harm them. They have absorbed too much from the horror genre of Hollywood films. Jesus assures you that when you expel demons "nothing shall harm you." Because of his name, we can be guaranteed of Satan's defeat. We are promised that the powers of darkness submit to us and are under our feet because of the name of Jesus. We can expect the same results as Christ, but we cannot take the credit or glory. Humility is the best antidote and most powerful weapon against Satan. We give thanks and rejoice, for deliverance brings salvation.

A final critique will be used to construct a Wesleyan theology and practice of deliverance. We will roughly use the Wesleyan way of salvation (*via salutis*) as a framework for much of the theological heavy lifting, beginning with baptism.

Yes to Renouncing Satan

Our Baptismal Vows of Renunciation: An Exposition

I have been in deliverance and exorcism ministry for nearly four decades. When I tell some Christians about my ministry, occasionally a few are perplexed, terror-struck, or scandalized. To some, it is not an "official" or "real" ministry of the church. And worse, to some, it is an unprofessional, self-appointed, fanatical concoction practiced by certain backwoods snake-handling types. Of course, I am quick to remind them of the ministry of Christ and his disciples and of the baptismal vows of the church for the last two-thousand years. They involve a renouncing of Satan.

Our focus is on the *baptismal vow of renunciation*, which is usually situated at the front end of the rite. Spiritual warfare and deliverance are not eccentric novelties to be practiced by a few specialists or fanatics. Resisting evil, including deliverance and exorcism, has been preparatory for one's baptism and initiation into the church for centuries. Deliverance is sacramental. In addition, vows to resist the devil have also been instrumental for Christians seeking to renew their baptism for a deeper walk in holiness.

When we speak of deliverance, we are speaking of warring against evil. Paul exhorts us "to clothe ourselves in Christ and not to satisfy our evil desires" (Rom 13:14). Scripture is replete with injunctions to resist evil and walk in the Spirit. Spiritual warfare, repentance, deliverance, and sanctification begin with the call *to renounce* the devil and his works. Practices such as these begin with our baptismal vows. Consequently, in our commitment to resist evil and do good, we should return to our baptismal vows as a theological foundation that grounds and informs our Christian praxis. Deliverance is a sacramental act. Simply put, remember your baptism!

Remember your vows of baptism to renounce Satan, all spiritual forces of wickedness, and their works. If you are a Christian and were baptized, either you, your parents, your godparent(s), or sponsor(s) took baptismal vows. Several of those vows were affirmations in response to various questions about one's faith. Across denominational lines, these affirmations are similar and often involve faith in God (Father, Son, and Holy Spirit) as expressed in the Apostles' Creed, faith in Jesus Christ as Savior, a profession of Christian faith contained in the Holy Scriptures, and a pledge of faithfulness to Christ's holy church. Along with these vows of Christian affirmation, there are also *vows of renunciation*. We are asked to renounce Satan and his works. For example, in the Anglican Rite for candidates who can speak for themselves, these questions are presented followed by the appropriate *renunciations*, along with an anointing and prayer for exorcism:

> **Question**: Do you renounce the devil and all the spiritual forces of wickedness that rebel against God?
> **Answer: I renounce them.**
> **Question**: Do you renounce the empty promises and deadly deceits of this world that corrupt and destroy the creatures of God?
> **Answer: I renounce them.**
> **Question**: Do you renounce the sinful desires of the flesh that draw you from the love of God?
> **Answer: I renounce them.**
> **The Celebrant prays over the Candidate(s) and may anoint each Candidate with the Oil of Exorcism, saying,** "Almighty God deliver you from the powers of darkness and evil and lead you into the light and obedience of the kingdom of his Son Jesus Christ our Lord. **Amen.**" (Book of Common Prayer, 2019)[2]

With some exceptions, these renunciations are fairly similar across Christian traditions. They involve renouncing Satan, all demonic forces, their evil works, and the entirety of sin. What do such renunciations mean to the church and to us personally? What is meant by Satan, evil, and renouncing? Do we take our vows seriously? What do we mean when asked if we renounce the devil, demons, and their works? Who are the devil and his demons?

Who Is Satan? What Are Demons?

Let us review in further depth the question of the existence of Satan and fallen angels. Do they exist as created personal angelic entities? Are Satan and the hordes of hell abstractions or real beings? Is Satan merely a metaphor, figurative language for systemic evil, a metonymy, or a synecdoche for all evil? There have also been several streams of interpretation, mostly over the last century, that have identified Satan more metaphorically and systemically, for example, in the work of Walter Wink or Robert Linthicum, among others. Under those models, the demonic are not spirit-beings that tempt individuals, but they exist in systems, usually social and political systems. I do not discount these

2. Anglican Church of North America, *Book of Common Prayer 2019*.

impersonal, psychologically abstract, or socio-systemic interpretations of Satan and evil. Such constructs should be included in our broad hermeneutic of the demonic. Personal evil can work collectively as a system, as the fallen angels collaborated in revolt against heaven, and as they collaborate through large scale sin like racism or abortion. Yet even in such cases, the evil is not merely an abstract system but is undergirded by "principalities and powers," which in their scriptural context refer to systems of demons. The demonic works on both levels, personal and systemic.

The existence of the devil is more than just figurative. Jesus was not casting metaphors out of people. In the letters of the New Testament, when we are encouraged to resist the devil or evil, we are not commanded to resist figurative language, abstractions, a synecdoche, or even a political system so that it "will flee from us." Nor are we called to beware of Satan, who roams around like a "roaring metaphor or trope seeking someone to devour." A lion is indeed a metaphor and an appropriate one, though its scriptural purpose is not to claim that Satan is a metaphor, but to compare his destructive work to a vicious predator that can ruthlessly destroy and devour its prey. I am not a verbal and plenary literalist, but I will take the genre as it presents itself and interpret it in its plain sense.

Both Scripture and Christian tradition have identified Satan as a fallen, evil angel, thus a being with agency and intelligence. Furthermore, that being chose to rebel against God and become morally evil. By misusing his freedom and perverting his will, the devil became the "author" of evil, the father of lies. Evil is not ontologically real but a distortion or falsification of what is real. It is a privation of the good that God has created. God did not create evil. Rebellion did. As the father of lies, the deprivation of truth, Satan is bent on deception and malevolence, as is the rest of the demonic hosts. Prominent figures of the Great Tradition, such as Justin Martyr, Irenaeus, Tertullian, Clement of Alexandria, Origen, Basil, Gregory of Nyssa, Chrysostom, Jerome, Augustine, Maximus the Confessor, Anselm, Aquinas, Luther, Calvin, Wesley, C.S. Lewis, and others, infer similarly and often wrote practically on spiritual warfare against the devil.

What Does it Mean to Renounce Satan?

Now that we have established what or who "Satan" refers to, what does it mean to "renounce Satan?" The baptismal vow of renunciation has several echoes in Scripture, where many have had to confront the evil one. From the beginning, the devil has been the adversary of both God and humanity. Michael and his angels defeated Satan and his hordes when they attempted a coup in heaven (Rev 12). The prideful, rebellious angels were given no place in heaven and were cast out and banished to the earth.

Satan disguises himself in many forms to tempt humanity. In the beginning in the garden, he came as a cunning serpent that beguiled our primal parents into distrusting God. They revolted against his command, believing the Almighty was withholding some good from them in paradise. They believed a lie that with the knowledge of good and evil they would become like God and could trust in themselves. Adam and Eve did not renounce Satan but acquiesced, as people have throughout human history. Renouncing the devil, at least in part, would have involved condemning and rejecting the tempter's lies that attempt to undermine the goodness and faithfulness of God and refusing his counterfeit offer of blissful autonomy.

Later in Scripture, Moses, by the power of God, confronted Pharaoh, resisted the injustice of slavery, and delivered his people from bondage. Tertullian understood Moses' confrontation with Pharaoh to be a confrontation with the devil. In the leanness of the desert, the liberated Israelites were tempted not to trust the God who delivered them but to return to Egypt and serve false gods. Many did not resist the devil and died off in the wilderness. It would be the next generation led by Joshua that would renounce idolatry and unbelief and enter the promised land.

In the New Testament, Christ comes as the last Adam. Where Adam failed against the devil, Christ succeeded. In the desert and in the Garden of Gethsemane, Christ was tempted with covetousness, pride, autonomy, power, and vainglory. He renounced the devil, resisted temptation, and stood on the Word of God (Matt 4; 26:36–46). When tempted to choose his will over the Father's, he denied himself and went to the cross. He died on the cross for our sins and defeated sin, Satan, and death. Throughout his ministry, we find Christ confronting and expelling the kingdom of darkness by doing good, casting out demons, and empowering his disciples to do the same (Matt 10:7–8). Likewise, we find the apostles in the book of Acts carrying out Christ's deliverance ministry (Acts 16:16–18).

Paul exhorts us in Ephesians "to be strong in the Lord's power" and "put on his armor so that we can stand against the devil's evil strategies." We find a representative list of those strategies in Galatians 5:19–21 marked as the "works of the flesh." The proper response is "to crucify the flesh" (v. 24). James gives us the direct command to oppose the devil and his works: "Submit yourselves to God. Resist the devil, and he will flee from you" (Jas 4:7). In this one verse, we find a theological summation of spiritual warfare. The injunction is given by James within the larger context of prayer, humility, and true repentance, which are instrumental to renouncing Satan and drawing near to God (Jas 4:8–10). Baptismal renunciation of Satan and sin is a call to radical humility, to reject Satan, to life-changing repentance that shuns the ways of the world (v. 4), and to receive God's gift of grace to follow Christ in righteousness.

Finally, John the Revelator shows us Christ returning to the world to destroy the power of the antichrist, the beast, the false prophet, and Satan. They are thrown into the lake of fire along with death and Hades (Revelation 20). As all things are becoming new, the history of the old creation culminates with the defeat and judgment of Satan and his demons and all the works of evil, both systemic and personal. Satan was defeated and judged at the cross and receives his sentence with Christ's return.

The practice of confronting and renouncing the devil was incorporated into the baptismal rite of the early church. Tertullian and Basil claimed the renunciation vow originated in apostolic tradition, though it is difficult to substantiate. The standard dating is between the late second and third centuries. We first see the renunciation vows in Hippolytus' *The Apostolic Tradition* (before 235). Tertullian (155–220) also claimed it in his day *(De Spectaculis*, circa 197 and *De Corona* 3, circa 201), as did Cyril of Jerusalem in his *Catechetical Lectures* (circa 350).

In many cases, as with Cyril, sanctified oil, representing the presence and power of the Spirit, was applied after renouncing Satan but prior to the baptismal confession and again following the baptismal act. We also see the renunciation in the baptismal rites in the *Apostolic Constitutions* (late fourth century), in the *Missale Gallicanum Vetis* (circa third century), in the Sarum Rite (eleventh century) in the West, and throughout the liturgical history of the Roman Catholic Church. It is later adopted in the Lutheran and Anglican Rites as well. In the Eastern Orthodox Rite, not only is there a baptismal renunciation of the devil, but there is also a prayer of exorcism over the candidate. In the baptismal liturgy of the Orthodox Church in America, there are three exorcisms that precede the vows of renunciation (OCA, 2012).[3] The witness of the early Fathers was clear that in baptism and conversion there needed to be a radical shift in allegiance from the devil and his works to Christ and his kingdom. Baptismal renunciation announced and sealed that shift.

Today, our understanding of renunciation found in the baptismal liturgy needs to be as radical as it was traditionally. We are condemning and rejecting Satan, his minions, and their abominable works. We will no longer ally with his depraved will or ways. Instead, we turn our full devotion to Christ as Lord and make a vow of radical commitment to his kingdom. In some modern mainline Protestant liturgies, such as the Presbyterian,

---

3. My granddaughter Costanza's baptism was in an OCA church where my wife Mariuccia is a member.

Methodist, Christian Reformed, and some forms of the Anglican Rite, the direct renunciation of Satan or the devil has been removed. In the case of my denomination, the United Methodist Church, the renunciation was included in Wesley's original *Sunday Service*. It was retained in the MEC hymnal from 1905 and in the Methodist hymnals of 1935 and 1966.

In the 1989 *United Methodist Hymnal*, however, the direct reference to Satan was removed and replaced with "the spiritual forces of wickedness" and "the evil powers of this world." Following this renunciation, the minister asks, "Do you accept the freedom and power God gives you to resist evil, injustice, and oppression in whatever forms they present themselves?" "Injustice and oppression" are listed alongside "evil" and may even modify or define evil in this context. Granted this version, to its credit, did add, from the early baptismal tradition, the anointing with oil, the laying on of hands, and an epiclesis. At the time of writing this book, it is good to see that the Transitional Book of Doctrine and Discipline of the newly formed Global Methodist Church has reinserted the renunciation vow into the baptismal rite.[4]

The change in the *United Methodist Hymnal* may seem minuscule at first. The phrases "spiritual forces of wickedness" and "evil powers of this world" may *seem* synonymous with "Satan," but not necessarily by all interpretations. "Injustice and oppression" certainly seem like things we should oppose. Yet the vagary of this language does not help us. These phrases can mean anything today depending on one's socio-political context. And everything is politicized. We live in an age where it is easy to hold to a deflationary folk view of evil that lacks a clear, robust theology. Our common view tends to locate evil in others and not in us, and usually only points to some extreme form, like Hitler and Nazi Germany. Evil has taken on more of a relative, socio-political guise. Depending on whom you ask, "evil, injustice, and oppression" may mean the Democratic Party, Hillary Clinton, and any voice supporting LGBT or CRT. For others, evil may mean the Republican Party, Donald Trump, and any voice supporting nationalism or capitalism.

In our world today, evil is in the eye of the beholder. Absolutes are censured, and surely evil in the ontic form of fallen angels has been debunked and discredited by modernity. Thus, the removal of the direct reference to Satan in the liturgy for some can be interpreted as the removal of personal evil as embodied and summed up emblematically in Scripture and the Christian tradition as "Satan and his works." Evil becomes depersonalized not only apart from Satan but also from me and you. The biblical and traditional context for understanding evil is removed or at least demythologized, softened, or perhaps replaced by the latest iteration of one group's object of scorn.

4. Global Methodist Church, "Transitional Book," 26.

However, the church's sacramental renunciation of evil is specifically a rejection of Satan, his rebellion against God, and his temptation of the whole human race to do likewise. Thus, in our commitment to resist evil, we should return to the roots of our baptismal vows. At the core of spiritual warfare, repentance, deliverance, sanctification, and similar practices is the pledge to renounce Satan and his works and to surrender our sole allegiance to Christ and his Lordship. In this way, we remember, reinforce, and renew our baptism. As Wesleyans, deliverance begins in *prevenient grace* with our baptismal vows. God delivers us out of darkness and initiates us into his kingdom of light. Wesley received and administered the Anglican vows of the baptismal rite. What further did Wesley have to say about baptism and deliverance?

Wesley, Baptism, and Deliverance

Sacramentally, deliverance from evil begins with baptism. Wesley understood baptism as *both* sacramental and evangelical. To comprehend Wesley's conjunctive view of baptism, it is necessary to grasp both his sacramental and evangelical views on baptism, the nature of their distinctions, and how Wesley attempted to hold them together in a larger soteriological framework that was fashioned to foster holiness. On one hand, Wesley held a high church, sacramental view of baptism and baptismal regeneration that he inherited from Anglicanism, which received it from Rome.

On the other hand, Wesley, following his Aldersgate experience in 1738, adopted an evangelical perspective that still valued infant and adult baptism as an outward sign but further insisted on the inward grace of regeneration that is solely ministered by the Spirit. In his own case as a youth and in the instances of many around him, he realized that one often sinned away the grace received in infant baptism and needed subsequently to be born again. Wesley's journal entry for May 24, 1738, gives account of Aldersgate and a brief overview of the years leading up to the experience. Wesley begins that entry referencing his infant baptism, later gradual fall into outward sin, and his quest for holiness.

Here, he is obviously interpreting and rethinking his infant baptism in light of his recent conversion experience: "I believe, till I was about ten years old I had not sinned away that 'washing of the Holy Ghost' which was given me in baptism . . . "[5] Wesley's theology and practice of baptism were developed over time as he attempted to hold these two views conjunctively

---

5. J. Wesley, "Journal Entry for May 24, 1738," 98.

in tension but not without ambiguity at times.[6] Again, the main thrust and benefit of grace, whether baptismal (prevenient) or regenerational was *deliverance* from all sin and holiness or perfect love.

Wesley on the Benefits of Baptism

In "A Treatise on Baptism" Wesley enumerates five benefits of baptism. He defines baptism as "the initiatory sacrament, which enters us into covenant with God. It was instituted by Christ, who alone has power to institute a proper sacrament, a sign, a seal, pledge, and means of grace, perpetually obligatory of all Christians."[7] Baptism, as a sign and means of grace, initiates a person into a covenant with God in which they partake of five basic benefits. The first benefit is "the washing away the guilt of original sin, by the application of the merits of Christ's death."[8] Wesley applied this to all in Adam, including infants. The inconsistency in this claim is that, elsewhere, Wesley attributed the removal of guilt from original sin to prevenient grace as an unconditional benefit.[9] Maddox reasons that by Wesley omitting the guilt as "damning" from Samuel Wesley's original work, he contended that the guilt "was universally cancelled at birth by Prevenient Grace."[10]

Likewise, Collins points out that for Wesley the "soteriological significance" of infant baptism "was diminished somewhat by his understanding of prevenient grace" that removes the penalty of eternal death for original sin.[11] More so, this unconditional benefit of the atonement indicates two things. First, that baptism is not juridically essential, nor did Wesley insist on it necessarily for salvation (i.e., the unbaptized regenerated Quaker).[12]

6. Scholars debate whether Wesley's views were consistent, altered, contradictory, or ambiguous. See chapter 1 of Felton's *Gift of Water* for more on this conversation, as well as a detailed treatment of other facets of Wesley's practice of baptism. See also Maddox, *Responsible Grace*, 221–24, for the sacramental versus evangelical debate regarding baptism, the weight placed on various editions of his published works on baptism, and Wesley's consistency regarding these two views. See also Williams, *John Wesley's Theology*, 116–22.

7. J. Wesley, "Treatise on Baptism," 188.

8. J. Wesley, "Treatise on Baptism," 190.

9. J. Wesley, "Letter from John Wesley to John Mason, November 21, 1776," 453. "Therefore no infant ever was or will be sent to hell for the guilt of Adam's sin seeing it is cancelled by the righteousness of God as soon as they are sent into the world."

10. Maddox, *Responsible Grace*, 224.

11. Collins, *Theology of John Wesley*, 264.

12. J. Wesley, "Journal Entry for Oct. 16, 1756," 387. Early Methodists attracted many Quakers. Wesley did not believe these converts were damned because they were not baptized. However, since baptism is commanded as well as the testimony of a good

Second, that our representation in Christ extends greater grace through universal atonement over the universal condemnation in Adam. Although the punishment of death is passed onto all through the disobedience of one man, the obedience of one righteous man brought righteousness and life to all (Rom 5:18).[13]

So, in one instance Wesley attributes deliverance from original guilt with baptism. And in another, he attributes it to universal prevenient grace. This latter view may be implied in his *Treatise on Baptism*. While Anglican and later Methodist baptismal vows speak of renunciation of evil, Wesley in his *Treatise on Baptism* does not mention that infants are delivered from the condemnation of the devil when they are washed of original guilt. Where Wesley is silent, I assert that the defeat of Satan is connected to our baptism into the death of Christ that destroys the claims and power of sin and delivers us from death (Romans 6).

The second benefit is New Testament circumcision: baptism brings one into covenant with God. For Wesley, this New Testament covenant is one in which God promises to "give them a new heart and a new spirit, to sprinkle clean water upon them;" a reality "of which the baptismal is only a figure."[14] Here, Wesley is making a distinction between the 'renewal of the heart,' which is an inward work of the Spirit, and 'baptism,' which is a 'figure' that represents or points to inner renewal. The third and fourth benefits confer admission into the Church, or membership in the body of Christ, and adoption into the family of God for those born of water and of the Spirit.[15] Again, Wesley makes a distinction between the outward sign (water) and the inward grace (Spirit).

In this way, Wesley often uses the term "baptism" in two senses. One is pejorative, the mere outward sign of the water, which alone is ineffective. The other is the proper sense, baptism as the sacrament that joins the outward sign of water with the inward grace of the Spirit. Wesley illustrates, "By water then, as a means, the water of baptism, we are regenerated or born again; whence it is called by the Apostle, 'the washing of regeneration.' Our

---

conscience from a new convert (1 Pet 3:21), Wesley baptized Quakers who came into the Methodist fold.

13. Note that an atonement which is for all, or a universal atonement, is different than universalism or universal salvation, which instead declares that all are saved. Christ's death for all provides unconditional benefits, such as prevenient grace that restores a degree of freedom to respond to God's grace and also removes Adamic guilt. Thus, death is merited due to our own sin and not that of Adam. Also, universal atonement means that Christ died for all, so that whoever believes in him will have eternal life.

14. J. Wesley, "Treatise on Baptism," 191.

15. J. Wesley, "Treatise on Baptism," 191–92.

Church therefore ascribes no greater virtue to baptism than Christ himself has done. Nor does she ascribe it to the outward washing, but to the inward grace, which, added thereto, makes it a sacrament. Herein a principle of grace is infused, which will not be wholly taken away, unless we quench the Holy Spirit of God by long-continued wickedness."[16]

Wesley insisted that the outward washing of the water alone does not result in the "washing of regeneration." It is the infusion of grace by the power of the Spirit through the elements of the water that makes it a regenerating holy act, a sacrament. Neither the water nor the practice can do the work by itself or together (an *ex opere operato*), the inward work of grace by the Spirit's power is essential to work the efficacy of regeneration.[17] The two aspects, water and the Spirit, though not synonymous, nor always joined, need to work together in the sacrament. Thus, the delivering power of God is not in the water nor in the act alone but in the power of the Spirit.

Finally, with the fifth benefit, "we are heirs of the kingdom of heaven" and to all the promises of God. All these benefits are provided "in baptism, the ordinary instrument of our justification."[18] Although debated, Wesley maintained throughout his ministry the importance and normativity of baptism and its need to be linked with deliverance and regeneration. The sacrament proper contains both the outward sign and the inward grace, and thus, only in this sense is regeneration connected with baptism, not as an outward sign alone. However, he did not equate the two; neither did the Church of England. In his sermon "The New Birth," the language is unequivocal:

> First, it follows, that baptism is not the new birth: They are not one and the same thing. Many indeed seem to imagine that they are just the same; at least, they speak as if they thought so . . . Certainly it is not by any within these kingdoms, whether of the established Church, or dissenting from it. The judgment of the latter is clearly declared in their large Catechism: -Q. "What are the parts of a sacrament? A. the parts of a sacrament are tow: The one an outward and sensible sign; the other, an inward and spiritual grace, thereby signified. -Q What is baptism? A. Baptism is a sacrament, wherein Christ hath ordained the washing with water, to be a sign and seal of regeneration by his Spirit."

16. J. Wesley, "Treatise on Baptism," 192.

17. J. Wesley, "New Birth," 74. Wesley uses the phrase, "an act of man, purifying the body," for the external visible washing of the water. According to Felton in *Gift of Water*, 33, and I concur, "Wesley thoroughly repudiated any interpretation of baptism which implied an *ex opere operato* view."

18. J. Wesley, "Treatise on Baptism," 191.

Here it is manifest, baptism, the sign, is spoken of as distinct
from regeneration the thing signified.[19]

Not only are baptism and the new birth not the same, but also the new
birth "does not always accompany baptism."[20] They do not constantly go
together. A man may possibly be "born of water," and yet not be "born of the
Spirit." There may sometimes be the outward sign, where there is not the inward grace. I do not speak about infants: "It is certain our Church supposes
that all who are baptized in their infancy are at the same time born again;
and it is allowed that the whole office for the Baptism of Infants proceeds
upon this supposition."[21] Wesley consistently affirmed this distinction between the new birth and adult baptism.

However, Wesley acknowledged that infant baptism, as an initiatory
sacrament, was the "ordinary way" one was initiated in Christ and regenerating grace. Yet, as an initiatory work, infant baptism was not a seal that
completed regeneration or salvation. Wesley observed that many baptized
as infants sinned away their baptismal grace, like he did at ten years of age,
and needed the new birth. Wesley responds to the one who relies on their
infant baptism, "Lean no more on the staff of that broken reed, that ye were
born again in baptism. Who denies that ye were then made children of God,
and heirs of the kingdom of heaven? But not withstanding this, ye are now
children of the devil."[22] Wesley encountered many who claimed baptism in
word but denied it by their deeds, and did not have the marks of new birth,
which are "power over outward sin," faith, hope, and love.[23] The fruit of the
Spirit, rather than water, signifies the true mark of regeneration.

Increasingly, over time, in emphasizing the distinction between the
new birth and water baptism, he put more weight on the transformation
of the new birth over the outward sign and even over the incipient regeneration received in infant baptism. The new birth sufficiently effected the
change needed to go on to perfection, which was always the goal.[24] Again,
the chief benefit of grace is perfect "love, excluding all sin," deliverance.
Wesley understood that grace begins preveniently at baptism, is realized
more in regeneration, and is fully realized in entire sanctification, when we

19. J. Wesley, "New Birth," 196.

20. J. Wesley, "New Birth," 197.

21. J. Wesley, "New Birth," 197.

22. J. Wesley, "Marks of the New Birth," 430.

23. J. Wesley, "Marks of the New Birth," 221–22; cf. J. Wesley, "New Birth," in 200;
see J. Wesley, "Marks of New Birth," 428.

24. See Maddox, *Responsible Grace*, 222, 224, especially Wesley's editing of the *Sunday Service* in these regards.

are delivered from inbred sin. In baptism and baptismal renewal, we need to stress the *renunciation of Satan* and his works. Wesley did not underscore this aspect of baptism, but it needs to be recovered. Renunciation is a historical element to the baptismal rite, a significant component in our baptismal vow, and a practice that characterizes our remaining lifelong journey of repentance and warfare against sin and evil.

The Connection Between Repenting Grace and Deliverance

Much of what we discovered in the previous chapters about Wesley and casting out demons is not found in his didactic writing[25] but in his *Journals* and *Letters*, which come from his experience. He simply never wrote a treatise, essay, or sermon on expelling evil spirits. However, he encountered them in ministry. It is in his journal entries and letters that he gives detailed accounts, and it is there that we can unearth an underlying practical or operating theology on deliverance and exorcism. Thus, much of what we gather from Wesley on the subject is extracted and extrapolated from his *de facto* "operational" theology.

Upon analyzing the recorded accounts of deliverance in his *Journals* and *Letters*, one notices that most of these encounters occur during or coincide with an individual's repentance. During those instances of repentance, some demonization is manifestly evident in certain cases, such as the woman who had to be physically restrained during deliverance. This event from Wesley's October 1, 1763, entry was discussed in chapter 3. Prior to Wesley's arrival, she was already presenting many demonic manifestations and was suicidal. Wesley was called on to minister to her. After prolonged labor and warfare with the evil spirits, she repented, was delivered, and restored.

In her case, as in most, deliverance and repentance coincided. There was a connection and a correlation. Deliverance begins to manifest with convicting and repenting grace within the Wesleyan way of salvation. In other circumstances, when there were not any previous manifestations, Wesley would preach in the open-air, and the conviction produced by the Word of God would drop people to the ground as "thunderstruck." As the conviction mounted, demonic phenomena would emerge to the surface between soul and body, releasing torturous screams, convulsions, and bodily contortions. Wesley noted that an internal clash was erupting between the sin-sick soul seeking repentance and liberty and the desperate devils seeking to maintain oppression and control. After much prayer, repenting, and yielding to the liberating work of the Spirit, the person would be released

25. In his teaching material such as his sermons, essays, and treatises.

and restored. Again, in both examples given, deliverance is connected and coincides with the repentance phase of salvation.

For Wesley, "convincing" or "convicting" grace means "repentance," resulting in "deliverance from the heart of stone."[26] Conviction and repentance of sin and deliverance are joined as cause and effect. Conviction leads to repentance that leads to deliverance, deliverance from sin *and* the demonic. When writing sermons, tracts, or essays, Wesley did *not* emphasize the demonic aspect of repentance and deliverance as he does in his *Journals* and *Letters*. Repentance is the grounds for breaking the hold of sin and Satan and leads to freedom. From a practitioner's standpoint, he or she should be vigilant that the period of repentance is when deliverance is at times required and should be ministered. Ministers need to be equipped and prepared to discern and seize the moment. Imaginably, putting more emphasis on this fact would have led Wesley to be more intentional, proactive, and direct in his approach to the demonic. A Wesleyan standardization for casting out demons perhaps would have produced more didactic material on the subject, as well. Nonetheless, there is much to gain from what he has recorded.

What can *we* learn about deliverance dynamics from Wesley's experiences? Chiefly, it is during conviction and repentance that the demons surface. However, in the case of the physically bound woman who had been manifesting for some time, during conviction and repentance, the manifestations increased, worsened, and came to a head prior to release and restoration. Further, we learn from Wesley that the demonic strongholds are associated with and attached to sin. This particular woman was shackled to every type of sin from hatred, a spirit of murder, unbelief, rage, blasphemy and a whole host of diabolical dispositions. She also acted in irregular ways that would not be interpreted as normal human behavior, such as displaying preternatural strength that could not be physically restrained. Sin and Satan worked together.

When conviction of sin occurred, the evil spirits were stirred up and awakened. When conviction augmented and the soul surrendered, then the demons began to surface, the manifestations proportionally increased, and conditions exacerbated. When the individual fully permitted the convicting grace of the Spirit to have its way, then godly sorrow was birthed, and repentance began to grow. As the person desired to surrender and turn completely to the grace-filled work of God, the repentance was completed, and the tie with the evil spirits was severed. At that point the demons were evicted. They could no longer abide in a repentant heart that cried out in

26. J. Wesley, "Working Out Our Own Salvation," 509.

faith to Christ for deliverance and salvation. Wesley identified an essential correlation between repentance of sin and deliverance from the demonic.

When a person under conviction, often presenting the demonic by shaking and shuddering, begins to seek repentance and relief, Wesley identified these struggles as the "chief times at which Satan is cast out."[27] The struggle of conviction and repentance was due to a fighting within where the sword of the Spirit was "wounding and healing" the sinner simultaneously. They were "struck through, as with a sword, and fell trembling to the ground."[28] Through convicting and repenting grace, "God was present, both to wound and to heal."[29] What or who was being wounded? The war is against God's enemies, the devil, and sin. Christ came to destroy the power of sin and Satan (Rom 6:6; 1 John 3:7). Let us examine in more depth the correlation between sin and the demonic.

The Connection Between Sin and the Demonic

Wesley admittedly recognized that when persons were under conviction and manifesting the demonic that Satan was being cast out. What he failed to see and incorporate into his theology and routinize in his ministry is that often the evicted demons were originally *permitted* to attach to the soul when the individual *surrendered* to the demonic voice of temptation and *yielded* to commit the sin. And most likely the sin became habitual. Sin opened the door to the demonic!

The demon that was being cast out had to enter the person at some point prior. How? How did it enter the person's world and begin to influence them? Temptation and sin were crouching at the door, knocking to enter (Gen 4:7). The person did not resist the temptation but opened the door, and sin entered. Eventually, sin does not have to knock. The person seeks after sin and invites it into the house. Soon, the evil spirit attached to the sin enters in as well.[30]

Admittedly, because one commits a sin does not necessarily signify that one needs deliverance from a demon. However, continual unrepented practice of a sin may open the door to greater bondage and permit a demon(s) to gain residence, since sin is connected or attached to the tempter, Satan. Satan is the tempter behind sin (Gen 3:1; Job 1–2; Matt 4; Luke 22:3,31; Rev

27. J. Wesley, "Journal Entry for July 19, 1759," 502.

28. J. Wesley, "Journal Entry for July 30, 1739," 213.

29. J. Wesley, "Journal Entry for April 16, 1773," 490.

30. For a full, systematic exposition of sin and the demonic, as well as thorough teaching and training in deliverance ministry, see Bellini, *X-Manual.*

12:9). Sin is the device Satan employs to gain influence and demonize the soul. Demonization refers to the degree of influence or control, not necessarily possession, the enemy has over a person. And influence is apparent when a temptation is successful; that is, it results in sin. Sins committed reveal the influence of the devil over a person or degrees of demonization.

As we learned from the renunciation vows in the baptismal rite, the early church understood the correlation between sin and demonic influence. Hence, catechumens, or young believers in training, went through exorcism prior to and during baptism. In that rite, they renounced sin and the powers of darkness. The priest would pray prayers of deliverance over them and exorcise the devil. The sacrament of baptism is connected to the washing away of sin, but the rite of exorcism within the rite of baptism deals with the devil and his power over the person. Both sin *and* the demonic needed to be addressed. And so today the need is the same, deliverance from sin *and* the demonic.

Let us explore the connection further. Simply, Satan is the author of temptation, and temptation can lead to sin. If one continues to practice sin in an area, it can open the door to a demonic *attachment* in which Satan has a stronghold of influence in the person's life.[31] At that point, any ten-

---

31. Ephesians 4:27 speaks to giving Satan a foothold in our life. As opposed to demonic possession, which is rare, demonization involves degrees of influence. Those demonic influences are attachments. They are "attached" or related to a particular sin that the demon represents and peddles to the weak soul. The influence is not total. It is not possession but in degrees and in a particular area. For example, one can be an unbeliever or even a believer and be addicted to alcohol, the sin of drunkenness. The rest of their life may be in order. They function fine and virtuously at work, in their marriage and family, and are otherwise productive members of society. They attend church, read their Bible, and pray regularly. However, in this one area, they have fallen. Initially it was a transgression here and there. But over time sin compounded into uncontrolled demonic activity, and the gratification system of the brain was highjacked. And the neuroscience of addiction takes over physiology, while the demons torment the soul. A few nights of transgression snowballed into a demonic attachment and an addiction, which resulted in further collateral damage as it ultimately began to impact the marriage and family. This is the evolution of sin and the destructive path it takes. Thus, an attachment is the influence of a demon that is attached to a particular sin that in turn attaches itself to the thoughts, emotions, and will of a person. Of course, the language of attachment is not physical or literal but more spiritual and metaphorical used to explain the dynamics of the will, sin, and the demonic. Examine 1 Corinthians 10:20. Paul told the Corinthians that when they were sacrificing to an idol, they were not only committing the sin of idolatry. He made it clear that they were making an offering to demons. They were partaking of the cup and table of demons (1 Cor 1:21). Further, they were fellowshipping with and worshiping demons through their sin. Some sin is not merely transgression against God, but also demon worship. Sin is actually submission to the demon behind the temptation and the sin.

When Jesus was tempted by the devil (Matt 4), Satan tempted Jesus to bow down and worship him. The temptation of idolatry was twofold, worship a false god and worship the

sion of temptation disappears. Sin and the enemy are no longer resisted. Freely invited in, they both find a resting place in the soul. Sin is like a chain that attaches the soul to the enemy. The enemy holds the chains of sin, and if the individual takes the bait at the end of the chain, a bond begins to form between the will of the person, the sin, and the enemy that offers the temptation.[32] We are commanded in Ephesians 4:27 to not give any place or opportunity to the devil.

Wesleyan Grace and the Will

We can draw a game-breaking conclusion learning from the dynamics between the will, sin, and the demonic. The will is the key to *bondage or deliverance*. God permits Satan to tempt us, as he did Job and even Christ. Neither God nor Satan force us to sin. Sin originates with our will, our decision. Sin is the result of a free moral agent willingly choosing to transgress the moral law of God by commission or omission (1 John 3:4). God created humanity with the freedom to choose. Even under the fall, God restores a measure of liberty and power to choose as a benefit of his prevenient grace. God grants us grace to see the good (conscience) and grace to choose it. We are called to respond to his prevenient grace. Our perspective is decidedly Wesleyan.

Wesley did not view God's co-operant free grace as irresistible and thus domineering and coercing the will to respond.[33] The "prevenient" (Latin—

---

devil, who is the false god. Of course, Jesus resisted the sin of idolatry on both counts. But it is evident that sin can lead not only to demonic influence but also to demon worship.

Many religious, occultic, and sexual practices today are nothing less than demon worship. Satan is the god of this world (2 Cor 4:4; 1 John 5:19; Rev 12:9); many worship him directly and fully aware, and many more worship him indirectly and unaware.

32. We can be tempted by our own fallen flesh as well as by the devil (Jas 1:14). However, I believe indirectly or directly at some point the flesh was tempted by the devil regarding that particular sin. Once the enemy gets in someone's mind, the flesh can be taught how to be tempted all on its own. The flesh learns to feed itself. So, Satan may not be directly involved in *every* temptation, but I believe that he is either directly or indirectly, and either immediately or remotely, connected to a particular temptation and sin.

Satan is the father of lies (John 8:44), and all temptation is a lie; therefore, the enemy is directly or indirectly and immediately or remotely connected with temptation and sin. 1 John 3:8 states, "The one who does what is sinful is of the devil, because the devil has been sinning from the beginning." Sin connects us to the enemy, directly or indirectly. So directly or indirectly all temptation and sin find their origin in the evil one. When we sin, it is connected to the work of the enemy. Nonetheless, we are directly responsible for how we respond to temptation. The reason the Son of God appeared was to destroy the devil's work."

33. Collins' term for it. Collins, *Theology of John Wesley*, 76. Collins is emphatic, and rightly so, to note that God takes the initiative, less we fall into a semi-Pelagian synergism. God's grace is *freely* given (Protestant emphasis) and enables by grace our

prevenire) in prevenient grace means "to go or come before" or "precedes."[34] "To precede" characterizes all God's grace toward us, from prevenient to justifying to sanctifying to glorifying. God's grace goes ahead of us. Wesley defines prevenient grace as "the first wish to please God, the first dawn of light concerning his will, and the first slight, transient conviction of having sinned against him."[35]

God's grace, by definition, goes *before* us. God initiates. He makes the first move. Wesley proclaims, "the very first motion of good is from above, as well as the power which conducts it to the end."[36] God's co-operant free grace restores some measure of liberty to enable us to respond to God's will in obedience and participation. God freely moves toward us with the intent of our cooperation or free response (Phil 2:12–13). Wesley simply put it this way: "First, God works; therefore you *can* work: Secondly, God works, therefore you *must* work."[37] Our will is empowered to respond in obedience by God's preceding grace. Thus, the will is key to our agency and our humanity (the moral image of God). And we will see that it is key to bondage or deliverance.

God created us in his moral image as moral agents. That, by definition, means that we are free to choose and own our decisions and consequences. Wesley viewed reason, affection, and freedom as "essential; to a moral agent."[38] God is not the author of evil. He gives us the grace to respond freely to his will. It is a "responsible" grace as Wesley scholar Randy Maddox so aptly put it.[39] However, God will not violate our will, and neither can sin nor the devil.[40] We must give permission for salvation or sin to take root. I call it *the law of the will* or agency. It seems to be a law in the Spirit that our freewill is intrinsic to who we are as moral beings, and it is essential for us to choose and be responsible for our own moral decisions. A will that is

---

response (Catholic emphasis), 292–93. Collins' conjunctive view of Catholic and Protestant emphases parallels that of Starkey. See Starkey, *Work*, 116–20.

34. Collins, *Theology of John Wesley*, 76.

35. Collins, *Theology of John Wesley*, 76.

36. J. Wesley, "Working Out Our Own Salvation," 509.

37. J. Wesley, "Working Out Our Own Salvation," 511.

38. J. Wesley, "General Spread of the Gospel," 280.

39. Maddox, *Responsible Grace*, 141–56.

40. The Lord indeed acts in many ways in our life contrary to what we desire or will. But we have the choice to accept his will, reject it, or even live in denial. God is free to do as he wills. Yet, we have a very limited parameter of choice that exists within limitations, the limits of God's nature and will, our human nature and ability, time, space, personal history, etc. Our free moral choice has its heavy limits and restrictions, yet, it is a choice nonetheless, and God grants it to us and does not violate it. Nor will he allow Satan to violate it. Under God's permission, the devil tempts us, but he cannot force us to yield.

not free (that cannot do otherwise) cannot choose, nor can it be morally responsible. As free moral agents, we are tempted to do evil. Though Satan tempts us, we cannot blame the devil if we yield to sin. Nor can we blame God. In the garden, our primordial parents tried to blame God, the serpent, and each other. It did not work then, and it does not work now.

The Connection Between the Will and the Demonic

In contrast to our Calvinist friends, Wesley understood God's free co-operant grace as not irresistible and one that requires a free response. Though Wesley did not contend that humans have the *natural* or innate ability to respond to God as in (semi-)Pelagianism.[41] Technically, no one is in a state of pure nature devoid of God's grace unless they sinned it way. Wesley penned, "no man is in a state of mere nature; there is no man, unless he has quenched the Spirit, that is wholly devoid of the grace of God." But concerning "preventing grace," "every man has a greater or less measure of this, which waiteth not for the call of man."[42] So it goes when we sin, we yield our will freely to the power of the darkness, both to the transgression and the evil one. Sin and Satan then hold the will in bondage. When sin is committed over an extended time as a factor of **intensity, frequency, duration, and across generations**, the power and authority of sin and darkness increase. These markers are standard for measuring behavior in Applied Behavior Analysis.

What I am labeling as *the law of the will* is simple and direct. Divine or demonic authority over the will is proportional to submission of the will. Control or authority is relative to submission. Whatever you submit to has a degree of authority or influence over you (John 8:34; Rom 6:16–18; 2 Pet 2:19). We can submit to sin and Satan, or we can submit to the Lordship of Christ. To the degree one submits to sin, the demonic, or Christ, to that degree sin, the demonic, or Christ has authority over that person's will. I am incorporating a Wesleyan understanding of free co-operant grace, human free moral agency, and the definition and nature of sin into a larger understanding of the mechanics of demonic bondage and deliverance.

For deliverance to occur, the will must be turned in repentance (repenting grace) from serving sin and Satan to serving God. Liberation and recovery of the will are instrumental to true repentance and deliverance.

41. Named after Pelagius (355–420) who held that humanity did not inherit original sin and was inherently good by nature. Thus, they could freely exercise their will to do what is good and right.

42. J. Wesley, "Working Out Our Own Salvation," 512.

Of course, victory is accomplished by the grace and power of God, but it also requires the will to cooperate and respond. Further, the prayers and intercession of the saints (deliverance ministry) can aid the individual's will with more grace. Deliverance begins to manifest with a recovery of agency.

I am taking the next step that, in my view, Wesley should have taken in the process. Wesley identified that during times of conviction and repentance persons would often convulse and manifest because these were the "chief times at which Satan is cast out."[43] In other words, repentance is the ground and time for deliverance to emerge. Repentance is turning the mind and will from sin and Satan to God. With repentance, the cooperation of the will to serve the enemy has been broken. The legal ground for sin and Satan to remain has been shattered. The recovery of the will to serve the Lord is being restored (Rom 6:15–22). During the season of repentance, whether related to justification or entire sanctification, we can proactively intercede for the seeker and participate with the Holy Spirit by actively confronting the devil(s) directly and driving him out. Wesley did not pick up on this strategic piece.

Christ Gives You Authority to Cast Out Demons

Wesley wrote considerably on repentance (and faith) leading to justification and the believer's repentance leading to entire sanctification. Repentance is a vital spiritual discipline on the way of salvation (*via salutis*). Repentance is also a strategic time for deliverance, either prior to salvation or on the way to perfection (entire sanctification). It is a strategic time because with repentance, the will is being convicted to renounce sin and the work of Satan. Grace is ripening the heart to be rid of one's sins (justification) or inbred sin (entire sanctification). With true repentance, the legal ground for sin and Satan to remain is broken. Both can be cast out by the authority and power of the name of Jesus.

You may ask, "Why do *I* have to cast the demon out? Since God takes away the sin, cannot he also remove the devil?" Yes, God has already destroyed the power of sin and Satan at the cross. But we are to appropriate the power of the finished work of the cross and resist sin and the devil. God does not resist sin or Satan for us. He commands us to do so. God has objectively already defeated the devil. We need to receive that objective work and appropriate it subjectively in our lives. In Luke 10:19–20, Jesus told his disciples, "I give you authority to trample on snakes (demons)." Clearly, Christ could do it himself and has done it at the cross. Jesus said, "It is finished"

43. J. Wesley, "Journal Entry for July 19, 1759," 502.

(John 19:30). What is finished? Sin is finished! Satan is finished! Death is finished! Salvation is finished!

Jesus already defeated the devil (John 12:31; 16:11; Col 2:15; Heb 2:14; 1 Jn 3:7). The provision has been made. But now, he calls us to resist the devil and cast him out. James 4:7 commands us "to resist the devil, and he will flee from us." "Resist" is an implied second person command. (You) resist the devil. Not God. You! He calls you to do it. *You,* not God, need to put on the armor of God to war against Satan. *You* have been called. *You* have been drafted to war. *You* have been armed and equipped for battle. *You* have been given authority in the name that is above every name. Every knee, including Satan's knee shall bow. All power and authority have been given to Christ, who gives you authority. Now, you go in his name!

7

A Wesleyan Framework and Strategy for Deliverance Ministry Today

SUMMARY OF LESSONS LEARNED FROM WESLEY

We have critically examined Wesley regarding deliverance and are situated to apply his understanding and methods to a Wesleyan theological framework for deliverance. What would characterize such a framework? In the previous chapters, we highlighted that both Scripture and Wesley assume a spirit-worldview. This seems necessary to account for evil spirit-beings and engagement in a spiritual war. In addition, a Wesleyan perspective would embrace a robust practical theology of the Holy Spirit the divine agent, working God's grace in us from prevenient to sanctifying grace and onto glorifying grace. Not only the Spirit works full salvation in our heart, but he also is our divine agent of assurance as well. We can *know* by the witness of the Spirit the work that God is doing and has done in us, a spiritual empiricism. We can experience the knowledge of God through the light shed by the Spirit of God. We can even discern the forces of darkness that war against our souls.

Spiritual warfare begins at baptism, as we renounce Satan and his works in our vows. Prevenient grace draws us closer to God, leading to convincing grace. The power of sin and Satan is broken by repentance and faith in Christ. We participate in the process of deliverance by casting out any influence of the devil over one's life. Jesus has given us his name as a weapon of warfare. Therefore, in a war that is not against flesh and blood but against invisible cohorts of demons, we can discern both the strategy of the enemy and the battle call of the Lord of Hosts and the nature of our spiritual weaponry. God has equipped the saints with the sword of the Spirit (the Word of God), truth, righteousness, salvation, peace, faith, the name and the blood of Jesus, prayer, worship, and thanksgiving, among others. Wesley encouraged early Methodists to put on the whole armor of God and steadfastly resist the strategies of the devil.[1]

METHODS OF DELIVERANCE

Wesley and early Methodists exhibited a steadfast prowess in spiritual battle for the souls of others. As we noted, Wesley's *Journals* and *Letters* are replete with encounters with diabolical spiritual powers. Whether outdoors during open-air preaching, at prayer meetings, or in people's homes, repentant souls under conviction sought deliverance while assailed by hell's assassins. *Indirect means* of confrontation include *hearing the Word, prayer, repentance, worship,* and *faith.* These means are indirect because one is not confronting and addressing Satan directly. Wesley also called these *ordinary* means that anyone can use who is not gifted. The ordinary-extraordinary distinction is not biblical because everyone is given a gift(s) of the Spirit. However, one has indirect means at their disposal as well as more direct means, like using the name and authority of Jesus that has been given to *all* believers to cast out demons. Both indirect and direct means, including one's gifts, should be used by the church in spiritual warfare and deliverance ministry.

THE WILL IS KEY

We noted in detail the significance of the will or agency in Wesleyan theology, specifically salvation (soteriology). God's grace goes ahead and bestows a measure of liberty to the will so that a moral agent may respond in obedience. For Wesley, God's grace is co-operant free grace. It is prevenient, meaning it goes first or ahead. And it restores freedom to the will to choose to cooperate. Wesleyan grace is not irresistible. Those who do not respond faithfully to God's grace resist God and can lose the grace that they have.[2] We are either going forward or backwards. Contrastingly, the Calvinist notion of grace is irresistible. God's grace works and secures salvation apart

---

1. J. Wesley, "Of Evil Angels," 379–80.

2. J. Wesley, "Scripture Way of Salvation," 49; John Wesley, "Repentance of Believers," 157, 165; and J. Wesley, "Working Out Your Own Salvation," 513.

from the will or working of the believer. Bound in our own depravity, we are only *free* to sin.

We appropriated a Wesleyan construal of grace and the will and applied it to deliverance from sin and Satan. During convicting and repenting grace, God is working on the will to free it from bondage. The will is strategic. Agency needs to be recovered so that the individual can receive grace and break ties with sin and Satan, turn towards the Lord, and receive grace to experience liberation. Thus, during the time of repentance (for justification or entire sanctification) the deliverance minister needs to intercede and stand in the gap for the person who is bound and begin to participate in their deliverance (a midwife if you will).[3] Of course, the Lord does the delivering, but his Spirit is working through the bound person and through the minister who is assisting to set the captive free. Deliverance ministry is an *intercessory* ministry in which we participate in the power and authority of God and assist the oppressed in the deliverance process. Through indirect and direct means, we war on behalf of the person against the forces of evil, while we exhort their will to cooperate with the Spirit of God, to find true repentance, and restoration.

Targeting and restoring the will or agency in repentance is essential. The will can give or take away the legal right for sin and Satan to remain. And repentance is the means that breaks the legal authority for sin and Satan to influence a person. In the practice of deliverance, I call these principles *the law of the will* and *the law of repentance*.

THE CROSS IS THE BASIS FOR DELIVERANCE

We did not discuss it much, though implied in all the Wesleyan way of salvation is the reality and necessity of the cross or the atonement for deliverance. I am using the phrase "the cross," throughout, as shorthand for the death,

---

3. Wesley identified the need, though remotely, for repentance prior to both crises experiences of justification and entire sanctification. Wesley taught the significance of repentance both prior to justification and to entire sanctification. The former is for unbelievers leading to salvation. The latter was a believer's repentance that begins when the believer is convicted by the Spirit of inbred, birth, or original sin that remains in the believer after justification and regeneration. They are not condemned by its presence because it is inherited, but they are held guilty if it remains in them, and they fall to it in temptation. Wesley believed that the regenerated believer still has the presence of sin, but the power of sin is broken. The regenerated can resist temptation and live above sin. In fact, for Wesley, that is the norm. In entire sanctification, one is delivered from the presence of remaining inbred sin. See J. Wesley, "Working Out Your Own Salvation," 599; J. Wesley, "On Sin in Believers," 145–56; and J. Wesley, "Repentance of Believers," 157–70; and J. Wesley, "Scripture Way of Salvation," 49.

burial, and resurrection of Jesus Christ and all that those events accomplished, specifically, the defeat of sin, guilt, death, hell, Satan, and his angels. Wesley held that "nothing in the Christian system is of greater consequence than the doctrine of the atonement."[4] "Christ and him crucified" is the foundation and supply for our salvation from prevenient to glorifying grace. A sizeable portion of his writing alludes to the objective and subjective or consequential dimensions of the atonement, such as appropriating its benefits. It is not a stretch to conclude that Wesley's entire *via salutis* (way of salvation) is rooted in the benefits of the cross or the atonement. Thus, without the cross there can be no deliverance or salvation, *the law of the cross*.

During one incident, Wesley was preaching on the *atonement*, which led to conviction and deliverance.[5] "In the evening I was again pressed in spirit to declare, that 'Christ gave himself a ransom for all.' And almost before we called upon him to set to his seal, he answered. One was so wounded by the sword of the Spirit, that you would have imagined she could not live a moment. But immediately his abundant kindness was showed, and she sang of his righteousness."[6]

Christ was given as a *ransom* for us all. Deliverance was secured at the cross by Jesus Christ, the Son of God who defeated our enemies. This model or emphasis of the atonement is known as *Christus Victor* (Christ the Victor).[7] Christ delivered humanity from sin and death by defeating the power of the devil through the power of the cross. On the cross, the King of kings and the Lord of lords destroyed the power of the enemy and delivered his people from the kingdom of darkness and into the kingdom of light. The efficient cause of deliverance begins and ends at the cross. The basis, authority, and power for all deliverance and exorcism is grounded in the finished work of the cross. If we are to be effective in spiritual warfare and deliverance ministry, we must forever settle this fact in our hearts and minds. Casting out a demon is not based on one's faith or ability to do so. We do not contend for victory in a deliverance session. Satan was defeated and the victory was won at the cross. We merely implement Christ's victory.

4. J. Wesley, "Letter to Mary Bishop," 297–98.

5. "Christ gave himself a ransom for all" often indicates a type of atonement model called the Ransom Theory or Christ the Victor (*Christus Victor*). It is debatable whether that was Wesley's preferred atonement model, or penal substitution, or if he leaned on any one model. But we do find the theme of Christ the Victor in Wesley's writings. *Christus Victor* that Christ defeated sin, death, and the Devil is instrumental to an effective theology and practice of deliverance.

6. J. Wesley, "Journal Entry for April 17, 1739," 188–89.

7. Aulen, *Christus Victor*, 1–15.

As Wesleyans, we are familiar with Wesley's writing on the saving and sanctifying grace that was purchased at Calvary. However, we often do not make the connection between the work of the cross and its implications for deliverance and victory. Let us briefly examine the potent dynamics of the cross and their direct assault on and defeat of the powers of darkness. Jesus died for our sins as a fact in history, regardless of our subjective experience of whether we feel forgiven. It was accomplished objectively.[8] It is finished. When Jesus died for our sins, he also took the *sinner* with him to the cross (Rom 6:1–7; Eph 2:6). Thus, when Jesus died, we died. When Jesus was buried, we were buried. When he arose, we arose. When he ascended into heaven, we ascended. All provisions for salvation have been made by Christ at the cross. We receive and experience this objective reality subjectively once we believe. *Subjective* here means a reality that we receive and experience personally. When we believe the gospel, the Spirit applies what has been provided by Christ objectively in history to our hearts subjectively. We personally experience death to the old self and victory over Satan.

The Spirit works from the objective ground of the cross and applies the experience of deliverance and victory to our lives.[9] The Spirit works in unison with the cross. What Jesus did on the cross, the Spirit applies to our hearts. He bears witness and implements, or puts into effect, the work of the cross in our lives. The Spirit makes the cross real to us. He lifts it off the pages of history and Scripture and applies it to our hearts. The Spirit leads us to Christ; that is the Spirit's ministry. The Spirit does not bear witness to himself but to Christ and his work (John 14:26; 15:26; 16:13–15). The Spirit leads us to the cross and applies it to our lives. He executes this ministry as the Spirit of Truth. He leads us and guides us into truth about our sin, truth about Christ, and truth about our need for a Savior.

When Christ died, he took sin, the sinner, guilt, shame, and death upon himself at the cross. Romans 6:6 claims, "we [the sinner] were crucified with him." There on the cross, he condemned our sin in his own body, tasting death for all (Rom 6; 8:2–3). In condemning our sin in his own flesh, he pronounced a judgment upon it. Sin is condemned. And he took our

---

8. When I speak of the objectivity of the atonement, I do not mean in the Calvinist sense where all salvation is accomplished and secured for the elect, and they can never fall away, since salvation has been objectively accomplished in Christ's death. By objective I mean that Christ died in history for the sins of all people. It is a finished fact. All that is necessary for salvation is accomplished. This objective fact is *realized subjectively* in each person who receives Christ, walks out the Christian life by the power of the Spirit, and finishes the race well. The provision is complete and for all. Whosoever desires to partake of it may through repentance and faith given by God's grace.

9. See Starkey's explanation of the Holy Spirit's administration of the saving work of Christ in Wesley. Starkey, *Work*, 34.

condemnation on himself.[10] Jesus put our sin to death in his own body, and he also judged it. Sin has been condemned and defeated.

Additionally, the power of the devil has been destroyed at the cross (Heb 2:14). When Jesus died, death could not hold him (Acts 2:24). He broke its grip. Jesus conquered death by death, as the Eastern Orthodox Easter liturgy proclaims. He defeated death at its own game, and thus stripped Satan of his power. John 16:11 declares that "the prince of darkness has been judged." Christ's death was the defeat and judgment of both sin and Satan (John 12:31). He "disarmed the spiritual rulers and authorities. He shamed them publicly by his victory over them on the cross" (NLT Col 2:15).

Finally, after taking captivity captive, he took the keys of hell and death and is waiting for the end of time when he will administer Satan's eternal sentence in the lake of fire. Hell and death will be thrown in the fiery lake as well (Rev 20:10, 14). Thus, the cross put an end to the power of sin, death, hell, and Satan. Good theology brings good results. To be effective in deliverance one cannot fear Satan because one knows that he is a defeated foe. We need to fix it in our mind's eye that sin and the devil were judged and defeated on the cross. The devil is a defeated foe, awaiting his final sentencing. When we go into a deliverance session, we do not look for victory. We do not look for victory or deliverance in what we do, say, feel, or experience. The subjective practice and experience of deliverance is grounded and based on the objective historical finished work of the cross that Christ already accomplished. We merely draw from it, enforce it, and execute it. I call this principle *the law of the cross*.

JESUS GIVE US AUTHORITY IN HIS NAME

Now with the foundation laid, we can move to the practical piece of casting out the devil. As we noted, Wesley employed an indirect method. He supplicated the Lord on behalf of the bound, asking for their deliverance. He did not *directly* confront Satan. However, as we learned, Jesus gave us his authority in his name to cast out demons (Luke 10:19–20), *the law of authority*. This is the charismatic 'update' and 'upgrade' to our Methodism 1.0.[11] We learned from Scripture and the Charismatic movement that God

10. For an examination of Wesley's thought on the atonement, its objective and subjective dimensions, see Collins, *Theology of John Wesley,* 103–10.

11. The great tradition of the church from the apostles to today has also affirmed the invisible and visible nature of creation. Many traditions have practiced exorcism and deliverance through their rites. While most have incorporated it into their baptismal liturgy, exorcism continues to be a *charism* in the modern church. Roman Catholicism and Eastern Orthodoxy have practiced their exorcism rites unbroken since their

gives us the authority and assignment of expelling the demonic. Casting out demons is our job. Sure, the Lord can do it himself, as he can do all the work of the ministry. However, in his grace and wisdom, he chooses to use us and allow us to participate in his mission. Ultimately, it is Jesus who casts out the demons when we use the power of attorney of his name. The authority and power are his. Make no mistake. And Satan knows that fact!

We have been equipped, as the disciples were, with the name of Jesus to *directly* drive out evil spirits. There is no magic formula to the practice, but it does require faith in Christ and in his name, as the sons of Sceva learned the hard way (Acts 19:11–20). It may sound something like this: "I bind the spirit of fear from Joe's mind, in the name of Jesus! I take authority over the tormenting voices of terror and fear that plague and oppress him in the night! In Jesus' name, I command them to loosen their grip and leave him now, never to return. And I ask, Lord, that you would fill Joe with your Holy Spirit and perfect peace to guard and protect his mind from all fear and devices of the devil, in Jesus' name, Amen." This example represents a *direct* method or way to confront Satan, using the authority of the name of Jesus. I address the demon directly and take authority over it. I know the demon is already defeated and judged by Christ at the cross. I am standing on the finished work of the cross and enforcing its application in this situation.

I would only confront the demon once the person has truly repented. Remember, repentance recovers and restores the will and breaks the legal ground for sin and Satan to remain. The bound person is put in a place where they must stand on the finished work of the cross and enforce its application in their life, as well. Sure, Satan is defeated. The devil knows that, but if an individual is ignorant of Satan's defeat and gives him control through sin, then Satan will remain. He will continue to influence the

---

incipience. Pentecostal-Charismatic and global Christianity of all stripes also recognize deliverance ministry as normative. Pentecostalism and the Charismatic movement of the twentieth century did much to restore the deliverance ministry back to the church.

Groundbreaking deliverance ministers like Smith Wigglesworth, Lester Sumrall, William Branham, A. A. Allen, Derek Prince, Frank Hammond, C. Peter Wagner, and Charles Kraft, to name a few, brought casting out demons into the mainstream of Spirit-filled ministry. Many like evangelist Lester Sumrall had no teacher but learned deliverance when he was confronted on the southeast Asian mission field by demon possessed and oppressed persons. Taught on the spot by the Holy Spirit, he was flying the plane while building his practice.

These pioneers helped to make deliverance a normative practice for PCRs. Like much of what is written in the field, their teaching came out of years of experience of applying their authority in Christ to expel demons. Much of the Wesleyan movement and mainline Protestantism missed out on the last one hundred years of the impact of the PCR movement and the power, teaching, and experience of these anointed men and women of God. We have much catching up to do.

person's life based on the (legal) grounds that the person has given him their will (*the law of the will*). And God permits it. So, it is imperative that the person lines up with the work of the cross and walks in its victory. The cross is the basis of our deliverance victory over sin and Satan, *the law of the cross*.

THE FOUR LAWS OF DELIVERANCE[12]

At this point, we can summarize all our learning related to a Wesleyan theology and practice of deliverance and distill it into some basic memorable and practical principles or laws. In this section, I will briefly highlight "Four Laws of Deliverance" that I have crafted in the Wesleyan tradition and used in deliverance ministry over the years. I have found these to be essential to successful deliverance: *the Law of the Cross, the Law of the Will, the Law of Repentance, and the Law of Authority*. These spiritual "laws" are simplified operating principles that can be used to discern and overcome the work of the enemy in one's own life and in ministry. Above we sketched out and unpacked each of these four laws.[13] The following is a review.

The Law of the Cross

Training people for deliverance, I discovered that many are fearful of casting out demons because they do not know where or how to begin. They assume that they are going into a battle alone against one of the most powerful agents in the created universe. However, they have begun with a faulty premise. The battle is not ours, but it belongs to the Lord. The battle was already fought and won on our behalf at the cross of Calvary. The cross is the place where sin, death, and Satan have been defeated and is our grounds, basis, power, and authority for deliverance (e.g., Rom 6:1–7, 8:3; Heb 2:14; and 1 John 3:8).

As Jesus declared on the cross, "It is finished" (John 19:30). What Christ meant was that sin is finished! Death is finished! Satan is finished! And the work of salvation is finished! Deliverance begins here with the finished work of the cross. Sin, Satan, and his demonic hordes have been vanquished. We are working from this objective fact that needs to be applied and implemented subjectively when we face the enemy in warfare or in deliverance. We are merely enforcing Christ's victory with the authority he has given us in his name. However, contra charismatic inclinations, even

---

12. This section is paraphrased from Bellini, *X-Manual*.

13. Not meant as a rigid formula but key points to remember.

though the work of salvation is finished, and Satan is defeated, the church will still go through trials, tribulations, adverse circumstances, and (righteous) suffering (Luke 9:21–27; John 16:33; Rom 8:17; Phil 1:29; Jas 1:2; 1 Pet 1:6; 4:12).[14] We resist unrealistic triumphalism.

It is imperative when casting out demons that one does not trust in do-it-yourself strategies, peculiar methods, spiritual experiences, thoughts, or feelings. Our faith and confidence must be in the completed work of the cross *alone*. The cross is primary. Our subjective ideas and experience are secondary at best. We are not "defeating" Satan in the deliverance encounter. If we think victory depends on us, then Satan has already won the battle. He will convince us to look at the one bound, at ourselves, our feelings, our lack of faith, our fear, evil manifestations, or any intimidating or distracting tactic that will keep us from ministering in Christ's authority based on the work of the cross. Do not look at your feet. Keep your eyes on Christ and walk on the water. The grounds for an effective deliverance ministry begin at the cross where evil has been dealt a death blow. If we are to be effective in spiritual warfare and deliverance ministry, we must forever settle this fact in our hearts and minds.

The cross alone is our solid basis for deliverance and exorcism. It is imperative to be utterly convicted that when you begin a deliverance session you are beginning from a place of victory. You are not struggling to attain victory. You start with victory. The battle has already been won!

The Law of the Will (Agency)

The law of the will is simple and direct. Authority over the will is proportional to submission of the will. Whatever you submit to has a degree of

---

14. There is an influence in the PCR movement stemming from the health and wealth (prosperity) gospel and the positive confession movement that claims that believers do not have to suffer, face adversity, or anything "negative." Of course, this is against Scripture, as listed above. The center of the gospel is the message of the cross which involves sacrifice and suffering. We are called to take up our own cross daily as a prerequisite to follow Christ and be his disciple. Christ's cross signified death for the sins of the world. Our cross is different, though it also involves sacrifice and suffering. We deny ourselves and lose our lives in order to gain them in eternity. Losing your entire life is sacrifice. Sacrifice always involves suffering, suffering from self-denial, resisting sin, Satan, and the world, opposition, and persecution. Virtually all the apostles suffered persecution and martyrdom. The early church went through great adversity and persecution, and they thought it an honor to do so because it means they were following after Christ. The servant is not greater than the master. Our cross and suffering are not salvific or atonement worthy, but it is part of the sacrifice required of us (our reasonable service) in order to be Christ's disciple. It is not a Savior's cross but a disciple's cross.

authority or control over you (John 8:34; Rom 6:16–18; 2 Pet 2:19). Submit to rage, then it will control you to some degree. Submit to lust, then it will control you. We can submit to sin and Satan, or we can submit to the Lordship of Christ. To the degree one submits to sin, the demonic, or Christ, to that degree sin, the demonic or Christ has authority over that person's will. Neither God nor the devil will violate your will regarding your choice for good or evil. Rather, God will not violate your will. He honors your freedom and personhood. And the devil *cannot* violate your will. God will not permit it. It is a law of the Spirit that I call *the law of the will*. Sin and Satan need our consent to enter and dwell.

If someone is bound by the devil, it is imperative that the person comes to a place where he or she wants to be set free. They must be willing. That is part of the *law of the will* and the bottom-line question. Jesus asked the paralytic in John 5:6, "Do you really want to be healed?" Some say they want to be healed or delivered, but in their heart of hearts they are comfortable in their situation and do not want to get up and walk, even after thirty-eight years of bondage, a learned helplessness. People who are bound may not be able to free themselves, but they can express a desire and willingness to be free. By the prevenient grace of God, they can commit to recovering their will or agency where it has been enslaved. A desire to recover the will is the first step toward deliverance.

What I am calling *the law of the will* or agency is direct. The authority that sin and the devil have in one's life is proportional to one's submission to sin and the enemy. The same is true with Christ's manifest authority in our life.[15] It is proportional to our submission to his Lordship. By God's prevenient grace, a measure of freedom has been restored so we can respond to God's will by obeying or disobeying. Whatever we submit to has a degree of authority or control over us (John 8:34; Rom 6:16–18; 2 Pet 2:19). We can submit to sin and Satan, or we can submit to the Lordship of Christ.

To the degree one submits to sin and the demonic or to Christ, sin and the demonic or Christ has authority over that person. By degree, I mean the relative *duration, frequency,* and *intensity* of submission. Rarely will one encounter someone who is "possessed." Rather, one will find that the enemy

---

15. In deliverance, we want our confession of the name of Jesus to be more than a magic formula or mere words recited. Our lives submitted to the Lordship of Christ need to back our use of his name to cast out demons. When we submit and walk in Christ's authority it begins to manifest in our lives. It becomes a reality. We see this authority in Christ when he walked by those who were demonized. At his mere presence, the demons would manifest, moan, and cry out for mercy. His very presence subdued the gates of hell. *Manifest authority* is what is needed to cast out demons. We can carry such authority by being obedient to Christ and letting him have full control over every area of our lives.

has a *certain degree of influence* over an area(s) of a person's life. In deliverance, Christ has come to set the person free from sin and recover his or her agency to serve righteousness (Rom 6:15–23). However, Christ will not violate a person's will. The bound person must desire and want to be set free. Even if bound, there must be a willingness to turn to Christ and yield to the process of deliverance.

The Law of Repentance

Wesley firmly stated, "Repentance frequently means an inward change of mind from sin to holiness."[16] Repentance (*metanoia*- Greek) means to turn the mind so as to turn one's life. In repentance, one turns from sin and self to God. We turn from self-centered and self-directing living to God-centered and God-directed living. Repentance begins when the Spirit of God convicts us of sin, and we begin to see sin as God sees it, and not how we want to see it. "To confess" sin in the Greek (*homologia*) means "to say the same thing" (1 John 1:7–9). We say what God says about our sin without rationalizing or excusing it. We see and say what God sees and says about the sin. It is evil and worthy of eternal damnation. When we repent and confess our sin, we must turn from sin and surrender fully to God. Anything less is insufficient. Sin and Satan are unmerciful.

True repentance involves *ceasing* from sin. We no longer give sin the slightest permission in our lives to serve it. We demonstrate that we are truly repentant when we show the fruit of repentance, which is twofold. First, we no longer practice the sin. Second, we practice righteousness, the opposite of sin (Matt 3). True repentance means we no longer fall into *repent and repeat*. *Repent and repeat* is the vicious, tormenting cycle one is dragged through when their repentance is either imperfect, incomplete, insincere, unfinished, or false. The person is under the conviction of the law (God's Word) that the thought or practice is wrong, but they cannot free themselves from its grip. Even if for a time they find some reprieve, inevitably temptation arises, and they succumb to the sin and fall back into slavery. Sin can be relentless! At the same time, repentance is often a process, and God supplies the grace needed for true repentance if we persevere.

Wesley recognized this dreaded cycle of *repent and repeat* as indicative of one who is still in "bondage and fear." In his sermon "The Spirit of Bondage and Adoption," Wesley writes on one bound in sin, "[T]he more he frets against it, the more it prevails; he may bite, but he cannot break his chain. Thus, he toils without end, repenting and sinning and repenting and

16. J. Wesley, "Repentance of Believers," 157.

sinning, till at length the poor, sinful, helpless, wretch is at his wit's end, and can barely groan, 'O wretched man that I am! Who can deliver me from this body of death?'"[17]

The provision for victory is at the cross, but the victory of the cross must be received subjectively in one's life, beginning with repentance. We need to make Christ's death our own (Rom 6:6,11). The word "repentance" involves a radical change of mind that involves a radical change of life, a 180-degree turn. It implies turning from a life governed by self and turning to God and a God-governed life. God calls the shots, not self. Repentance means that we have decided to *cease* from sin and give it no more consent to enter our lives.[18] We yield to God's repenting grace. We will no longer bargain and compromise with sin's insidious ways and fall into the endless cycle of *repent and repeat*. No more attempts at sin-management. Sin management results in sin managing us! Allow the Spirit to lay the ax to the roots of sin. Repentance and forgiveness of sin break Satan's "legal right" and enslaving power to keep us chained to his influence.

John the Baptist preached that repentance means to 'straighten out the crooked ways' (Matt 3:3). Christ wants to live in us, but we must first repent. Repentance prepares the way for Christ and deliverance. It straightens out and levels our crooked will. In repentance, our ways are measured by the standard of God's holy Word (Matt 7:13–14). The high places of pride need to be leveled. The low places of brokenness need to be built up (Luke 3:5). It is imperative to know that the unrepentant heart cannot be delivered from the demonic. A kingdom divided will not stand. Satan will not cast out Satan. Also, one bound with a certain sin cannot cast that same sin out of another person because Satan will not cast out Satan. Repentance is an essential practice that must precede deliverance if the power of sin and Satan are to be broken in an individual's life. Seeking and finding true repentance, which is a gift from God, is vital to deliverance. Prior to deliverance, prayer and fasting as a "means of grace" can assist in receiving the power to truly repent and be delivered from sin and Satan.

Humility and holiness are indispensable to effective deliverance ministry. James 4:6–10 are signature verses for spiritual warfare. "Submit yourself to God, and resist the devil, and he will flee from you." Yes, but first receive the grace to do so. And he only gives grace to the humble. St. James ties humility in with repentance from the sin of double mindedness, a divided loyalty. Thus, we are commanded to humble ourselves before the mighty

---

17. J. Wesley, "Spirit of Bondage and Adoption," 104.
18. J. Wesley, "Scripture Way of Salvation," 48.

hand of God, then we will be given grace to resist the devil. Humility is a prerequisite for both repentance and deliverance.

Remember, sin cannot cast out sin. Flesh cannot cast out flesh. Satan will not cast out Satan, because a kingdom divided against itself cannot stand. If we have anger within our heart, how will we cast out anger in another? The log in our own eye prevents us. In fact, our anger actually assists in the mission of Satan. Don't feed your flesh, and don't feed the devils. On the other hand, purity attracts true spiritual authority. Holiness is needed to fight against unholiness in a holy war. Humility and holiness of heart and life are essential for effective warfare.

The Law of Authority

When casting out demons, we do not confront Satan in our own power, knowledge, or goodness. We are no match for angels, even fallen ones. We will surely be defeated. We come in the name of the Lord Jesus Christ. There is no name higher in heaven and earth. At the name of Jesus, every knee will bow, even the demons will bow. He created all things. He conquered sin, death, and the devil. He will create a new heaven and a new earth. There is no one higher. And to think that his authority and his name have been given to us to defeat and cast out devils (Mark 16:17; Luke 10:19). Using a figure of speech, Christ has given us a 'power of attorney' to use his authority and name to cast out demons. Jesus cast out demons by his own authority. His disciples cast out demons in his name, and we are to cast out demons in the same manner.

Preaching and teaching the kingdom, healing the sick, *and* casting out devils (Matt 10:7–8) is a missional formula that one finds throughout the synoptic Gospels (Matthew, Mark, and Luke). It defines Jesus' evangelistic ministry. It defined the disciple's ministry and the ministry of the early church.[19] However, it is absent from the ministry of the church today. These core practices were identified with "fully preaching the gospel" (Rom 15:19, Heb 2:4), not just in word but in demonstration of the Spirit and power (1 Cor 2:4, 4:20). If we are not casting out devils, we are not fully preaching the gospel. The church has been given the keys to bind the devil and all the gates of hell. They cannot prevail against us. With Christ's power and authority, expressed in the name of Jesus, we can overcome devils and drive them out. Based on the finished work of the cross, we can claim and execute Christ's victory over sin, death, and the devil.

---

19. See Twelftree, *Jesus the Exorcist*, 130–74, and *Name of Jesus*, 209–78.

CONCLUSION

The kingdom of God is here! Deliverance is a sign that the kingdom has come! Casting out demons was central to the core *non-verbal practices* of ministering the kingdom. Deliverance is a demonstration that the kingdom has indeed come (Luke 11:20). Just as Yahweh judged Pharaoh with the "finger of God" by sending plagues to deliver the Hebrews (Ex 8:19), so also Jesus came with the "finger of God" to point out and judge the works of the devil and deliver his people from sin and death.

Without deliverance and exorcism, so many people would still be bound in sin by the devil. Many still suffer needlessly, however, because of the church's unbelief, fear, and lack of understanding regarding our authority in Christ and the healing practice of deliverance. I encourage you to pray and ask Christ to fill you with his power and authority to minister healing and deliverance to those who are broken and in captivity.

8

The C1–13 Deliverance Assessment Instrument

HOW DO I KNOW WHEN SOMEONE NEEDS DELIVERANCE?[1]

Throughout this book, one may be asking the obvious question, "How do I know when someone needs deliverance?" You may be working with a person who seems troubled and possibly bound by a demon. Do they really have a demon? Do they need deliverance? How do I know? How can I be sure? I developed a psycho-spiritual assessment instrument for that very purpose to ascertain demonization. The C1–13 (Colossians 1:13) assessment instrument can help to determine whether an individual needs deliverance. It should be filled out by the leader of the deliverance team who asks the seeker questions. The assessment follows an interview format. Prior to the assessment, there is a 10 Point Checklist to ensure the seeker is *ready* to take the assessment. When the assessment is finished, it is scored. Results are evaluated by the scoring key at the end of the assessment. Based on the information, a decision can be made how to proceed, whether deliverance is needed or not. Many are not ready for deliverance. At times an emergency may arise, and there is no time to come through the C1–13 protocol. An *emergency deliverance session* may be done on the spot. A formal deliverance session using the C1–13 protocol (or proper diagnosis and procedure) can be done at a later scheduled date.

1. These sections are paraphrased from Bellini, *X-Manual*.

EMERGENCY AND FORMAL DELIVERANCE SESSIONS

Let me unpack what I mean by *emergency deliverance session*.[2] I am making a distinction between an *emergency situation* that is ministered immediately, on-the-spot, and a *formal deliverance session(s)* that involves a formal protocol (the C1–13) of preparation, prayer, fasting, testing, scheduling, and deliverance. An emergency situation arises in the moment or when one can afford no time to waste for various reasons. The situation demands immediate attention. On one hand, the emergency session (ER) is like non-elective ER surgery. On the other hand, the formal deliverance session is like getting tested and if needed scheduling an elective surgery.

Both situations exist. There are ER deliverance sessions *and* scheduled formal deliverance sessions. We need to be prepared for both. In the case of ER and formal deliverance sessions, both will need to apply the *4 Laws of Deliverance*, the *5-Step Method of Deliverance* (found below), and post-deliverance follow-up with *Truth Therapy* (referenced below). Only in the case of the *formal session* (not ER) will one go through the entire C1–13 protocol.

For example, if someone experiences chest pains and needs ER heart surgery, we do not schedule them for a visit in five months. However, if the situation is not an ER situation, we can schedule an appointment. Similarly, with a non-ER deliverance case, we can run through much of the protocol (the C1–13) first and make sure deliverance is truly needed.

We need to make sure that what we think is the problem is really the problem. Treating a problem that is not the problem can result in malpractice and further harm done. The C1–13 protocol is an instrument that helps ascertain the real problem. We are dealing with people's lives and are liable before God and humanity and should take our work seriously, professionally, and carefully. The consequences can be spiritual, moral, psychological, sociological, and legal.

Because of the gravity of the circumstances, what I am attempting in deliverance and healing ministry is to legitimize, standardize, and professionalize what is often a hit or miss, shoot from the hip, anecdotally led ministry, which often leads to excesses, malpractice, and further harm. If there is any field and practice that needs quality control, it is deliverance ministry. Since deliverance and divine healing are working with spiritual and medical categories, such as health and wholeness, I draw from a medical model as well as from a spiritual one. We are seeking to integrate the best

---

2. The following distinction and explanation of ER and formal deliverance services was inspired by a conversation I had with Candy Gunther Brown, a description of which can be found in *X-Manual*.

from the sciences and combine them with the best theological practices to establish effective, careful, tested, and credible integrated models and practices of deliverance and healing.

Thus, in "diagnosing" and treating spiritual problems like deliverance, we are attempting to develop thorough, sophisticated procedures and protocols that cover all the bases and incorporate the learning, methods, and approaches from all relevant fields. Hence, medical model diagnostic testing is simulated in the instruments and strategies that I have developed. We are not "medically" treating people, but we are drawing from the medical model by testing, caring for, and practicing at the optimal level.

I created the C1–13 instrument as a protocol to address the problem thoroughly, professionally, and spiritually as well as to integrate treatment from other fields. Often in my ministry I have found that prior treatment in areas like mental health, followed up with deliverance and healing if needed, have been more effective than *deliverance alone*. Undergoing the C1–13 testing also helps the diagnostic (elimination) process in discerning etiology (causes) for more effective treatment. I have witnessed much abuse in this area of diagnosis, especially around mental health. It is too easy to jump the gun, demonize, and attempt to cast out things that may be better treated elsewise. I have seen too many people walk away more damaged after a deliverance session than they were before. Treatment and other care from the medical and psychological fields and even from pastoral ministry should precede any deliverance.

So, let me qualify that deliverance *often needs to be a last resort.* I believe in emergency situations when deliverance needs to be immediate, and not initially go through the protocol that I prescribe. Sometimes a case may be urgent, and the person is ripe and ready. There is no time for a lengthy protocol. I have been in that situation as a pastor, revivalist, and deliverance minister countless times. It is also the case that ER was the only way Wesley exercised deliverance. Since then, we have professionalized and refined the pastoral counseling ministry.

A deliverance minister or team should be prepared to take on ER (emergency) situations which require immediate attention, treatment, and ministry. They should also be prepared to minister a formal deliverance session that goes through the extensive C1–13 protocol. ER situations often but not always occur with unbelievers in evangelistic settings where the gospel is proclaimed with signs and wonders. Signs and wonders (including deliverance) are non-verbal proclamations and demonstrations of the kingdom and the gospel and should be standard in ministering the gospel. Deliverance and healing happen as the Spirit leads and, at times when needed, can bypass protocols (i.e., happen spontaneously and not in a scheduled session with standardized practices).

In a worship service or prayer meeting, when demons sometimes manifest on the spot, or a person is in dire need and should be taken to a private deliverance room, we need to follow the Spirit's lead and minister to the person. But there should still be a *follow-up appointment* for the more formal and standardized approach to deliverance. The protocol will help the deliverance team be more thorough and effective and catch anything that might have been missed. In my experience, most of the prerequisites from the 10 Point Checklist have already been met prior to one filling out the C1–13. Having a person who goes through an emergency deliverance session later go through the protocol is more of a both/and rather than an either/or.

The standardization (the C1–13) I created is to prevent abuse and excess, but I do not want the protocol to become the problem it was meant to solve. A deliverance team needs to use wisdom and prayerful discernment in making the call as to when to practice deliverance. In summary, I am making the distinction in deliverance situations between "ER, non-elective surgery" situations and "scheduled, non-elective tests and surgery" that is emergency deliverance and scheduled deliverance sessions. *There are both emergency and formal deliverance session(s).* The Holy Spirit, discernment, the particular case, and the circumstances will determine which is needed. All emergency sessions should still be followed up with a formal session and its protocol. *The C1–13 is protocol for a formal deliverance session.*

INTRODUCTION TO THE C1–13 INSTRUMENT

When does someone need a deliverance session? Many ministries approach this question differently. My approach is integrative using the best resources that the Spirit and the sciences can afford. Thus, you need sharp discernment, the inner witness of the Holy Spirit, and an effective assessment instrument, as you pray about a particular case.[3] In addition, the testimony of the seeker concerning their own oppression is very helpful.

I developed the C1–13 assessment instrument, named from Colossians 1:13, several years ago for ministry use. My intent was to develop

---

3. The inner witness is when God's Spirit directly bears witness with our spirit about the truth (John 14–16, 15:26; Rom 8:14–16; Heb 10:15; 1 John 2:20, 27). Or simply, the Spirit tells us the truth about a matter. The witness is immediate, direct, and self-evident. It is often a still small knowing or voice that leads the believer into truth. It is our sixth sense, or spiritual sense by which we know God and discern good and evil.

something more sophisticated and accurate beyond the usual inventory checklists offered at the back of many pop-deliverance books. The C1–13 is modeled after instruments developed and used in the soft sciences, like psychology. The C1–13 probability assessment is a qualitative and quantitative research instrument that evaluates the *probability* of the need for deliverance. No instrument is 100 percent accurate. After the person takes the assessment, the results are not absolute but *probable*. Thus, discernment must be employed. Read over the C1–13 several times until you understand it before administering.

The C1–13 measures the *degree of demonization and bondage* to a sinful practice. The instrument also evaluates the need for deliverance, utilizing a score that will indicate whether deliverance is probably needed or not needed. This instrument seeks to identify areas of bondage and to ascertain the degree of bondage in a particular area. The instrument is based on the understanding that to the degree one submits to an area or practice, to that degree the sinful practice has authority or control over one's will. This proportional relationship between submission and control is, as you now know, *the law of the will*. Sin and the demonic have control over an individual to the degree he/she submits to them.

One of the main goals of deliverance is the liberation of the will, the recovery of agency, which is recovering one's humanity. Agency, the self, a sense of personhood and dignity, and one's humanity need to be restored. Recovery begins by taking authority in the name of Jesus over the powers that hold one's will in captivity, resulting in a will that is liberated. At that juncture, a liberated will can respond to grace, believe in Christ, and choose righteousness. Satan may tempt us, but we have the responsibility and choice to resist him, and he will flee (James 4:7).

The C1–13 instrument is broken up into five sections: **Personal Information, Inventory of Prior Treatment of the Problem, 10 Point Checklist, the Assessment Inventory, and the Score Sheet.** The first three sections are intended to gather information to form a comprehensive picture of the problem and document prior treatment. Treatment from other fields may involve medical treatment, psychiatric care, clinical therapy, pastoral counseling, spiritual direction, or even small group accountability. The premise is that a formal scheduled deliverance session is often a *last resort* to alleviating symptoms and solving the problem. Other prescribed spiritual measures and prescribed healthcare treatment need to be considered holistically and prior to a formal deliverance session. This sequencing assists in the diagnostic process.

These first three sections assist in locating missing pieces in a comprehensive plan of treatment and refer seekers to other types of treatment prior to participating in a deliverance session. If a seeker has any items unchecked on the 10 Point Checklist, they are to address those *prior* to continuing with the deliverance assessment process.

The final two sections of the C1–13 instrument are the actual assessment inventory and the score sheet, which is a worksheet for tallying up the composite score and evaluating the score for the need for deliverance. At the end of the C1–13, there is a key that evaluates the score. The key lets you know if the person probably needs deliverance or not.

The assessment inventory is divided into eight categories or clusters/classes of sinful practices, with an itemized list of practices under each category. The eight categories or clusters of sinful practices are: occult, mental health-related, addictive, sexual, criminal, religious, family of origin, and other.[4]

The person taking the assessment marks each practice that they or a family member is or has been involved with. Family member involvement (generational) may impact all members and can open the door to the demonic for the entire family, so it must be identified (Exod 20:5; Deut 5:9). The assessment scores each practice in relationship to four variables: generational, frequency, duration, and intensity of practice. From these four scores a composite score (Bondage Composite, or BC) is derived. The BC score is then evaluated in terms of the probable need for deliverance.

There are two notable distinctions made in this instrument. The first is that mental disorders are *not* demonic in themselves. The second is that deliverance is different from exorcism. These two points you have already learned. First, it is important to recognize that mental disorders are not demonic in themselves, but they can impair the person in a way that can open the door to demonic attack and demonization. Thus, there is an awareness inventory under section 2 of the assessment that helps the seeker to identify current mental health issues that may render one *susceptible* to certain sinful and demonic practices.

---

4. Here are some of the evil spirits affiliated with each cluster or class of sin. The list is not exhaustive. Occult: spirits of divination, witchcraft, Jezebel, necromancing, prognostication, and others. Evil spirits can take advantage of mental health disorders: spirits of murder, control, Python, lawlessness, deception, fear, and others. Addiction: rejection, reproach, Ahab, violation, fear, witchcraft. Sexual: spirits of pride, idolatry, Leviathan, Jezebel, lawlessness, murder, Python, abuse, violation, confusion, perversion, rejection, reproach, Molech, and covetousness. Criminal: spirits of fear, murder, lawlessness, deception, rejection, abuse, confusion, and others. Religious: spirits of deception, idolatry, adultery, witchcraft in various local forms, Python, Jezebel, doctrines of devils, confusion, fear, among others. Family of Origin: spirits of rejection, reproach, guilt and shame, Python, Jezebel, Moloch, addiction, Leviathan, abuse, lawlessness, deception, idolatry, murder, and others.

The awareness inventory does not contribute to the actual scoring for demonization but is used for critical self-awareness. The awareness inventory is not factored into the overall score for demonization, because demons and mental disorder are *not* synonymous. The inventory makes one aware that a mental disorder can make them vulnerable to demonic attack. Following this awareness inventory is the *actual* inventory of related sinful practices that are to be scored.

When deemed necessary, proper psychiatric treatment and counseling must precede any assessment of deliverance. Give a referral! Don't counsel beyond your credentialing and capacity! Often, many confuse mental disorders for the demonic.[5] I have watched too many people unsuccessfully try to cast out schizophrenia, rather than treat the disorder psychiatrically, minister inner healing, and then cast out spirits (if there are any) that attacked the individual due to the disorder. When mental healthcare professionals properly treat the mental disorder, it often becomes clearer what is a clinical issue and what is a demonic issue. If a mental health issue is detected and treatment has not been prescribed yet, then a person first should be referred to a mental health professional.

Second, it is also significant to note that this assessment makes a distinction between deliverance and exorcism. The former involves degrees of demonic influence and can occur in believers. The latter is rare, involves demonic possession, and cannot occur in believers. The former involves degrees of demonization and control, while the latter involves total demonization and control. However, both deliverance and exorcism are handled in the same manner. The 4 Laws of Deliverance apply to both. Exorcism is just a more intense and involved version of deliverance because it is dealing with possession.

Although this instrument seeks to assess areas and degrees of demonization, again, not every Christian challenge or trial involves a direct encounter with a demon or needs intercessory deliverance. The normative way to deal with sin and evil is through resisting temptation, sin, and the devil with the power God gives us. The Lord has thoroughly equipped the church with a variety of weapons for the battle. For instance, God gives us power in his name, the Scriptures, humility, thanksgiving, prayer, the keys to bind and loose, fasting, the gifts of the Spirit, his armor, worship, his blood, the cross, and his presence to do battle with sin and evil. In our everyday struggles with evil, we are called to take up our cross daily and put

---

5. For a rationale for differentiating between mental disorder and the demonic, see Bellini, *Unleashed!*; *Cerulean Soul*; and *X-Manual*.

to death our flesh and its passions and temptations (Gal 5:24). The cross is our basis for deliverance.

There are occasions, however, when we fall. If anyone does sin, we have an advocate in Jesus Christ (1 John 2:1). We are called to come to the throne of mercy (Heb 4:16), confess, and repent of our sins. If we turn away from our sin and toward God, God will forgive us, and the blood of Jesus Christ cleanses us from all unrighteousness (1 John 1:7–9). Yet, there are instances following sin and repentance where one cannot break the cycle. A door to the demonic has been opened. In other cases of advanced and progressive transgression, one continues in a sin or sins, opens the door to the demonic, is oppressed, and needs assistance through the ministry of deliverance in order to be liberated.

When ministering deliverance, it is important that deliverance is ministered by church leadership that has been *trained, certified, installed,* and *recognized* in this area. Deliverance needs to be ministered in teams of two or more for safety and effectiveness. Also, there needs to be pre- and post-work that contributes to the overall deliverance and healing process. I recommend this book, of course, *The X-Manual,* and *Truth Therapy* (Peter Bellini, Wipf and Stock) or a similar work, like *Deliverance and Inner Healing* by John Loren Sandford and Mark Sandford. The pre- and post-work involves teaching, counseling, repentance, confession, faith and forgiveness, inner healing, renewing the mind with the Word of God, accountability, prayer, and discipleship.

It is also essential to approach deliverance and healing holistically. Utilize all necessary means and treatment available that can work together comprehensively. For example, a healthy diet, daily exercise, deep breathing, good and sufficient sleep, counseling, and medication when needed can work well together with prayer to minister healing to people struggling with depression and anxiety. If a person is on medication, do not counsel them to stop treatment. Let all doctor prescribed treatment be assessed by the doctor alone. Leave medical counsel, diagnosis, and prescribing to the medical professionals.

The C1–13 Integrative Deliverance Needs Assessment[1]

Can be filled out by the client, minister, or deliverance team leader in an interview format.

Personal Information
Name _____
Address _____ Ph # _____
Sex ( ) M ( ) F Age _____
Marital Status: ( ) Single ( ) Married ( ) Divorced ( ) Remarried ( ) Widowed
Profession _____

Your parents' status:
( ) Single ( ) Married ( ) Divorced ( ) Divorced and Remarried ( ) Widowed

Number of children and ages _____
Currently in Counseling ( ) Y N ( ) For how long? _____
Currently taking meds ( ) Y N ( ) Names of med_____
How long on meds _____
How many hours of sleep do you get a night? _____
Have you gained ( ) or lost ( ) more than give pounds in the last month?
Have you experienced loss of appetite ( ) or increased appetite ( ) lately?
Do you have constipation ( ) or diarrhea ( ) in the last month?
Have you experienced lately loss of interest in things you once enjoyed ( )?
Have you experienced any of the following: a strange invisible presence ( ), hearing voices in your head ( ), strange sights or sounds in your house ( ), thoughts that someone or something is watching you ( ), moments of blanking or blacking out.

1. Taken from Bellini, *X-Manual.*

Have you had odd experiences lately, such as nightmares ( ), accidents ( ), sudden significant financial loss ( ), irregular fights with family members ( ), explosive fits of rage ( ), other _____?
Any other mental health issues in your family, past or present?

Faith Information
Do you currently attend a local church? ( ) Y ( ) N Name_____
_____
How long attended? _____
Do you profess saving faith in Jesus Christ? ( ) Y ( ) N
Salvation? Date _____
Have you been baptized in the Holy Spirit? ( ) Y ( ) N Date_____

Are you familiar with phenomena such as the work of the Spirit, angels, and even demons? ( ) Y ( ) N
Do you have a time of regular prayer and Bible Study? ( ) Y ( ) N How much time? _____
Are you involved in any ministry? _____
For how long? _____

Reason for this Deliverance Appointment
Description of problem and symptoms _____
_____

Is there a family history of this problem? ( ) Y ( ) N Explain_____
_____

Inventory of prior treatment of the problem
Since deliverance is a type of healing, it is often helpful to think of deliverance in terms of wholeness and health. Issues of health are often treated holistically and comprehensively from an integrated approach that affords the best resources from faith and science. Thus, it can be helpful and effective to approach certain problems and issues with multiple types of treatment that impact body, mind, emotions, and spirit. Indicate which types of treatment you have used or are currently using.

What other forms of treatment for the problem have you used? Mark (X) and fill in blanks.

__ Repentance. How long _____ Results _____
   What type _____

__ Medical. How long _____ Results _____
   What type _____

__ Counseling. How long _____ Results _____
   What type _____

__ Support group. How long _____ Results _____
   What type _____

__ Prison or jail. How long _____ Results _____
   What type _____

__ Recovery group (AA, NA) How long _____ Results _____
   What type _____

__ Medication. How long _____ Results _____
   What type _____

__ Prayer group. How long _____ Results _____
   What type _____

__ Prior deliverance. How long _____ Results _____
   What type _____,

__ Confession and forgiveness. How long _____ Results _____
   What type _____

__ Diet. What type _____ How long _____ Results _____

__ Exercise. What type _____ How long _____ Results _____

__ Sleep therapy. How long _____ Results _____
   What type _____

__ Other lifestyle changes. How long _____ Results _____
   What type _____

__ Other: _____

10 Point Checklist

Read each of the ten statements. If the statement describes you, and you still found no relief or change in your condition, then mark a check in the brackets. If you mark a check by *all* ten statements, then you qualify for deliverance. If you have left any statements unchecked, you need to have those addressed with the proper professional (general physician, psychiatrist, therapist, or pastor) *before* continuing with the inventory assessment. Note, you *cannot* continue with the deliverance assessment if you have *any* unchecked items on any of the 10 statements.

1. Confessing sin, repentance and faith, forgiveness, accountability, participation in worship, inner healing, prayer, and discipleship groups are not breaking the cycles of sin or oppression in an area. ( )

2. Attempts at prayer, fasting, and spiritual warfare, and those by other intercessors, are not breaking the cycles of sin or oppression in the area. ( )

3. You addressed your beliefs and practices, especially questionable ones, with your pastor or spiritual leadership in your church. ( )

4. Leadership discerns demonic presence and influence in your life. ( )

5. You sense demonic influence in your life. ( )

6. You visited a physician, therapist, or other mental health professional for evaluation. ( )

7. Treatment such as counseling, medication, diet, exercise, rehabilitation, recovery group, or other form of treatment is not working. ( )

8. You feel helpless in one or more area(s) and struggle at times to perform daily functions. ( )

9. You have been seen by professionals (medical, pastoral, or other) about your problem(s). ( )

10. After trying other means of help, deliverance is often seen as a last resort. ( )

Follow-up: Identify each numbered question that you did not check. Find that number below for follow-up instructions. For example, if you left numbers 6 and 9 unchecked, then go to numbers 6 and 9 below and follow the instructions for each. After you have followed through with the instructions on each question and can eventually check all 10 statements, then you can proceed with the assessment.

1. You need repentance and faith in that area of sin. Take time to follow up in this area. Participate in spiritual disciplines, the means of grace, confession of sin, repentance and faith, forgiveness, accountability with one or more people, worship service, inner healing, or a discipleship group.

2. You may need to pray, fast, and execute spiritual warfare, as well as approach intercessors on your behalf to do the same. Take the time to follow up in this area.

3. Take time to meet with your pastor or spiritual leadership to address your specific beliefs and practices and have them evaluated by Scripture, especially any questionable ones. Transformation of beliefs can lead to

transformation of life and practice. Christian catechesis, conversion, and discipleship are all necessary for right belief, worship, and practice.

4. You need to make an appointment with leadership for prayer, discernment, and inner healing. Intercessors, prophets, spiritual directors, and counselors, among other qualified leadership, can assist you in hearing the voice of God and discerning God's direction and will for your life.

5. Take time to discern in prayer if you are battling an evil spirit(s).

6. Schedule an appointment with a therapist or other mental health professional to be evaluated concerning the problem.

7. Receive proper treatment from the proper professional (medical, mental health, social worker, sponsor, nutritionist, trainer, recovery etc.).

8. You may not need deliverance. Confide with a counselor, spiritual director, confidant, or accountability group or partner to make sure you are being open and honest about personal struggles in your life.

9. Discuss your problem with the proper professional: pastor, medical doctor, specialist, or mental health professional.

10. Have the problem addressed according to the follow-up instructions given in 1–9.

If you have checked *all* ten statements, then proceed to take the Inventory Assessment to determine the probability for deliverance. If you have any unchecked statements, then you should *not* continue with the assessment. Those areas need professional follow-up prior to proceeding further with this assessment. Do *not* take the Inventory Assessment until you have had those areas addressed by a medical professional, psychiatrist, therapist, pastor, or other appropriate professional. Only proceed with the Inventory Assessment after checking off *all* ten statements.

The Inventory Assessment

INVENTORY OF PRACTICES

There is no formula, metric, or scientific test to discern with absolute precision the presence of demonization. Detecting demonization is a spiritual process. One can discern from Scripture, the Holy Spirit, and the fruit in one's life whether deliverance is needed. However, the spiritual process of discernment can be aided by a qualitative analysis of one's behavior as well as a cross-evaluation with other disciplines in the hard and soft sciences, such as general medical practice, psychiatry, or clinical therapy.

This inventory is a tool that assists the spiritual discernment process by working in concert with other professional fields while analyzing behavior that is considered sinful and possibly demonic according to the Christian Scriptures. The C1–13 assumes cooperation with other professional fields and as a last resort assesses the probability and need for deliverance based on practices or fruit and the frequency, duration, and intensity of the practice. The inventory identifies doors of evil influence that may require deliverance. Not all the practices implicate immediate demonization. The scoring following the inventory, along with the 10 Point Checklist above, can ascertain the probability of demonization.

*Practices indicated in the inventory by an asterisk can be highly traumatic and open doors to the demonic immediately and may not need to occur frequently but sometimes just once. Scoring is determined by the experience of the person taking the assessment.

Check off any of the following influences or practices that involve you or your family. Only check a sinful practice once. Do not check the same sinful practice twice.

1. Occult Practices (spirits of divination, witchcraft, Jezebel, necromancing, prognostication, and others):

    __ Witchcraft of any form

    __ Curses: cursing or cursed

    __ Inner vows, pacts, and covenants

    __ Curses: history of inexplicable systemic accidents, tragedies, or misfortunes

    __ Sacrifices

    __ Ouija board

    __ Crystals, charms, amulet use

    __ Numerology

    __ Fortune telling

    __ Hypnotism: giver or receiver

    __ Macumba, Santeria, Umbanda, Candomble

    __ Tarot cards

    __ Kabbalah

    __ Trances

    __ Evil eye or similar curses

    __ Books, music, movies, or other forms depicting the occult

    __ Freemasonry or secret societies

    __ Levitation

    __ ESP, telekinesis

    __ Witchcraft medicine, witch doctoring, shamanism

    __ Alchemy (modern type involving magic)

    __ Mind-reading

    __ Automatic writing

    __ Horror movies, violent and gore related movies

    __ Astrology, zodiac

    __ Séance

    __ Satanism*

    __ Wicca

__ Esotericism

__ Vampirism

__ Crystal ball use

__ Table lifting or other telekinesis

__ Black Magic or magic of any type

__ Divination

__ Gang vows or rituals

__ Astral projection or out of body experiences

__ Channeling

__ Spirit guides or mediums

__ Kundalini associated with certain forms of yoga

__ Clairvoyance

__ Sacrifices*

__ Role playing games involving other gods' or spirits' demonic practices

__ Necrophilia, necromancy

__ Contacting the dead or use of mediums

__ Palm read or reading, palmistry

__ Reiki, energy healing or other types of healing

__ Covenants, vows, oaths, pacts to any spirit or deity

__ Psychics

__ Regular involuntary movement, twitches, jerks, speech, blinking, cursing, scratching, and other tic-like behaviors not diagnosed or explained as Tourette Syndrome

__ Do you possess paraphernalia related to the occult: books, movies, games, music, or any objects that have been used for non-Christian religious purposes, like masks, idols, statues, fetish objects, etc., or for any of the above purposes? (Acts 19:18–19)

__ Gnostic type practices

__ Summoning spirits, demons, the dead, or any non-physical beings*

__ Role-play games involving any of the above

__ Other paraphernalia

__ Animal abuse

__ Any summons of gods or goddesses

__ Other occult practices_____

List not exhaustive. See Christian Bible.

2. Destructive Practices (related to mental disorders):

NOTE: *It is important to recognize that mental disorders are not demonic in themselves, but they can impair the person in a way that can open the door to demonic attack and demonization. When necessary, proper psychiatric treatment and counseling must precede any assessment of deliverance. Often many confuse mental disorder for the demonic. Once a mental disorder is properly treated by mental healthcare professionals, it often becomes clearer what is a clinical issue and what is a demonic issue. If a mental health issue is detected and treatment has not been prescribed yet, then seek help from a mental health professional.*

Check the following mental health issues to determine the susceptibility to unwanted or destructive practices. These items are not part of identifying and scoring practices used to assess the probability of the need for deliverance. Checked items create an awareness of vulnerability to certain practices. This list identifies mental health issues that may or may not be collaterally related to practices that need deliverance. Mental disorders alone are not necessarily demonic.

Awareness Inventory of Mental Disorders and Susceptibility

__ Minor Depression diagnosis from a professional

__ Major Depression diagnosis from a professional

__ DSM-5 on Major Depressive Disorder. If one has five of the following nine symptoms daily:

__ depressed mood or irritable most of the day, nearly every day, as indicated by either subjective report (e.g., feels sad or empty) or observation made by others (e.g., appears tearful)

__ decreased interest or pleasure in most activities, most of each day

__ significant weight change (5 percent) or change in appetite

__ change in sleep: insomnia or hypersomnia

__ change in activity: psychomotor agitation or retardation

__ fatigue or loss of energy

__ guilt/worthlessness: Feelings of worthlessness or excessive or inappropriate guilt

__ concentration: diminished ability to think or concentrate, or more indecisiveness

__ suicidality: Thoughts of death or suicide, or has suicide plan

__ Mood Disorder/Bipolar diagnosis from a professional

__ Schizophrenia diagnosis from a professional

__ Panic or panic attacks

__ Anxiety Disorder diagnosis from a professional

__ DSM 5—The presence of excessive anxiety and worry about a variety of topics, events, or activities. Worry occurs more often than not for at least six months and is clearly excessive. The individual experiences at least three characteristic symptoms including:

__ restlessness or feeling keyed up or on edge

__ being easily fatigued; always tired

__ difficulty concentrating or mind going blank

__ difficulty focusing

__ irritability; easily disturbed

__ muscle tension

__ and sleep disturbance

__ ADD diagnosis from a professional

__ ADHD diagnosis from a professional

__ OCD—compulsions or compulsive behavior—diagnosis from a professional

__ ODD—oppositional, defiant—diagnosis from a professional

__ Hearing voices

__ Trauma* (from any number of incidents of war, abuse, or other)

__ Racing thoughts

__ Involuntary movements such as tics related to Tourette Syndrome—diagnosis from a professional

__ Very difficult to focus

Susceptible to Destructive Practices: These items are to be identified and scored to assess probability for the need of deliverance. Spirits of murder, control, Python, lawlessness, deception, fear, and others can be related to this category of sinful practices. Score the following items:

___ Suicidal (ideation, plans, or attempts)

___ Death wish (want to die)

___ Self-mutilation or cutting

___ Curses—cursing or cursed

___ Inner vows, pacts, alliances, and covenants

___ Compulsions or compulsive behavior

___ Thoughts and feelings of rejection or low self esteem

___ Hallucinations, irrational paranoia, or hearing voices not related to treated Schizophrenia. These symptoms should first be assessed by a mental health professional.

___ Feelings and thoughts of hopelessness, worthlessness, and helplessness

___Violent behavior toward self or others

___ Lying or stealing

___ Promiscuity

___ Criminal behavior (See section #5)

___ Vertigo, dizziness, or involuntary movement or manifestation not related to other somatic or mental health issues

___ Night terrors/violent nightmares

___ Fear (undifferentiated)

___ Fear of people, crowds, death, the opposite sex, the dark, future, sickness or disease, or any other specific type

___ Obsession(s)

___ Any addictive behaviors (See section 3)

___ Other unwanted or destructive practice. See Christian Bible.

3. Addictions/Addictive Practices (see chapter 4 of *The X-Manual*: rejection, reproach, Ahab, violation, fear, witchcraft):

___ Alcohol, drunkenness

___ Prescription Drugs_____

__ Illegal drugs _____

__ Marijuana, hashish, opium

__ Heroin

__ LSD, hallucinogenics, N-Bombs

__ Krokodil

__ Methamphetamines, crystal meth

__ Opioids of any sort like Gray Death, Fentanyl, Pink AH-7921, and others

__ Flakka, bath salts

__ Ecstasy

__ Molly

__ Anabolic steroids

__ Crack cocaine, cocaine

__ Pornography

__ Cigarettes

__ Sexual addictions

__ Gambling

__ Excessive, compulsive or needless spending or spending sprees

__ Obsessive and compulsive internet use

__ Internet chatting, dating, sexting, or encounters for sexual or illicit purposes

__ Other_____

List not exhaustive. See Christian Bible.

4. Sexual Practices (often connected with spirits of pride, idolatry, Leviathan, Jezebel, lawlessness, murder, Python, abuse, violation, confusion, perversion, rejection, reproach, Ashtoreth, Molech, and covetousness):

__ Any sexual practice forbidden in Scripture (See Christian Bible.)

__ Gender dysphoria and related practices

__ Autoeroticism, masturbation

__ Polyamorous relationships

__ Pornography

__ Adultery*

__ Fornication*

__ Lust, covetousness

__ Incest—victim* or perpetrator*

__ Abuse of others*

__ Experienced sexual abuse*

__ Pedophilia*

__ Prostitution

__ Paraphilias

__ Necrophilia

__ BDSM

__ Soul tie(s)—connections between people that are not connections of the spirit but of the mind, will, emotions, and personalities. Between sexes they can be suggestive but not consummated, an emotional affair, though it can involve a physical tie, which binds the people together spirit, soul, and body (1 Cor 6:15–18). A soul tie is not a normal, healthy friendship, but a connection that is out of order and sinful, often based on power, control, manipulation, and emotional satisfaction. It is an over-attached relationship.

__ Incubus, succubus, or sexual experience with a presence in dreams or awake at night

__ Voyeurism, stripping or watching, or exhibitionism

__ Bestiality*

__ Rape* or was raped*

__ I molest* or I was molested*

__ Perverse forms of sex or sexuality

__ Confusion around one's gender or sex (may not be demonic itself but may invite demonic attack)

__ Sex paraphernalia, objects, files, books, videos, games, etc. related to pornography or sexual abuse

__ Other_____

List not exhaustive. See Christian Bible.

5. Criminal Practices (often connected with spirits of fear, murder, lawlessness, deception, rejection, abuse, confusion, and others):

__ Theft, forcible entry

__ Murder*, homicide, manslaughter

__ False witness, perjury

__ Assault or battery of any kind

__ Racketeering

__ Extortion, conspiracy, or treason

__ Manslaughter*

__ Homicide*

__ Gang affiliation and activity

__ Abortion*

__ Fraud _____

__ Drug use, sales

__ Prostitution

__ Incarcerated

__ Experienced physical, mental, verbal, or sexual abuse

__ Sex trafficking/trafficked* or working in the sex trafficking industry*

__ Other_____

List not exhaustive. See Christian Bible.

6. Religious Practices:

Note: Religious affiliations do not always necessitate demonization and the need for deliverance. As a religious affiliation facilitates beliefs and practices contrary to Scripture, it can open the door to sin that in turn can open the door to the demonic. However, it is significant to note that some religious affiliations' teachings about the nature and activity of God or moral conduct may parallel or be in line with the teaching of Scripture, and not be sinful or demonic.

For example, a religion may teach that God created the universe, or that stealing, lying, and adultery are forbidden practices. Sinful practices and potential doors to the demonic are identified by Christian Scripture. World and folk religions, beliefs, practices, and forms claiming to be "Christian," new religious movements, cults, and various spiritual movements that foster unbiblical beliefs and practices, can not only be sinful but can also open the door to the demonic.[1]

Sinful religious practices can be connected to spirits of deception, idolatry, adultery, witchcraft in various local forms, Python, Molech, Ashtaroth, Jezebel, doctrines of devils, confusion, and fear, among others. These items are to be identified and scored to assess probability for the need of deliverance. Score the following items:

__ Idolatry: Prayer, use of artifacts in magic or worship, communication, or a specific practice or devotion to any god besides the God of the Christian Scriptures

__ Transcendental Meditation or other forms of meditation that involve other gods including self

__ Doctrine of devils and seducing spirits: World religions, indigenous religions, or Christian syncretistic religions with unbiblical teachings and practices, for example Baha'ism, any polytheistic or animistic religions, and others. Can include false doctrines held within a Christian denomination or by an individual unrelated to any movement

__ Cultic manipulation, control, and abuse found in "Christian" cults, such as Mormonism, Jehovah's Witnesses, Unification Church (the Moonies), Boston Movement, Christadelphians, Rosicrucian, or others

__ Cultic manipulation, control, and abuse found in non-Christian cults, such as Scientology, Eckankar, Twelve Tribes, EST (the Forum), the Family, NXIVM, and others

__ Religions, syncretism, folk religions, or spirituality that uses sorcery, channeling, fetishes, spells, enchanted objects, or any other means to conjure, communicate, contact, gain power, or be influenced by spirits or the spirit realm, such as New Age, paganism, Wicca, shamanism, Satanism, Freemasonry, secret societies, paganism, Course in Miracles, Umbanda, Macumba, malocchio, distinu, Santeria, Yoruba, orichas, Voodoo or other similar forms and practices. Acts 19:18–19

---

1 According to sociologist William Bainbridge, "A cult movement is a deviant religious organization with novel beliefs and practices." Bainbridge, *Sociology of Religious Movements*, 24. Due to pejorative examples and connotations of the word *cult*, this particular use of cult derived from sociology and anthropology of religion is not in current use as much as "new religious movements." However, this instrument is claiming that both new religious movements and the more limited, pejorative understanding of cult need to be examined for beliefs and practices and weighed out culturally through critical contextualization in light of Scripture.

__ Legalism of any sort, whether Christian or non-Christian religion

__ Doctrines and practices of racism and racial supremacy, regardless of race

__ Practices of witchcraft

__ Book of Urantia

__ Umbanda, Candomble

__ Freemasonry and secret societies

__ Necromancy

__ Trances

__ Reiki

__ Hearing voices not explained by mental disorder

__ Night terrors

__ Sleep paralysis (demons riding the person)

__ Curses: given or received

__ Inner vows or covenants

__ Conjuring spirits

__ Spirit possession (intentional or unintentional)

__ Talking to spirits

__ Sacrifices

__ Covenant or alliances made to any spirit or god besides the God of Christian Scripture

__ See occult practices

__ Ancestor worship (beyond honoring) that involves devotion as unto God or covenants and alliances made

__ Paraphernalia related to religious practices

__ Other

List is not exhaustive. See Christian Bible.

7. Family of Origin Practices (see the other categories for related demonic activity; often connected with spirits of rejection, reproach, guilt and shame, Python, Jezebel, Moloch, addiction, Leviathan, abuse, lawlessness, deception, idolatry, murder, and others). In this section, if

you marked a particular sinful practice in another previous category, then you may mark it here as well.

__ Occult_____

__ Addiction _____

__ Sinful or destructive practices related to mental disorder _____

__ Criminal acts _____

__ Unbiblical religious belief practice_____

__ Sexual sin _____

__ Divorce

__ Abortion or survivor of one*

__ Curses—cursing or cursed

__ Inner vows, pacts, and covenants

__ Rejection issues, orphaned, abandoned. Other rejection issues.

__ Trauma of any type

__ Prone to systemic accidents, injuries, sickness, miscarriage, financial crises, premature death etc.

__ Incest*

__ Rebellion

__ Disobedience to parents

__ Abuse (sexual, physical, mental, or verbal)

__ Other _____

List not exhaustive. See Christian Bible

8. Other Sinful Practices:

__ Pride

__ Jealousy

__ Lust

__ Laziness or sloth

__ Envy

__ Greed

__ Gossip, slander, backbiting

__ Condemnation

__ Judging, judgmental

__ Unforgiveness

__ Hatred

__ Spirit of fear of future, others, the opposite sex, heights, closed spaces, death, sin, insanity, water, going outside, and other objects of fear

__ Competition

__ Rebellion

__ Idolatry

__ Anger or rage

__ Swearing/cursing

__ Drunkenness

__ Gluttony

__ Malice

__ Blasphemy

__ Profanity

__ Taking God's name in vain

__ Lying, false witness, deceit

__ Heresy

__ Division, schism

__ Legalism

__ Bitterness

__ Experienced familial, marital, short or long-term abuse of any type

__ Books, movies, games, music, or other forms that depict sinful practices that have influenced your thoughts and behavior

__ Other _____

List not exhaustive. See Christian Bible.

EVALUATION OF EACH PRACTICE:

Score each practice that was flagged in the inventory of practices by assigning a numerical value (1 to 5) to each of the four areas of assessment (generational, duration, frequency, and intensity). The total score represents the Bondage Composite. Note some practices need only occur once to open the door to the demonic and require deliverance.

GENERATIONAL—OVER HOW MANY GENERATIONS HAS IT BEEN PRACTICED?

1. First generation
2. 2 generations
3. 3 generations
4. 4 generations
5. 5 generations

DURATION—HOW LONG HAS IT BEEN PRACTICED?

1. Less than 3 months
2. 3 months to a year
3. At least a year
4. 1–5 years
5. More than 5 years

FREQUENCY—HOW FREQUENTLY HAS IT BEEN PRACTICED?

1. A few times a year
2. Once a week to once a month
3. 3 times a week
4. Daily
5. More than 3 times a day

INTENSITY—HOW INTENSELY HAS IT BEEN PRACTICED?

1. Practice with little interest and passion

2. Practice with some interest and passion

3. Practice with moderate interest and passion

4. Practice with high interest and passion

5. Practice with intense commitment and passion

SCORESHEET

Type of Practice	Generational	Duration	Frequency	Intensity	BC Total

Evaluation of BQ Composite Score (the *Bondage Quotient)* for each practice and levels of demonization		
	0 –	No deliverance needed 0%
Level 1:	1–5	Need for repentance and faith with very low probable need for deliverance 0–20%
Level 2:	6–10	Repentance and faith needed with low to moderate probable need for deliverance 20%–50%
Level 3:	11–15	Need for deliverance is moderate to likely probable 50%–70%*
Level 4:	16–20	Need for deliverance is highly probable 70%–100%*
*Asterisk indicates probable need for deliverance		

LEGAL WAIVER FOR MINISTRY

RELEASE AND WAIVER OF LIABILITY

DISCLAIMER: THIS FORM DOES NOT CONSTITUE LEGAL ADVICE. ANYONE USING THIS FORM SHOULD DO SO ONLY WTH THE ADVICE OF THEIR OWN LEGAL COUNSEL.

Read before signing

IMPORTANT. READ CAREFULLY. This document affects your legal rights. You, the "Participant," must sign it whether you are an adult or minor, if you are participating in "Activities" (generally referred to as "Deliverance Ministry") facilitated by [CHURCH use actual legal entity] ("Facilitator").

Your parent or legal guardian must sign it also if you are a minor Participant (under 18 years of age.) The parent or guardian agrees to these terms individually and on behalf of the minor. Only a parent or legally appointed guardian may sign for a minor Participant. References in this agreement to "I" or "We" include all who sign below unless otherwise clearly indicated.

PARTICIPANT AGREEMENT (Including Acknowledgement and assumption of Risks, Agreements of Release and Indemnity, and Additional Provisions)

In consideration of the opportunity to participate in activities offered by Facilitator,

I, _____ the Participant (adult or minor), and,
(Please print name)

_____, the parent or legal guardian of a
(Please print name) minor Participant, understand,
acknowledge and agree as follows:

ACTIVITIES, HAZARDS AND RISKS

The various activities may include [LIST ACTIVITIES].

The hazards and risks (together referred to as "risks") associated with the various activities may include [LIST], as well as associated reasonably foreseeable risks.

Participant, and the parent or guardian of a minor Participant, acknowledge and understand that the description of the activities and risks described herein is not complete and that all activities, whether or not described, may be dangerous and may include risks which are inherent and cannot be reasonably avoided without changing the nature of the activity.

Facilitator has made no effort to determine, and accepts no responsibility for, medical, physical, or other qualifications or the suitability of Participant, or other participants, for the activities. [MAY NEED TO CHANGE THIS IF YOU DO BACKGROUND CHECKS, ETC.]

Participant, and the parent or guardian of a minor Participant, accepts full responsibility for determining Participant's medical, physical, or other qualifications or suitability for participating in the activities.

Participant, and the parent or guardian of a minor Participant, HEREBY CERTIFIES that the Participant, and the parent or guardian of a minor Participant has personal health insurance. Insurance company is

_____.

FIFTY GUIDELINES FOR DELIVERANCE

Note: There is no strict formula or science to deliverance. Deliverance comes from the grace of God, revealed in the finished work of Jesus Christ on the cross, through the power of the Holy Spirit. Deliverance is Spirit-led and occurs through the faith of the believer, as he or she trusts in and implements the authority of the name of Jesus, given to them by Christ. Although there is no strict formula or magic phrase for deliverance, there are Biblical and Spirit-led wisdom and principles that can guide the process. Here are some guidelines and wisdom one can use for deliverance:

1. After answering "True" on all 10 statements on the 10 Point Checklist, have the recipient fill out the release form. Remember not to administer deliverance if the person has not scored 10 on the Checklist. ____ Have them go over each area and repent individually for each sin. The person should take three to four weeks to do this while fasting. Also, both participant and team need to have fasted twenty-four hours prior to the session.

2. Assign the session to an available, well-trained, prepared, and certified deliverance team (of at least two people, preferably three or four, mixed sexes). ____

3. Recipient has filled out inventory, C1–13 assessment, and waiver forms. ____

4. Leadership has reviewed the results of the inventory and assessment with recipient. ____

5. Leadership has interviewed recipient about the problem, the inventory and assessment, the solution and deliverance procedures, and expectations. ____

6. It is good to have women take the lead with women and men with men. ____

7. Protect the dignity of the person above all. ____

8. Deliverance team with designated leader is prayed and fasted up. ____

9. Deliverance team has gone through a period of repentance, cleansing, and fasting over each area of sin identified by the C1–13. ____

10. Make sure deliverance team does not hinder the process in any way through improper dress, foul breath or odors, division, arguing, forcing of manifestations, or the like. Have breath mints and mouthwash in the deliverance room. ____

11. Set aside a special, private room for deliverance. ___

12. Have the following items available: Bibles, bottles of water, power or granola bars or healthy snack items, towels, tissues, a garbage can, praise and worship music, breath fresheners, and other useful items. ___

13. Saturate the room before, during, and after deliverance with prayer, praise, and worship. ___

14. Explain the process and ask permission at each juncture. ___

15. Set aside an initial time for worship and submission to God. ___

16. Plead the blood of Jesus over the room, the team, and the recipient. ___

17. Invite recipient to repent of all sins and renounce all practices from both the inventory and whatever comes to their mind. ___

18. Invite Jesus the Lion of the Tribe of Judah, the Dragon and Demon Slayer, into the room to release deliverance. ___

19. Ask for protection from warrior angels and release protection. ___

20. Bind all distractions and hindrances. ___

21. Bind and break powers over the area and the deliverance team. ___

22. Dismantle and deactivate all assignments and strategies of the enemy. ___

23. One person speaks at a time. Avoid confusion and distractions. ___

24. Expect the Spirit to reveal the gifts of the Spirit, especially discernment, healing, and words of knowledge and wisdom that will address names of spirits, types of afflictions, and strategies for victory (Ps. 107:20). ___

25. Ask permission from the person to lay on hands or for anything attempted. Lay hands lightly. ___

26. When necessary, explain the process and its procedures to the seeker as you proceed. ___

27. Be pastoral even over being prophetic. ___

28. One should lay hands with permission, in only appropriate places, and on the same sex. ___

29. Do not allow demons to manifest or speak. They are liars. ___

30. Go through the 5 Step Deliverance Method in chapter 8 ___

31. Address each spirit from the inventory or otherwise specifically by name and command it to come out in the name of Jesus. ____

32. Break and renounce each of these spirits in Jesus' name. ____

33. Curse the demonic powers with the blood of Jesus. ____

34. Declare over the candidate repeatedly that Jesus is Lord; Insist that the demons acknowledge it as well. ____

35. Remind Satan that all authority has been given to you in Jesus' name to bind him and cast him out. He has been judged. ____

36. Throughout the session, as led by the Spirit, invite the candidate to repent of various sins and to renounce them, as well as to confess Jesus as Lord. ____

37. Only raise your voice if the Spirit leads, but it is not necessary for deliverance. ____

38. Be led. Allow for others to speak and take the lead for a time if the Spirit leads. But stay focused. Watch out for distractions from the enemy through the seeker or the team. ____

39. Do no harm! Be attentive to the person's dignity and honor. Do not hurt, harm, embarrass, or shame the person. ____

40. Do not get physical in a way that can harm, hurt, or violate the person. Be gentle but bold. ____

41. Heaviness can harbor and manifest in the chest area. Pray over that area. ____

42. Demons often nestle in the spirit that impacts the stomach area. Pray over that area. ____

43. Do not struggle, wrestle, or contest with demons unnecessarily or for prolonged periods. The person is either ready for deliverance, or they are not. The deliverance team knows their authority in Christ, or they do not. ____

44. Continue to praise and worship Jesus throughout the session. Actually, Christ is the main focus during the deliverance session and not Satan. ____

45. If the person is not willing to repent, renounce each spirit, or surrender to the point of breakthrough, do not force their will, but discontinue the session for a later date when the recipient is more open or ready. ____

46. Close all open doors and seal them with the blood of Jesus. __

47. If the person has repented and is set free, invite the person to accept Christ as their Lord and Savior (if they have not already) and pray for the person to receive the infilling of the Holy Spirit where a vacancy has been created by the deliverance. ___

48. Plead the blood for cleansing over all who have participated. ___

49. Pray protection against backlash over each person and all that pertains to the covenant in their lives. ___

50. Schedule a follow-up session before leaving and begin discipleship in *The X-Manual* and *Truth Therapy* by Peter Bellini or a similar work. Other recommended reading: *Deliverance and Inner Healing*, John and Mark Sandford; *Christianity with Power*, Charles Kraft; *The Bondage Breaker, Victory over the Darkness, Who am I in Christ, Freedom From Addiction*, and other titles, Neil Anderson; *Deliverance from Evil Spirits*, Francis MacNutt; *Biblical Guidebook to Deliverance*, Randy Clark; *How to Cast Out Demons*, Doris Wagner; *Demons: the Answer Book*, Lester Sumrall; *Deliverance and Spiritual Warfare Manual*, John Eckhardt; *Handbook for Spiritual Warfare*, Ed Murphy, among others. ___

THE TEN MOST ASKED QUESTIONS ABOUT DELIVERANCE

1. *Can anyone cast out demons?* No. Unbelievers cannot. But a believer who knows their authority in Christ can. All believers have the authority to cast out demons and should receive training. Only local church trained, certified, and appointed people should engage in this very sensitive ministry. Deliverance is not the wild, wild west. We don't need self-appointed cowboys to shoot up Dodge. Proper training is essential. See chapter 4, "Qualifications for Deliverance" in *The X-Manual* by Peter Bellini.

2. *Can a Christian have a demon?* A Christian cannot be *possessed* by a demon. However, a Christian can be *influenced* by a demon, beginning with temptation leading to sin, leading to oppression and a stronghold or demonic attachment in an area of their life. An example of a believer needing deliverance was Peter when he told Christ he did not have to go to the cross. Jesus knew Satan was speaking through Peter (Matt 16:23, Mark 8:33, Luke 4:8). The same disciple who said just prior, "You are the Christ, the Son of the living God" (Matt 16:16). Peter had

a spirit of fear, and Satan spoke through him. He was not possessed, but the devil clearly had a degree of influence on him.

Judas was one of the twelve who preached Christ and worked miracles. Christ said to his disciples that their names were written in heaven, indicating that the disciples were believers. (Luke 10:20). Nonetheless, Satan entered into Judas and used him to betray Christ (Luke 22:3; John 13:2, 27). Randy Clark cites two other cases in which believers needed deliverance, the woman disabled for eighteen years (Luke 13:10–17) and the Syrophoenician woman's daughter (Mark 7:24–30).[2] It is noteworthy that many of the demons Christ cast out were in God's house (Mark 1:23,39; Luke 4:33).

Also, there are some ministers who say you should not minister deliverance to an unbeliever, because if they are not converted, seven more demons will come back. This is true in a sense if the person does not repent and submit to Christ's lordship. But deliverance absolutely should be ministered to unbelievers upon their *repentance and submission* to Christ, as taught in this book, for both believer and unbeliever. Deliverance is evangelistic and part of conversion, like it was for the Gadarene man. Deliverance is a sign and wonder that aids conversion and proclaims the gospel to others (see the Gadarene man, Matt 8, Mark 5, and Luke 8). We should not forbid it. It is an instrumental component of power evangelism.

3. *During deliverance, should we ask demons questions, like asking them their names?* This is a controversial subject. Some ministries do and some do not. I personally do not prefer to ask demons questions. They are all liars. They are worse than talking with *some* teenagers. My experience has been that this is an effective distraction of the devil to lead people down a rabbit trail. Ministers can easily get off-track and lose the goal, which is liberation, not a conversation. Demons will make any excuse not to leave. They are like trying to put your six- and eight-year-old to bed at night. They run and hide. They make excuses. They want water, food, their favorite toy, this, or that. Anything but to go to bed. You cannot reason with them. You cannot reason with demons (Of course, that is the only similarity between them). There is only one biblical occurrence where Christ asked the demons their names (Legion) when ministering to the Gadarene man. In other instances, he told the demons to be silent (Mark 1:34; Luke 4:41). He also did not allow the demons to manifest uncontrollably or hurt a person.

2. Clark, *Biblical Guidebook to Deliverance*, 53–55. See also Arnold, *Three Crucial Questions*, 73–142.

One of our goals is to protect the seeker. They are not a subject for experimentation. Try not to permit demons to speak, manifest, or harm the person. Be bold and tell the evil spirit to be silent. Ministers ask demons questions because they are looking for clues and information that can help the deliverance process. The rationale is that if they know the name of the demon, then they have authority over it. This conclusion is erroneous. You already have authority over the demon in Jesus' name. Do not look to Satan for clues and information for deliverance. Rely on the Spirit and not demons.

If demons are willing to give you "insight," how much more is the Holy Spirit? The Holy Spirit will lead you. He will reveal the names of demons and other information if necessary. Also, you have the C1–13 that has already disclosed the type of demons that you will be facing.

I try not to get caught up in constructing a formal, sophisticated taxonomy or naming of demons when Scripture is not that clear or exhaustive on the matter.[3] Occasionally, Scripture will reference the name of a demon, but many ministers seem to go beyond Scripture. They have gone over the top with a name for every demon. Some get as creative as they would be if they were naming their own newborn son or daughter. "Honey, let's buy a demon name book and pick it out together." It may make people sound more "spiritual," but maybe bordering on the "spooky spiritual." We Spirit-filled types are often labeled as flaky, and some of that stereotype is warranted. I call it "spiritual granola" in charismatic churches: too many fruits, nuts, and flakes.

Let us not become superstitious, mythical, spiritualists, overdramatic, or extrabiblical. And we will become just that if we major in minors and get off-track. It is all about *Jesus Christ, repentance of sin,* and *forgiveness and salvation as revealed in Scripture by the Holy Spirit.*

We charismatics have often gone overboard on self-styled spiritual experiences that go beyond the simple boundaries that I expressed. Our Christian life looks more like a Marvel Universe movie than the scriptural life of Christ. Too many Dr. Stranges in the house. We do not have to be able to name a demon in order to cast it out. They respond fine to "devil," just like the person next to me turns toward me when I say, "Hey, you." I do not have to be specific. If the Spirit or Scripture gives a specific name to a demon, then so will I.

4. *Should we allow deliverance during worship services?* To protect the privacy and dignity of the seeker and the congregants, I would suggest not doing public deliverance sessions. Train your altar team to

3

take the seeker to a special room designated for deliverance if demonic manifestation should emerge. Remember that demons can attack the innocent, like children, who cannot defend themselves. They should not be exposed to that environment.

5. *Can I address the devil directly or must I ask the Lord to do it on my behalf?* I think either way is scriptural. I use both approaches, depending on how I am led. We are given the authority to do both. Christ clearly commanded the disciples to cast out demons. So, the believer can directly address the devil to come out in the name of Jesus. The believer can also say to the devil, "The Lord rebuke you, Satan." Most often I address the devil directly with boldness and authority. Even then, let your words be scriptural, few, and authoritative (see Jesus in Matt 4). We are not there for a tea party. And we are not there in pride to mock the devil. Even Michael the Archangel did not do so (Jude 1:9). We cannot beat the devil by being like the devil. Be humble!

6. *What if the demon(s) does not come out?* There can be many reasons for resistance. It is not uncommon. A seeker's spiritual pipes are already clogged; that is why they came to you for spiritual Drano. Possibly, the seeker has not truly or thoroughly repented. Perhaps the deliverance team was not fully prepared and walking in manifest authority. During a session, there can be stuck points or blocks. Satan can create these as well as the seeker. The seeker can become fearful. Pray for peace. Seek to soothe their fear. Explain the process and what is occurring.

   At times, the seeker may quit resisting the devil. This can happen because they are not aware that they are no longer resisting. Go back to coaching them to resist. Also, the seeker may stop resisting because he/she is tired. Deliverance is spiritually, physically, mentally, and emotionally grueling for all parties. Take a break for a couple minutes if necessary but stay on track. If the person has repented and is open, and the team is on-point, then the demon(s) should come out. Like a loose tooth, when it is ready, it will come out. When it is not ready, you can pull and pull, and it will not budge. When the apple is ripe, it falls. When the baby is ready, it can be delivered.

   Coach and push through stuck points. Like in childbirth, make sure the seeker is breathing properly and sufficiently, in through the nose and out through the mouth, and, when it becomes difficult, short quick breaths. Watch at stuck points during the 5 Steps, which is below in this chapter. Pay attention to when the block occurs during the 5 Steps. Pray for wisdom. Often you will be able to sense when and where the resistance is occurring. If the seeker or the team are exhausted, even after breaks, reschedule if necessary. If it is a chain of demons, they may not always come out in one session. You may need several sessions, depending on progress.

Beware of a *false or premature* deliverance. A false deliverance occurs when the manifestations have subsided, but the demon has hidden for cover deep within the flesh. The demon wants to go undetected, so that it can remain attached to the person. Therefore, it hides in silence undetected. The demon plays dead. The witness of the Spirit and discernment of spirits from a seasoned deliverance minister can easily pick this up. At this point, once one starts to pursue the demon aggressively, then it is forced to manifest. I always make one final aggressive pursuit before finishing a session to make sure the house is clean.

Another clever tactic is when the demon blows smoke to distract you and cause you to abort and prematurely end the session. Watch out for this trick. The devil uses it often. Once I was casting a demon out of a young woman. She was manifesting and writhing on the ground. Then she started to complain that I was hurting her, even though no one was touching her. She did not seem to be lying. She appeared to be in real agony. The evil spirit was actually causing the pain throughout her body to prevent further deliverance. It was hoping she would throw in the towel and quit the session. The devil was also tempting those present to feel sorry for her so we would quit. We took authority over the pain. I was not buying that cheap trick and pressed on until she was delivered. The young woman received Christ as her savior that night!

7. *How do I cast out demons?* There is no one exact formula. But we simply cast out demons with a command to leave the person in the name of Jesus. When the person is ready, we say, for example, "Spirit of fear, I command you to come out of Joe in Jesus' name." Just use the cross, faith, authority, and the name of Jesus. Continue reading for more details.

8. *How do I know if someone has a demon?*[4] This type of knowledge with certainty can be tricky. The deliverance team and the seeker can know directly by the inner witness[5] and the gift of discerning of spirits[6], and

---

4. See chapter 4 from Bellini, *X- Manual*, and have the seeker take the C1–13.

5. The inner witness is when God's Spirit directly bears witness with our spirit about the truth (John 14–16, 15:26; Rom 8:14–16; Heb 10:15; 1 John 2:20, 27). The witness is immediate, direct, and self-evident. It is often a still small knowing or voice that leads the believer into truth. It is our sixth sense, or spiritual sense by which we discern good and evil.

6. Discerning of spirits is a gift that allows one to detect and identify spirits (good

indirectly by demonic manifestations (presentations), sinful practices, seeker's testimony, and the C1–13. Demonic manifestations may include, but are not limited to: involuntary twitches or bodily movement not explained medically; eyes rolling back to the whites; cursing and blaspheming; rage and supernatural strength; scratching, cutting, or self-mutilation; speaking in a different voice; a foul scent; hissing; jerks, twitching, contortions, bloating, an abnormal swelling in a part of the body that when prayed for moves; bodily pain; slithering on the ground; yawning; repetitive licking of the lips or sticking out of the tongue; eyes change color or grow darker; growling; a sudden increase in strength that comes with rage; levitation; vomiting and others. The eyes are also a good indicator. Focus on them. Remember that these bodily activities can also be explained, at times, by other causes. Thus, we ask for medical evaluation prior.

Of course, these manifestations (presentations) are not all listed in the Bible and are debatable in themselves. The Bible does not give us much detail about these phenomena. That is why we make the connection with the demonic through sinful behavior that can be observed. I have witnessed these manifestations, and they were correlated with the demonic due to the behavior associated with the person. I also trusted the inner witness of the Spirit and the gift of discerning of spirits. Here, I rely on my years of deliverance ministry experience.

Our strategy is integrative and incorporate the biomedical and psychological models of explanation as well. We should verify that these manifestations, presentations, or symptoms cannot be explained otherwise by medical science. Refer to a medical professional when necessary. Even have one present if possible. After medical treatment, if the manifestations persist, then the seeker may need deliverance.

9. *What is the difference between oppression and possession and deliverance and exorcism?*[7] Unbelievers can be oppressed or possessed. Believers cannot be possessed, only oppressed. Deliverance is for degrees

---

and evil) through spiritual perception that can involve hearing, seeing, smell, or feeling. For me it works with the inner witness and allows me to pick up on demonic signals, identify the type of demon, track its movements, uncover demonic spirits when they hide in a person, and know when they have left a person.

My spiritual perception usually operates through spiritual sight and feeling. I see and feel demonic presences. For me discerning of spirits coupled with the inner witness is like a cross between a demonic GPS tracking system, a "demonoscopy," a DRI (Demonic Resonance Imaging), and a demon-seeking drone or missile. I am using figurative language, of course. This gift operates as the Spirit wills (1 Cor 12:10–11).

7. See chapter 4 of Bellini, *X-Manual*, for details.

of demonic influence like oppression. Exorcism is for possession when the seeker no longer has agency to act freely. The method to liberate one who is oppressed or possessed is the same.

10. *How long or how many sessions does it take for a person to be liberated?* It depends on many variables. Has the seeker truly repented? Is the deliverance team truly on-point? How many demons are the team facing? What is the degree of demonization? Are the demons in chains and clusters? Deliverance can be immediate or progressive. Deliverance session(s) are finished when the person is free. We know one is free immediately by the inner witness of the Spirit through the team and the seeker. Those who have the gift of discerning of spirits can detect this immediately as well. We can also detect an immediate visible change in their countenance. Manifestations have ceased, and their countenance, *especially the eyes*, appear illuminated and lucid. The person will often weep and experience great joy. The evidence and signs are cumulative; freedom is not detected by merely one sign alone.

Wisdom. Do not rely on any one manifestation as a litmus test or indicator that one has been delivered. There is no single gauge that we turn to, but it is rather a cumulative witness of the Spirit, ceasing of manifestations over a period of time, a reversal in behavior, and the fruit of the Spirit. When I was a pastor, I had a congregant who always felt he had a demon. Even though I explained to him that the way of the cross was the normative way we are delivered from evil, he insisted on regular deliverance. He had learned this erroneous doctrine from his previous church.

He had another outlandish, quirky theory that he always knew when the demons left him because he would burp. No burp, no deliverance. That was his sign that he relied on absolutely. Nothing else. I should have given him Pepto-Bismol. For some it is vomiting, yawning, sighing, or crying. Eventually, I would not do sessions with him anymore. He ended up going weekly to another deliverance minister for his regular dose of Rolaids.

Be aware that the ceasing of a manifestation(s) in itself is not a clear sign of deliverance. A temporary ceasing of manifestations is an old trick of the devil.[8] Demons will retreat, go into hiding, and nestle

---

8. I was ministering deliverance to a non-denominational pastor who was bound in multiple areas of sexual addiction for quite some time. He was bound in one area since his teen years. The Spirit of God moved powerfully in our session and was breaking strongholds. The seeker had several strong manifestations, such as other voices, growling, screaming, and hissing. At one point, we had a major breakthrough, as spirits of perversion and confusion left, and the manifestations subsided. I regularly interviewed

deep in the soul so they cannot be detected. They go under the radar. Their goal in hiding is to convince you that the seeker has been delivered so you will quit the session too early. Watch out for demonic camouflaging. Don't abort the mission. Another indirect long-term way to know the person has been delivered is that they no longer practice that specific sin anymore.

In terms of numbers of sessions, there is no hard rule. Many times I have led deliverances that occur instantly. On one occasion, a mother brought her teenage son to the altar following my preaching. It was a revival service. She said her son was a practicing warlock and had been oppressed by spirits for quite some time. He wanted to be free.

I did not intend to cast the demons out of him at that moment. I went to lay hands on him while listening and waiting for the direction of the Holy Spirit. As soon as I laid hands on him, he flew horizontally backwards in the air and landed about fifteen feet from where I first laid hands. The ushers and I went to the ground with him to pray and to check how he was doing. I was thinking, we may have to take him into a room for deliverance, but he was already delivered. Lucid, in his right mind, weeping with joy and confessing Christ. No prayer, no repentance, and no deliverance session.

At a later date, the church followed up to make sure his deliverance was genuine. I know I said not to hold deliverance sessions during worship service. Well, I did not intend to, and really, we did not hold a deliverance session. God did it all by himself!

On the other hand, I know of a man who received prayer for nearly thirty years to deal with an issue of rage that afflicted him. He was abused as a child by his mother. His mother's violent anger was transferred to him. Later, after he married, he would manifest rage spontaneously and uncontrollably at his wife for no apparent reason. Screaming and physical abuse accompanied each episode.

---

the seeker at various strategic points.

After this breakthrough, I asked how he was doing. I knew we had a major victory, but I also knew by the Spirit that we were not finished. He said he felt peace and knew he was fully delivered and smiled. I discerned that the remaining demon went underground and was hiding. He would not manifest, and show his face, unless I realized that the work was not finished.

Well, praise God, we have the Holy Spirit who guides us in all truth. I told the pastor that we had had a big breakthrough and he felt peace, but we were not done yet. We still had to catch the biggest fish. He trusted me, and we went back to work. I commanded that devil to come out of hiding and show himself. It started to manifest, then I bound it, judged it, and cast it out. The pastor has been walking in freedom ever since. Glory to God!

Things began to turn around when he received a candid dream that a violent spirit was attached to him like a flat disc against his back and would not let him go. He cried out in the dream for help but could not be loosed. He would try to escape but the spirit would stay attached. In the dream, the Lord showed him to seek deliverance, and that, in deliverance the evil spirit would be cut in pieces and easily removed by the hand of God.

After decades of oppression, he found freedom after I held only two short sessions with him. Praise God! Why then? Why only two sessions? I do not know. He indicated that for the first time, he truly owned his actions, and his repentance was sincere, which is quite possible. Ultimately, only God knows. The bottom line was he was delivered from a generational spirit of rage and murder, a Jezebel spirit, and a spirit of Leviathan.

THE DELIVERANCE SESSION: THE 5-STEP METHOD

Preparation

1. Identify

2. Repent

3. Renounce

4. Expose and Bind

5. Judge and Evict

Preparation

- In order to protect confidentiality and the dignity of the seeker, deliverance should be done in private in a room set apart for such a ministry. The room should have comfortable chairs, even a couch. Have water and healthy snacks for post deliverance. Deliverance can be exhausting. There should be altar cloths and anointing oil available. Anoint the room and consecrate it for this special purpose. The oil is for the healing of deliverance. Anoint each member of the team and the seeker with oil before laying on hands. Some use crosses and Bibles in their session as symbols to mediate spiritual authority. Loose warring angels against the enemy and ministering angels to heal the seeker.

- Turn on light worship music and begin to worship and invoke the Lord Jesus Christ.[9] Magnify the Lord. Put God in the center. This is about the Lord, not the devil. Let this be an act of worship. Praise him. Give thanksgiving. Confess the various names of God. Worship him. Then, pray a prayer of adoration, invocation (invite Christ the Deliverer), and cleansing (for all). Pray a prayer against demonic backlash, covering each person, their families, possessions, and everything that pertains to the covenant with a hedge or firewall of protection and the blood of Jesus.

- Make sure the person keeps their eyes open (as best as possible) throughout the session. The eyes are the window of the soul (Matt 6:22). Regularly look into their eyes when you confront the devil. The eyes will often reflect the inner state of the person as they move from darkness to light.

The 5-Step Method[10]

1. **Identify**: Identify sins and demons from the C1–13 that need repentance and deliverance. Identifying is done by the team leader and the seeker. The team is also inviting the Holy Spirit to come and loose demonic strongholds and bring freedom. Throughout the session, the team needs to listen to the Holy Spirit who will manifest gifts, such as discerning of spirits, words of knowledge and wisdom, faith, and healing to lead the deliverance. He sends his Word to heal and deliver (Ps 107:20). *This process is to be spoken aloud.*

   a. Identify demons that are influencing the person. Taken from their C1–13 assessment and the leading of the Spirit.

   b. Identify degrees of demonization, C1–13.

   c. Identify sins committed by the person that have opened a door. Legal access.

9. We recount how David's worship drove out the demons of rage and torment from Saul (1 Sam 16:14, 23; 18:10; Ps 18:1) and how the armies of God routed the enemy through the praise of Judah (2 Chr 13:14–15; 20:20–24). Worship is a weapon of war.

10. In addition, feel free to pray ancient exorcism and deliverance prayers from St. Basil the Great and St. John Chrysostom or another form of prayer of deliverance. See Appendix in the back of the book.

d. Identify sins committed against the person that have opened a door. Legal access.[11]

e. Make sure the seeker is aware of each sin and/or demon that will be addressed.

f. Have them open their hearts, yield, and focus on Jesus Christ as Lord.

g. Make sure this step is complete before moving on to the next step. Interview the seeker to be certain.

2. **Repent:** Repentance is to be done by the seeker. The team is praying for the Spirit to convict. The team is also praying for an openness and willingness to repent on behalf of the seeker. They are also interceding for a release of the gift of repentance.

1. Confess aloud all the sins that have opened a door to the demonic, even generational sins.

2. Express aloud godly sorrow for each sin with the understanding that our sin deserves eternal punishment. Say what God's Word says about each sin. Use Scripture.

3. Express aloud a willingness to be set free from sin and demonic attachments.

4. Make a prayerful and intentional decision to cease from sinning, turn from them, and turn to God.

5. Submit aloud those areas to God, breaking all former legal access and authority of the devil. Humble and submit yourself to God.

6. Receive (and give) forgiveness and healing in those areas by faith. Release forgiveness to anyone who has wronged or hurt you. Receive forgiveness for the transgressions you have committed.

7. Following repentance, the X-Team will give the scriptural assurance that the seeker is forgiven.

8. Make sure this step is complete before moving on to the next step. Interview the seeker to be certain.

---

11. The deliverance team can pray repentance on behalf of the one who committed sins *against* the seeker. These sins specifically do not need repentance from the seeker but inner healing. Inner healing often loosens the demonic stronghold. Pray for Christ to transform the person's thoughts and self-talk regarding the event. Override the lies with the truth. If there have been sins committed against the person that subsequently led to the person committing willful sins, then one needs to repent of those sins.

3. **Renounce**: Both the seeker and the team will renounce aloud each sin and demon one at a time.

   1. Address and renounce every demonic tie, covenant, vow, curse, alliance, assignment practice, idol, false altar, ritual, and/or connection that has opened a legal door to these sins and strongholds. Use the C1-13 and the leading of the Spirit.

   2. Renounce and break each one of these connections. Shut every legal door of access in the name of Jesus.

   3. Apply the cross and plead the blood of Jesus over affected areas. Rom 8:3: sin is condemned and judged.

   4. Claim your right in Christ that Satan has no more legal grounds or access in your life.

   5. Repentance and renouncing break the legal ties with sin and Satan. With true repentance, there is legal ground to evict.

   6. With true repentance (ceasing of sin) and renouncing complete, the person is ready for demons to be exposed, bound, judged, and evicted.

   7. Make sure this step is complete before moving on to the next step. Interview the seeker to be certain.

4. **Expose and Bind:** Repentance has cancelled the legal ground of sin and demonic access. Renouncing each demon breaks the attachment. The will is no longer in cooperation with the demonic and is being recovered. It is time to expose, arrest, and bind the demon(s). The deliverance team and the seeker, as able, will go through these steps out loud.

   1. Look into the eyes of the person (the windows of the soul) when you bind, judge, and cast out demons. Keep looking in the eyes throughout. At times you will be able to follow the demons through manifestations (presentations) in the body and eyes. They often begin in the stomach area and move up out of the mouth and/or eyes. They often exit through the mouth or eyes.

   2. Call on Jesus the demon slayer to arise and slay the demonic with the sword (the Word) that proceeds from his mouth. It is a double-edged sword with truth as its point. One edge is mercy. The other edge is judgment. When the point of the sword of the Lord touches sin, it cuts between soul and spirit, giving mercy to the sinner and judgment to the devil.

3. Speak directly to the demon and cut off every demon, sin, and their work from the spirit of the person with the Sword of the Lord, the Word of God (Heb 4:12).

4. Ask the Lord to put the Finger of God on every evil spirit in the person. Command every demonic spirit to come out from hiding, to come to the light, to be revealed, and to be exposed (manifest) in Jesus' name.

5. Demons may manifest or come out from hiding at this point. Control the manifestations. We want to know they are emerging, but with no harm to the person.

6. Take authority over these demons. As they emerge, arrest and bind them one at a time in the name of Jesus. Since repentance has occurred, the demons have no legal right. They are to be arrested and bound.

7. Bind the strong man, the ruling spirit, and every other exposed demon that is revealed in the name of Jesus. The ruling spirit is the controlling or root demon. Sometimes this demon is at the end of the chain.

8. Make sure this step is complete before moving on to the next step. Interview the seeker to be certain.

5. **Judge and Evict:** God gives judgement to sin and Satan but gives mercy to seekers. Mercy triumphs over judgment (Jas 2:13)! Since the demons have been exposed, arrested, and bound, it is time for judgment and eviction. The deliverance team and the seeker, as able, will go through these steps audibly.

   1. Declare, according to John 16:11, that the Prince of this World is judged and defeated by the Finger of God. Pronounce his judgment in Jesus' name. Sin has been judged on the cross (Rom 8:3), and Satan has been judged on the cross (John 12:31; 16:11, 19:30; Heb 2:14–15; 1 John 3:8).

   2. Evict (cast out) every demon spirit by name, one by one in the name of Jesus. Break the chains. Break Satan's power. Drive out the enemy. Destroy his idols and tear down his altars.

   3. Cast into outer darkness every demonic power and render them harmless and void never to return. Seal the soul with the blood of Jesus in every area.

4. Pray that every open door be shut and sealed with the blood of Jesus.

5. Command angels with flaming swords to guard every portal of the soul from any demons returning to the person (Gen 3:24).

6. Pray for an infilling of the Holy Spirit and inner healing in every affected area.

7. Pray and intercede until there is a witness of the Spirit in the team and the seeker that the work is finished. Examine the eyes for lucidity, an absence of oppression, and the presence of the Lord. The seeker will usually express liberation through tears and expressions of joy. Everyone in the room should experience the peace of God (peace acts as umpire and makes the call, Col 3:15) to indicate the demon(s) has been expelled, victory has come, and Christ rules in the seeker's heart.

8. Provide any comfort, care, hospitality, word, food, etc. needed.

9. Make sure this step is complete to finish the session. Interview the seeker to be certain.

Is the Deliverance Session finished? 5 Point Checklist

1. All 5 steps have been completed as stated above. ( )

2. Every member of the deliverance team has an inner witness and/or a discerning of spirits that the work is finished and has peace. ( )

3. The seeker has an inner witness and/or a discerning of spirits that the work is finished and has peace. ( )

4. All demonic manifestations have ceased, and the person shows signs and testifies of salvation, love, peace, and/or joy. Their countenance has lifted. Eyes are lucid. ( )

5. The person is no longer walking in the sin(s) that opened the door to the demonic. The deliverance team needs to hold them accountable over the *next month* to observe whether there is any fruit. Checking off the *first 4 points* will indicate that the deliverance session is *finished.* The *5th point* determines that the deliverance is *complete.* If any of the first 4 points are not checked, then determine which of the 5 steps is incomplete and go back to that step. ( )

Follow-up

- I recommend pre-work preparation and post-work follow-up to accompany any deliverance session. See *The X-Manual, Unleashed,* and *Truth Therapy* by Peter Bellini, and similar works for direction. The newly delivered soul needs their mind renewed, the cracks in the soul healed, and their whole being filled with the Spirit. We do not want the demons to come back with seven more friends (Luke 11:26).

- This 5 Step process is based on the simple command from James 4:7–8 to "submit to God and resist the devil and he will flee from you," and to draw near to God and repent.

- The key is the law of the will. To whatever degree one has submitted one's will to a power (Christ, a sin, an evil spirit), to that degree it has authority over them. The will needs to be recovered. As one has submitted one's will as an instrument of disobedience and sin, to that degree one needs to submit to Christ and righteousness.

- Follow-up with a counselor, pastor, or deliverance minister.

- Follow-up with a covenant or discipleship group in the Wesleyan tradition for accountability, prayer, support, encouragement, and growth.

- **Home cleansing:** If needed, the deliverance team should go to the person's home for a cleansing. Take inventory of all demonic items. Make sure all demonic objects are permanently removed from the home. Play worship music in the house for at least twenty-four hours the day before the cleansing. Anoint the home, each room, door, doorway, bed, table, pets, etc. Also, anoint the outside of the house. Prayer-walk around the perimeter of the house. Use the 5-Step Method to identify sins and demons, repent of each sin, renounce each sin and demon, bind the demons, judge and evict them from the home and property into outer darkness.

9

A Wesleyan Gifts Assessment

An Instrument for Teaching and Identifying the Gifts of the Holy Spirit in your Ministry

TEACHING OUTLINE ON THE GIFTS OF THE SPIRIT

1. Unwrapping Your Spiritual Gifts!!!

   - Do all have spiritual gifts?

   - 1 Cor 12:7: but the manifestation of the Spirit is given to everyone to profit the body.

   - Who gives these gifts? See 1 Cor 12:11,18: All of these are the work of the one and the same Spirit. He gives to everyone as he wills.

2. Seven Purposes for the Gifts

   - 1 Cor 12:7: for the spiritual benefit of all

   - Eph 4:12–16: for the building up of the body

   - For the work of the ministry

- For the perfecting of the saints until we arrive at the unity of the faith
- 1 Pet 4:10–11: that God be glorified
- Hebrews 2:4: confirms the Word
- John 14:12: to fulfill the ministry of Christ

3. Spiritual Gifts v. Natural Talents

   a. Talents:
   - Inherited genetically
   - Used as self wills
   - Taught by natural means
   - Given by human birth
   - For human activities
   - Given to all people
   - Glorifies self or others
   - Can be done without the Holy Spirit
   - God can use them when consecrated to him

   b. Gifts of the Spirit:
   - Gifted by the Spirit
   - Used as Spirit wills
   - Given by Spirit baptism
   - Taught supernaturally
   - For ministry of body
   - Given to believers
   - Glorifies God
   - Accomplished by Holy Spirit

   c. God can use some natural talents when they are brought into submission to his will and consecrated for his purposes. The Holy Spirit can sanctify our talents for his kingdom goals.

4. What are the differences between the fruit and the gifts of the Spirit?

   a. Fruit:

- Mark of what a believer *is*
- Same in all believers
- Singular
- Involves character
- Fruit is an end in itself
- True mark of spirituality
- Eternal (love)
- Makes one holy

b. Gifts:

- Mark of what a believer *does*
- Differs in each
- Plural
- Involves charisma
- Gifts are a means to an end
- Not a mark of spirituality
- Temporal
- Do not make one holy

5. Are the gifts of the Spirit for Wesleyans too?

a. Yes! The (charismatic) gifts are given to all believers (1 Cor 12:7)

b. John Wesley was not a cessationist. You should not be either.

c. John Wesley operated in the gifts of the Spirit. You should as well.

d. Some Pentecostal and Charismatic Christians prioritize speaking in tongues over holiness when receiving the Baptism of the Spirit. As a result, some Methodist, Wesleyan, and Holiness Christians have *dismissed* the gifts of the Spirit to safeguard the priority of holiness. Dismissing the gifts, including speaking in tongues, is unscriptural and unnecessary. Methodists by nature are bent towards healing gifts.

e. The baptism or fullness of the Spirit involves both *fruit and gifts*. Fruit and gifts are not opposed. Receive them both!

f. Wesleyan Charismatics receive *both fruit and gifts* but put a priority on the fruit (of holiness).

g. Dear Wesleyan Christian, do you need a charismatic update and upgrade?

6. **The 6 Discernment Questions:** How do I know which gifts I have? Discernment. Answering "yes" to all six discernment questions is a strong indicator that you have that gift.

a. **Maturity Question:** Have you been apprenticed and trained in a one on one or small group setting with accountability in ministering this gift? Do you operate in this gift with the fruit of the Spirit, specifically love, gentleness, and self-control?

b. **Church Question**: Has God used you corporately in such a way, and has the body of Christ recognized and benefited from your gift?

c. **Resistance Question:** Have you been open, available, and willing when God has tried to use you in this area and have not resisted? Answering "Yes" to the other five questions and a "no" on the resistance question can still be a strong indicator that you have the gift in question. What is needed is a prayerful openness to being taught and used in this area.

d. **Leadership Question:** Has authorized (official, elected, licensed, certified, or ordained) church leadership recognized this gift in you and informed you of it? If not talk to church leadership about your gift.

e. **Proficiency Question:** Does this gift manifest often in you, and you feel confident operating in this gift, along with a feeling of satisfaction, or at least have a strong desire and drawing to minister in this gift?

f. **Discernment Question:** Have you prayerfully discerned if this desire is from God?

7. Evaluation of my gifts. How many discernment questions were affirmed for each gift?

a. 6—Very strong indicator

b. 5—Strong indicator

c. 4—Possible indicator

    d. 3—Uncertain indicator

    e. 2—Unlikely indicator

    f. 1—Highly unlikely indicator

8. What are the gifts of the Holy Spirit

    a. Identify the gifts from the following lists: Romans 12; 1 Corinthians 12; Ephesians 4. They are listed in the inventory as well.

    b. There are other gifts outside of those lists.

GIFTS ASSESSMENT FOR A CHARISMATIC UPGRADE

Note: Definitions of terms often come from Scripture and various church traditions. This assessment indicates only the Scripture reference and my definitions. This gift assessment instrument is in the Wesleyan tradition, which utilizes community discernment. Wesley expected God's gifts and grace for ministry in one's life to be evident among the people. There is an inward and outward witness of the Spirit to your gifting. The Spirit will bear witness with your spirit and those around you that you are called to ministry. Your ministry will bear fruit in the lives of others if it is from God. Also, in the Wesleyan tradition, this assessment evaluates for fruit (holiness) and not just gifts.

1. Word of Knowledge

Definition: Knowledge from God. Divine enlightenment or insight. Supernatural understanding that one could never have known or received naturally. Understanding or knowledge revealed by the Spirit of God. This gift allows one to have knowledge of a person(s) or situation(s) from the Holy Spirit that one could not have known through natural means.

Scripture: 1 Cor 12:8

Example: Reference John 4:17–18. Jesus knew that the Samaritan woman had five husbands. The knowledge was not known previously, nor was it acquired by natural means. It was revealed from above by the Spirit.

    Use: In solitary or corporate settings (where two or more are gathered) it is used by God to reveal understanding about a person and/or situation that requires God's intervention and ministry. The person with this gift may share revelatory knowledge that comes through a vision, a feeling, a knowing, an impression, a mental picture, or words to a person or persons for the purpose of deliverance, repentance, salvation, sanctification, healing, call, edification, or any other purpose the Spirit deems fit. A word of knowledge is illumination given to help one come to or grow in Christ. This gift, like, most gifts, can operate in concert with the other gifts of the Spirit. Those who are ministering in prayer for that person and/or situation can pray, exhort, edify, or offer comfort with supernatural insight.

Answer the following six questions:

c. Maturity Question: Have you been apprenticed and trained in a one-on-one or small group setting with accountability in ministering this gift? Do you operate in this gift with the fruit of the Spirit, specifically love, gentleness, and self-control? (Y) (N)

d. Church Question: Has God used you corporately in such a way, and has the body of Christ recognized and benefited from your gift? (Y) (N)

e. Resistance Question: Have you been open, available, and willing when God has tried to use you in this area and have not resisted? (Y) (N)

f. Leadership Question: Has authorized church leadership recognized this gift in you and told you so? (Y) (N)

g. Proficiency Question: Do you feel confident operating in this gift, along with a feeling of satisfaction, or at least have a strong desire and drawing to minister in this gift? (Y) (N)

h. Discernment Question: Have you prayerfully discerned if this is from God? (Y) (N)

Total number checked (Y)_____

2. Word of Wisdom

Definition: Wisdom from God; the sagacity and divine soundness of an action or decision, or judgment with regard to the application of experience, knowledge, and good judgment; a supernatural application of understanding for the future, and/or a supernatural endowed sense of how to apply understanding in what you do or don't do, or in what you say or don't say.

A word of wisdom is the way in which truth is applied, either in word or action. The practical application of truth as directed by the Spirit.

Scripture: 1 Cor 12:8

Example: Luke 21:15 says I will give you wisdom that your enemies will not be able to respond or resist. In 1 Kings 3:16–28 Solomon was given divine wisdom to determine who was the real mother of the baby, when he decided to cut the baby in half and give each woman half. Wisdom was given to Solomon to make a tough decision to discern the truth. See also Luke 20:1–8, 22–26 and Acts 10:9–20.

Use: God will give this gift to a person in a particular situation so they can understand *how* God would have them to be, do, say, or minister to a particular situation. Wisdom involves good judgment and sense from God. This gift may also be given as wisdom to someone for their personal use. This gift may also be given for a future situation as to 'what ought to be done' or 'how it ought to be done.' Often it is coupled with the Word of Knowledge and Prophecy, but it can manifest with the use of any gift since it reveals God's divine way that something should be done.

Answer the following six questions:

a. Maturity Question: Have you been apprenticed and trained in a one-on-one or small group setting with accountability in ministering this gift? Do you operate in this gift with the fruit of the Spirit, specifically love, gentleness, and self-control? (Y) (N)

b. Church Question: Has God used you corporately in such a way, and has the body of Christ recognized and benefited from your gift? (Y) (N)

c. Resistance Question: Have you been open, available, and willing when God has tried to use you in this area and have not resisted? (Y) (N)

d. Leadership Question: Has authorized church leadership recognized this gift in you and told you so? (Y) (N)

e. Proficiency Question: Do you feel confident operating in this gift, along with a feeling of satisfaction, or at least have a strong desire and drawing to minister in this gift? (Y) (N)

f. Discernment Question: Have you prayerfully discerned if this is from God? (Y) (N)

Total number checked (Y) _____

3. Discerning of Spirits

Definition: All believers are given common discernment through the light of the Scriptures and the work of the Spirit in their lives. The gift of discernment, or discerning of spirits, is beyond the ordinary or common measure given to believers because it is listed as a gift and not all have all the gifts. Also, it refers to identifying and distinguishing various spirits. One can identify spirits through any of the senses (sight, taste, touch, smell, or hearing) or by reason (intuition). This gift is the ability to know, judge, and/or sense in the spirit and understand the origin, nature, and/or purpose of spiritual activity (either divine, human, or satanic). The gift exceeds, in depth, what is known as "common discernment" which all believers have.

Scripture: 1 Cor 12:10

Example: In Acts 16:16–18, Paul recognized a spirit of divination in a women, even though in the natural world she was merely stating a truth that Paul was a man of God preaching the way of salvation. See Mark 2:8; 9:25–27; Acts 5:1–9; 13:8–10; 2 Kings 6:8–17; 1 Cor 14:29–32. There are many spirits (good and evil) mentioned in the Bible: e.g., a spirit of fear, bondage, antichrist, heaviness, love, power, wisdom, spirit of knowledge, and spirit of fear of the Lord etc. This gift enables ones to identify and distinguish the various spirits for the purpose of resisting evil and doing good.

Use: God gives this gift for the purpose of deliverance or intercession when a person or a situation is under the influence or stronghold of a particular demons(s). God gives this gift to prophets, deliverance ministers, and other ministers to identify and assess spiritual reality so that one may know properly how to respond to a particular situation. The gift equips one on how to combat a particular manifestation of evil or how to cooperate with a particular manifestation of the Spirit of God. A person with this gift will be able to tell if someone needs deliverance or what is the specific spirit at work in a situation, and what wisdom is needed to overthrow that spirit. They can also identify strongholds in an individual, a church, a city, or a nation. A person with this gift can often discern how God will move and manifest his Spirit, i.e., in joy, healing, or warfare, so that the body of Christ can be receptive and open to how God will move.

Answer the following six questions:

a. Maturity Question: Have you been apprenticed and trained in a one-on-one or small group setting with accountability in ministering this gift? Do you operate in this gift with the fruit of the Spirit, specifically love, gentleness, and self-control? (Y) (N)

b. Church Question: Has God used you corporately in such a way, and has the body of Christ recognized and benefited from your gift? (Y) (N)

c. Resistance Question: Have you been open, available, and willing when God has tried to use you in this area and have not resisted? (Y) (N)

d. Leadership Question: Has authorized church leadership recognized this gift in you and told you so? (Y) (N)

e. Proficiency Question: Do you feel confident operating in this gift, along with a feeling of satisfaction, or at least have a strong desire and drawing to minister in this gift? (Y) (N)

f. Discernment Question: Have you prayerfully discerned if this is from God? (Y) (N)

Total number checked (Y) _____

Prophecy

Definition: A divine message (inspired by God) for an individual(s), situation, place, or for the body of Christ that is biblical, and which edifies, exhorts, comforts, rebukes or casts the future. Some refer to preaching as the gift of prophecy. On some occasions prophecy can actually be preaching, but usually what we preach has a prophetic nature to it, but it does not mean it is prophecy itself. The one who prophecies is given a message directly from God and so often utters it in first person, though it can also be given in third person as well. Prophecy often calls people to repentance and holiness. All prophecy should be tested by the Scripture, its veracity and the fruit by which it is given and which it bears. Both deliverer and recipient of prophecy are required to test the spirits. Prophecy can be conditional, and if it is, it should be stated as such. Both giver and receiver of prophecy need to test the spirits.

Scripture: 1 Cor 12:10; 14:3

Example: All prophecy given today is subordinate to the closed canon of the Christian Scriptures, which are God's revelation and our touchstone for truth and all other 'words' or prophetic utterances that God may give. Isaiah 40 is a good example of prophecy as are God's messages to the 7 churches in Revelation. Some prophecy may predict the future as when Jesus foretold his death in John 2:18–22. See 1 Cor 14.

Use: God gives this gift to edify, exhort, or comfort his people. It is meant for the building up of the body. Prophecy is to be judged by the Scriptures. Prophecy should also be judged by the inner witness of the one giving the prophecy; the inner witness of the one receiving the prophecy; and by the fruit of the Spirit. Prophecy should always be tested objectively first by the Word and inwardly by two or three church authorities who are gifted in prophecy, as well as by the recipient. A person with this gift, when receiving the spirit of prophecy (often a 'welling' up or unction within), will speak out a message. Often the message is given in first person, from God's perspective, but it may not come in that form. Forms may vary. Biblical prophecy is usually connected to a call to repentance and holiness.

Answer the following six questions:

a. Maturity Question: Have you been apprenticed and trained in a one-on-one or small group setting with accountability in ministering this gift? Do you operate in this gift with the fruit of the Spirit, specifically love, gentleness, and self-control? (Y) (N)

b. Church Question: Has God used you corporately in such a way, and has the body of Christ recognized and benefited from your gift? (Y) (N)

c. Resistance Question: Have you been open, available, and willing when God has tried to use you in this area and have not resisted? (Y) (N)

d. Leadership Question: Has authorized church leadership recognized this gift in you and told you so? (Y) (N)

e. Proficiency Question: Do you feel confident operating in this gift, along with a feeling of satisfaction, or at least have a strong desire and drawing to minister in this gift? (Y) (N)

f. Discernment Question: Have you prayerfully discerned if this is from God? (Y) (N)

Total number checked (Y) _____

5. Tongues

Definition: a divine message in an unknown tongue for the body or an individual that is to be translated or interpreted in a known tongue. Different than an ecstatic personal prayer language which is not public prophecy but meant for personal devotion (See 1 Cor 14:2–4).

Scripture: 1 Cor 12:10; 1 Cor 14:2–4

Example: 1 Cor 14 provides a reference for the use of this gift. Examples are found in Acts 10:46; 19:6.

Use: It is used in the same manner as prophecy, as mentioned earlier. Tongues are meant for the building up of the body. Tongues should always be tested objectively by the Word first, and then by other prophetic authorities. See prophecy.

Answer the following six questions:

a. Maturity Question: Have you been apprenticed and trained in a one-on-one or small group setting with accountability in ministering this gift? Do you operate in this gift with the fruit of the Spirit, specifically love, gentleness, and self-control? (Y) (N)

b. Church Question: Has God used you corporately in such a way, and has the body of Christ recognized and benefited from your gift? (Y) (N)

c. Resistance Question: Have you been open, available, and willing when God has tried to use you in this area and have not resisted? (Y) (N)

d. Leadership Question: Has authorized church leadership recognized this gift in you and told you so? (Y) (N)

e. Proficiency Question: Do you feel confident operating in this gift, along with a feeling of satisfaction, or at least have a strong desire and drawing to minister in this gift? (Y) (N)

f. Discernment Question: Have you prayerfully discerned if this is from God? (Y) (N)

Total number checked (Y) _____

6. Interpretation of Tongues

Definition: An intelligible interpretation of a divine message that was originally given in an unknown prophetic tongue for the body or an individual. Tongues plus interpretation equals prophecy.

Scripture: 1 Cor 12: 10

Example: See 1 Cor 14.

Use: As discussed in tongues section, it is used in the same manner as prophecy.

Answer the following six questions:

a. Maturity Question: Have you been apprenticed and trained in a one-on-one or small group setting with accountability in ministering this gift? Do you operate in this gift with the fruit of the Spirit, specifically love, gentleness, and self-control? (Y) (N)

b. Church Question: Has God used you corporately in such a way, and has the body of Christ recognized and benefited from your gift? (Y) (N)

c. Resistance Question: Have you been open, available, and willing when God has tried to use you in this area and have not resisted? (Y) (N)

d. Leadership Question: Has authorized church leadership recognized this gift in you and told you so? (Y) (N)

e. Proficiency Question: Do you feel confident operating in this gift, along with a feeling of satisfaction, or at least have a strong desire and drawing to minister in this gift? (Y) (N)

f. Discernment Question: Have you prayerfully discerned if this is from God? (Y) (N)

Total number checked (Y) _____

7. Faith

Definition: All believers are given a measure of faith (common faith). The gift of faith is an extraordinary impartation of faith surpassing common or saving faith. The gift is given in a moment for believing the miraculous. Normally works in concert with the Working of Miracles and the Gifts of Healing.

Scripture: 1 Cor 12:9

Example: Acts 9:32–38 illustrates the gift of faith in operation when Peter prayed for Tabitha, and she was resurrected from the dead. Also, Daniel 6:18–23, the gift of faith enabled Daniel to remain in the den of the lions untouched, when God sent his angels to close their mouths. We also see this gift in operation when Peter walked on water, and when Joshua "stopped" the sun. These believers were given a gift of faith to believe the miraculous.

Use: This gift can be used in any circumstance of ministry, even in grave adversity or great need. God gives this gift, as all gifts are given, as he wills, for his purposes. The gift of faith is a special impartation of faith for specific purpose. For example, such a gift enables missionaries to drive on an empty tank of gas for 5 hrs. or to believe God to feed a whole orphanage with no available funds.

Answer the following six questions:

a. Maturity Question: Have you been apprenticed and trained in a one-on-one or small group setting with accountability in ministering this gift? Do you operate in this gift with the fruit of the Spirit, specifically love, gentleness, and self-control? (Y) (N)

b. Church Question: Has God used you corporately in such a way, and has the body of Christ recognized and benefited from your gift? (Y) (N)

c. Resistance Question: Have you been open, available, and willing when God has tried to use you in this area and have not resisted? (Y) (N)

d. Leadership Question: Has authorized church leadership recognized this gift in you and told you so? (Y) (N)

e. Proficiency Question: Do you feel confident operating in this gift, along with a feeling of satisfaction, or at least have a strong desire and drawing to minister in this gift? (Y) (N)

f. Discernment Question: Have you prayerfully discerned if this is from God? (Y) (N)

Total number checked (Y) _____

8. Working of Miracles

Definition: The divine power to perform acts that are beyond the ordinary function of the observable laws of nature and one's natural ability. In a broad sense all the scriptural demonstrations of God's supernatural power are miracles, but often the Bible lists miracles as separate from salvation, healing, and casting out of demons.

Scripture: 1 Cor 12:10

Example: In John 2:11 Jesus turns water into wine. Another working of miracles is found in John 6 when Jesus multiplied the five loaves and two fish to feed the multitude. Also see Exodus chapters 4–11 (the plagues) and 2 Kings 1:10; 2:6–15; 6:1–7 & 13:20–21.

Use: See the Faith section for details. The gift often accompanies the gift of faith to accomplish God's purposes. The gift is a divine impartation and operates as God wills.

Answer the following six questions:

a. Maturity Question: Have you been apprenticed and trained in a one-on-one or small group setting with accountability in ministering this gift? Do you operate in this gift with the fruit of the Spirit, specifically love, gentleness, and self-control? (Y) (N)

b. Church Question: Has God used you corporately in such a way, and has the body of Christ recognized and benefited from your gift? (Y) (N)

c. Resistance Question: Have you been open, available, and willing when God has tried to use you in this area and have not resisted? (Y) (N)

d. Leadership Question: Has authorized church leadership recognized this gift in you and told you so? (Y) (N)

e. Proficiency Question: Do you feel confident operating in this gift, along with a feeling of satisfaction, or at least have a strong desire and drawing to minister in this gift? (Y) (N)

f. Discernment Question: Have you prayerfully discerned if this is from God? (Y) (N)

Total number checked (Y) _____

9. Gifts of Healing

Definition: A divine impartation given in a moment or over time to heal any manner of sickness, disease, disorder, trauma, or dysfunction that may be physical, spiritual, mental, emotional, or otherwise, and even cast out demons. All believers can pray the prayer of faith and see the sick healed based on the atonement and promises of God. However, this gift is extraordinary and is different than the prayer of faith used to heal the sick. Actually, Jesus never prayed for persons to be healed. He commanded them to be healed. Jesus manifested the gifts of healing. These impartations enabled persons to touch even his garments and draw the healing out from him. Though one can pray using this gift, it often tangibly manifests in the one gifted and is released into the person in need. For example, one may find their hands burning or ignited with electricity or emitting oil, indicating that God has imparted the gift to be used to heal an ailment. This gift also includes deliverance, as deliverance is a form of healing. Evil spirits can be the cause of sickness and healing resulting from exorcism. Jesus healed all those who were oppressed of the devil, Acts 10:38 claims. The word "gifts" is plural indicating possibly many types of manifestations for a variety of ailments. Healing is also a divinely realized eschatological trajectory that begins and ends with resurrection. It can be immediate or a process or both. And at times can be different than curing. Healing can be spiritual, emotional, mental, physical, etc.

Scripture: 1 Cor 12:9

Example: This gift is seen in operation in Acts 3:1–9 when Peter & John told the man at the gate beautiful to get up & walk. There was no prayer, merely a commandment to be healed. The gift of healing was literally manifested through their words. Also Acts 19:11–12; Mk 5:23–30.

Use: As discussed in the Faith section, this gift is given as God wills as a special impartation for a great need. The gift is often used with the gift of faith or the working of miracles to accomplish God's purposes. Often evangelists, prophets, and apostles will have this gift, as well as other ministers.

Answer the following six questions:

    a. Maturity Question: Have you been apprenticed and trained in a one-on-one or small group setting with accountability in ministering this gift? Do you operate in this gift with the fruit of the Spirit, specifically love, gentleness, and self-control? (Y) (N)

    b. Church Question: Has God used you corporately in such a way, and has the body of Christ recognized and benefited from your gift? (Y) (N)

c. Resistance Question: Have you been open, available, and willing when God has tried to use you in this area and have not resisted? (Y) (N)

d. Leadership Question: Has authorized church leadership recognized this gift in you and told you so? (Y) (N)

e. Proficiency Question: Do you feel confident operating in this gift, along with a feeling of satisfaction, or at least have a strong desire and drawing to minister in this gift? (Y) (N)

f. Discernment Question: Have you prayerfully discerned if this is from God? (Y) (N)

Total number checked (Y) _____

10. Teaching/Teacher

Definition: A divine ability to understand and explain spiritual truth, comparing spiritual things with spiritual. The gift is often coupled with the Word of Knowledge for understanding the Scriptures. The gift should incorporate rigorous theological study but does not strictly rely only on human reason but reflects faith seeking understanding. Academic research should be submitted to Scripture, the teaching of the Church, the mission of God, and the anointing of the Spirit. Both academic rigor and revelation knowledge from the Spirit are needed and should work together in teaching.

Example: Rom 12:6. There are many Biblical examples of this gift. One is Jesus' Sermon on the Mount (Matt 5–7). Jesus did not teach as a natural man but as one having authority (Mk 1:21–22) see 1 Cor 2.

Use: A person with this gift is used to teach the Scriptures and spiritual truths to the body of Christ in a variety of settings, i.e., Seminary, Sunday School, small groups, worship service, seminars, training events etc. Often such a person will have a certain area in which they are called and gifted to teach, such as the gifts of the Spirit, healing, or church history. Others may have many areas of specialization This person has a deep desire to study the Word of God prayerfully and in the Spirit as well as utilizing academic and pastoral resources. A teacher is also gifted communicator, articulating, illustrating, and simplifying the deep truths of God.

Answer the following six questions:

a. Maturity Question: Have you been apprenticed and trained in a one-on-one or small group setting with accountability in ministering this gift? Do you operate in this gift with the fruit of the Spirit, specifically love, gentleness, and self-control? (Y) (N)

b. Church Question: Has God used you corporately in such a way, and has the body of Christ recognized and benefited from your gift? (Y) (N)

c. Resistance Question: Have you been open, available, and willing when God has tried to use you in this area and have not resisted? (Y) (N)

d. Leadership Question: Has authorized church leadership recognized this gift in you and told you so? (Y) (N)

e. Proficiency Question: Do you feel confident operating in this gift, along with a feeling of satisfaction, or at least have a strong desire and drawing to minister in this gift? (Y) (N)

f. Discernment Question: Have you prayerfully discerned if this is from God? (Y) (N)

Total number checked (Y) _____

11. Evangelism/Evangelist

Definition: A supernatural desire and ability to reach the lost with the gospel and/or to organize and equip the church to reach the lost with the Gospel. Transcends common evangelism in which all believers as witnesses are expected to participate in sharing the gospel. Evangelism can be verbal and non-verbal. Signs and wonders are a non-verbal proclamation and manifestation of the kingdom and should accompany all evangelism.

Scripture: Eph 4:11

Example: A significant portion of Acts contains accounts of evangelism beginning at Jerusalem in chapter 2 and continuing to the surrounding areas and then into Samaria in chapter 8 and then to the Gentiles in chapter 10. Throughout many of these chapters, we find Paul exercising the gift of evangelism to reach lost people groups.

Use: A person with this is gift is used in the marketplace, revival services, crusades, and other evangelistic forms of outreach, including open air preaching, friendship evangelism, cyber evangelism, servant evangelism, and personal faith sharing. Such a person has a brokenness for lost souls and is committed in prayer for their salvation. They long to reach persons with the Gospel. An evangelist is equipped also with the gifts of preaching, teaching, and often with the gifts of healing and word of knowledge to accompany the preached word. Jesus' evangelistic ministry, as well as that of the apostles, can be summed up as "teaching, preaching, and healing all that were oppressed."

Answer the following six questions:

a. Maturity Question: Have you been apprenticed and trained in a one-on-one or small group setting with accountability in ministering this gift? Do you operate in this gift with the fruit of the Spirit, specifically love, gentleness, and self-control? (Y) (N)

b. Church Question: Has God used you corporately in such a way, and has the body of Christ recognized and benefited from your gift? (Y) (N)

c. Resistance Question: Have you been open, available, and willing when God has tried to use you in this area and have not resisted? (Y) (N)

d. Leadership Question: Has authorized church leadership recognized this gift in you and told you so? (Y) (N)

e. Proficiency Question: Do you feel confident operating in this gift, along with a feeling of satisfaction, or at least have a strong desire and drawing to minister in this gift? (Y) (N)

f. Discernment Question: Have you prayerfully discerned if this is from God? (Y) (N)

Total number checked (Y) _____

12. Pastor, Shepherd, Lay Pastor, Disciple-Maker

Definition: An ability to lead, guide, train, nurture, and build up younger believers or new converts in the understanding of Scripture, the nature of servanthood, the life of the Spirit, growing in the image of Christ, and empowering believers to find and operate in their areas of giftedness. The pastoral call is apostolic in nature as he/she oversees a flock in every aspect of spiritual life. The pastor has the charge and authority to preach and teach the Word, minister sacraments, organize worship, raise up leaders, strategize and organize for administration and mission etc. Lay persons with a shepherding gift, depending on the denomination or ministry, may also be called and equipped to minister similarly as a pastor, performing many of the same functions.

Scripture: Eph 4:11

Example: We see this gift obviously manifested through Christ, as the Good Shepherd who called out the 12 and taught and equipped them for the ministry of the kingdom. We also see it in Paul who laid doctrinal, governmental, and ethical foundations for leaders and churches. See 1 and 2 Timothy.

Use: A shepherd has a desire to nurture and admonish believers in the faith. This person has also been discipled as well by a seasoned minister, for example Timothy under Paul. One called to be a shepherd is mature, stable, well-grounded in truth, discerning, submissive to authority, and has a pastor's heart for God's children. This person consistently manifests the fruit of the Spirit, and has the gifts of government, encouragement, teaching, and exhortation, among others. One may shepherd a church, a ministry, a small group, or one on one.

Answer the following six questions:

a. Maturity Question: Have you been apprenticed and trained in a one-on-one or small group setting with accountability in ministering this gift? Do you operate in this gift with the fruit of the Spirit, specifically love, gentleness, and self-control? (Y) (N)

b. Church Question: Has God used you corporately in such a way, and has the body of Christ recognized and benefited from your gift? (Y) (N)

c. Resistance Question: Have you been open, available, and willing when God has tried to use you in this area and have not resisted? (Y) (N)

d. Leadership Question: Has authorized church leadership recognized this gift in you and told you so? (Y) (N)

e. Proficiency Question: Do you feel confident operating in this gift, along with a feeling of satisfaction, or at least have a strong desire and drawing to minister in this gift? (Y) (N)

f. Discernment Question: Have you prayerfully discerned if this is from God? (Y) (N)

Total number checked (Y) _____

13. Exhortation

Definition: The divine ability to encourage, console, comfort, reprove, and motivate other believers in a spirit of meekness to obey God's will, fulfill God's purposes, and give God glory.

Scripture: Rom 12:8

Example: In Galatians 3:1, Paul exhorts the Galatians after they fell into legalism. "O foolish Galatians who hath bewitched you . . . be not entangled again with a yoke of bondage." In this letter Paul corrects, rebukes, and encourages the Galatian believers to trust in the message of grace, as they once did. In this letter, Paul exhibits many of the traits embedded in the gift of exhortation. Also see 1 Tim 2:1.

Use: One who exhorts is often given the Word of Knowledge and Wisdom for the purposes of exhortation. This gift enables one to minister and build up individuals or the body through correction, encouragement, and/or consolation. The gift is used in lay pastoral and pastoral ministry, especially in discipling, counseling, or visitation of the sick or home bound. This gift can also be used informally one to one as the Spirit leads. The evidence of true exhortation though will be that the Body of Christ will recognize the gift in you and benefit from it. Such a person often gets timely 'words' for others that minister faith, hope, love, and grace to the hearer.

Answer the following six questions:

    a. Maturity Question: Have you been apprenticed and trained in a one-on-one or small group setting with accountability in ministering this gift? Do you operate in this gift with the fruit of the Spirit, specifically love, gentleness, and self-control? (Y) (N)

    b. Church Question: Has God used you corporately in such a way, and has the body of Christ recognized and benefited from your gift? (Y) (N)

    c. Resistance Question: Have you been open, available, and willing when God has tried to use you in this area and have not resisted? (Y) (N)

    d. Leadership Question: Has authorized church leadership recognized this gift in you and told you so? (Y) (N)

  e. Proficiency Question: Do you feel confident operating in this gift, along with a feeling of satisfaction, or at least have a strong desire and drawing to minister in this gift? (Y) (N)

  f. Discernment Question: Have you prayerfully discerned if this is from God? (Y) (N)

Total number checked (Y) _____

14. Helps

Definition: A ministry of support and assistance needed to accomplish larger tasks and goals within the mission of God. The gift of helps is an ability (natural or supernatural) to enable and free others to use their gifts by organizing, working details, completing tasks, and doing the busy work of the ministry. This person comes alongside the frontline workers and assists them in accomplishing their ministry. This gift works in tandem with the gift of service and can also extend to ministries of compassion, e.g., feeding the hungry and disaster relief.

Scripture: 1 Cor 12:28

Example: Acts 6:1–4 describe how Deacons were set apart to serve and minister to the Gentile widows, while others were set apart for the preaching of the Word of God. 1 Cor 12:28 and Romans 16:9.

  Use: Such a gift is versatile and can be employed in numerous ways. Persons with this gift can be a pastors' assistant, secretary, trustee, administrator, armorbearer, usher, deacon etc. They have a heart to fill in the details so that other ministries can take place. Helpers have a desire to serve leadership and follow their vision in assisting in the preparation and implementation of ministries and program. Such a person is a "doer" and is usually orderly, systematic, and can work out details.

  Answer the following six questions:

  a. Maturity Question: Have you been apprenticed and trained in a one-on-one or small group setting with accountability in ministering this gift? Do you operate in this gift with the fruit of the Spirit, specifically love, gentleness, and self-control? (Y) (N)

  b. Church Question: Has God used you corporately in such a way, and has the body of Christ recognized and benefited from your gift? (Y) (N)

   c. Resistance Question: Have you been open, available, and willing when God has tried to use you in this area and have not resisted? (Y) (N)

   d. Leadership Question: Has authorized church leadership recognized this gift in you and told you so? (Y) (N)

   e. Proficiency Question: Do you feel confident operating in this gift, along with a feeling of satisfaction, or at least have a strong desire and drawing to minister in this gift? (Y) (N)

   f. Discernment Question: Have you prayerfully discerned if this is from God? (Y) (N)

Total number checked (Y) _____

15. Hospitality

Definition: A natural or divine ability to extend and give one's space, time, and/or resources, such as one's home, to others for the purpose of the Gospel. This person is often a non-anxious presence and carries the peace of God about them. Their presence is a safe, inviting space of God's grace and warm embrace.

Scripture: Rom 12:13

Example: Titus 1:8 speaks of being a lover of hospitality as a qualification for church leadership. Rom 12:13 speaks of being "given to hospitality." 1 Pet says "to be hospitable one to another." In 1 Kings 17:9 the Lord set apart a widow specifically to sustain the prophet Elijah, vv. 10–24. She welcomed him into her home and fed him. 1 Tim 5:10 speaks of widows, who would be cared for by the church, having lived a life of faithfulness and service including the lodging of strangers. In Matt 25:35, Jesus speaks of the faithful who saw him as a stranger and cared for him.

   Use: Such a gift is used to entertain and serve ministers, young converts, Bible studies, small group ministry, migrants, immigrants, refugees, the homeless, strangers, etc. A person with this gift has the desire to open their resources and their heart for the service of others. This person wants to offer their gifts, talents, and graces of love, patience, and goodness, serving, giving, cooking, and caring for the purposes of the Gospel. This gift enables the believer to express the inviting warmth, grace, and love of the Gospel to all people through serving persons. Also, this person can serve as an usher, greeter, or attendant in the local church, as the gift often operates in tandem with the gift of helps.

Answer the following six questions:

a. Maturity Question: Have you been apprenticed and trained in a one-on-one or small group setting with accountability in ministering this gift? Do you operate in this gift with the fruit of the Spirit, specifically love, gentleness, and self-control? (Y) (N)

b. Church Question: Has God used you corporately in such a way, and has the body of Christ recognized and benefited from your gift? (Y) (N)

c. Resistance Question: Have you been open, available, and willing when God has tried to use you in this area and have not resisted? (Y) (N)

d. Leadership Question: Has authorized church leadership recognized this gift in you and told you so? (Y) (N)

e. Proficiency Question: Do you feel confident operating in this gift, along with a feeling of satisfaction, or at least have a strong desire and drawing to minister in this gift? (Y) (N)

f. Discernment Question: Have you prayerfully discerned if this is from God? (Y) (N)

Total number checked (Y) _____

16. Service

Definition: A God-given desire and ability to offer oneself to take on acts of mercy, compassion, and outreach to serve the needy, the poor, the downtrodden, the excluded, and the oppressed. Service can include the distributing of food, clothes, and other resources to those in need. Service also includes the offering of one's skills on the mission field or in the life of the church as a doctor, teacher, carpenter, mechanic, nurse, etc. God can use someone who has a natural skill for the sake of Gospel ministry. One with this gift has a consistent flow of the fruit of the Spirit and a heart of a servant. This gift is also used in the visiting of widows, the fatherless, the sick, the imprisoned and the shut-in. It transcends the common service that all Christians are called to give.

Scripture: Rom 12:7

Example: 1 Tim 5:9–10 speaks of widows who have ministered as servants through good works, raising children, lodging strangers, washing the saint's feet and relieving the afflicted. In Luke 8:2–3, certain women had given themselves and their substance to Jesus' ministry. Jesus obviously had this gift as we see Him feeding the multitudes, curing the lepers, fellowshipping with undesirables, washing the feet of disciples, and ultimately offering up his life.

Use: This gift also can be employed in a variety of ways from serving in a food pantry, in a mission, in a nursing home, in a mentoring program to serving as a deacon(ness). Service can occur in the local church, the mission field, or at an outreach, or anywhere. A person with this gift has a heart abundant with love, compassion, mercy, and selflessness.

Answer the following six questions:

a. Maturity Question: Have you been apprenticed and trained in a one-on-one or small group setting with accountability in ministering this gift? Do you operate in this gift with the fruit of the Spirit, specifically love, gentleness, and self-control? (Y) (N)

b. Church Question: Has God used you corporately in such a way, and has the body of Christ recognized and benefited from your gift? (Y) (N)

c. Resistance Question: Have you been open, available, and willing when God has tried to use you in this area and have not resisted? (Y) (N)

d. Leadership Question: Has authorized church leadership recognized this gift in you and told you so? (Y) (N)

e. Proficiency Question: Do you feel confident operating in this gift, along with a feeling of satisfaction, or at least have a strong desire and drawing to minister in this gift? (Y) (N)

f. Discernment Question: Have you prayerfully discerned if this is from God? (Y) (N)

Total number checked (Y) _____

17. Giving

Definition: A divine endowment given to a person(s) or an organization to contribute material, financial, temporal needs, and resources for the work of the ministry in a spirit of cheerfulness and liberality. Transcends the common giving of tithes and offerings that is expected of all Christians. This person gives freely out of the abundant joy in their heart.

Scripture: Rom 12:8

Example: In the early church, believers gave all they had for the common need of the church and its members. See Acts 2,4, and 5. Collections and offerings were made by the wealthier members of the church to other churches that were in need. See Rom 15:25; 1 Cor 16:1–4; 2 Cor 8:4–15; 9:1–15. God endows some with great wealth that they can glorify God with it and be a blessing to others. Yet, one does not necessarily have to have wealth to have this gift. Many allow the wealth to pass through their hands and into the hands of others, as did John Wesley who supported Methodist Societies, clinics, loans, and other forms of relief but died with very little personal assets.

Use: This gift operates according to the principle that if you are faithful with the smaller things that have been given to you, God can bless you with greater things. Also, the spirit of giving is based on the gospel principle that if lose your life you will gain it (and vice versa). Giving is a gift but also a spirit imparted by God to be gracious and to seek the blessing of others. There are many areas and capacities that this gift can function wherever there is a need and the Spirit leads.

Answer the following six questions:

    a. Maturity Question: Have you been apprenticed and trained in a one-on-one or small group setting with accountability in ministering this gift? Do you operate in this gift with the fruit of the Spirit, specifically love, gentleness, and self-control? (Y) (N)

    b. Church Question: Has God used you corporately in such a way, and has the body of Christ recognized and benefited from your gift? (Y) (N)

    c. Resistance Question: Have you been open, available, and willing when God has tried to use you in this area and have not resisted? (Y) (N)

    d. Leadership Question: Has authorized church leadership recognized this gift in you and told you so? (Y) (N)

e. Proficiency Question: Do you feel confident operating in this gift, along with a feeling of satisfaction, or at least have a strong desire and drawing to minister in this gift? (Y) (N)

f. Discernment Question: Have you prayerfully discerned if this is from God? (Y) (N)

Total number checked (Y) _____

18. Administration and Government

Definition: A divine ability to do the operational, organizational, and business oriented tasks of the ministry. Often this is a natural talent that when consecrated to God can be used for the service of God, though it is often coupled with the word of wisdom as well. In certain offices of leadership, the person is gifted with divine vision to see what God sees. They also may walk in greater measure in God's manifest authority. They have wisdom, maturity, experience, and godly character, working well with a diversity of people.

Scripture: 1 Cor 12:28

Example: Even Jesus needed a treasurer for his ministry, a position which Judas fulfilled until he betrayed Jesus. 1 & 2 Timothy and Titus speak of leadership roles in the church whose work is also administrative. In the Old Testament, Aaron stood as a type of administrator for Moses, performing the operational aspect of Moses deliverance ministry in Egypt as well as priestly roles in the Tabernacle. Old Testament priests would have performed most of the administrative and business-related tasks of the ministry. Also, David's court consisted of administrative assistants.

Use: A person gifted in this area can serve in many capacities, such as trustee, board member, local church elder, pastor's administrative assistant, chairperson of a committee, or a team leader to name a few. The person with this gift has good organizational and analytical skills. They have a good sense of the acquisition and use of money for the service of the ministry. Such a person can make well thought out and far-sighted decisions yet is able to listen to others and consider the counsel of others. This person knows how to weigh out all the options and figure which is most beneficial to the kingdom, but also this person knows how to lean on God more than on their own understanding for resources, provisions, and wisdom.

Answer the following six questions:

a. Maturity Question: Have you been apprenticed and trained in a one-on-one or small group setting with accountability in ministering this gift? Do you operate in this gift with the fruit of the Spirit, specifically love, gentleness, and self-control? (Y) (N)

b. Church Question: Has God used you corporately in such a way, and has the body of Christ recognized and benefited from your gift? (Y) (N)

c. Resistance Question: Have you been open, available, and willing when God has tried to use you in this area and have not resisted? (Y) (N)

d. Leadership Question: Has authorized church leadership recognized this gift in you and told you so? (Y) (N)

e. Proficiency Question: Do you feel confident operating in this gift, along with a feeling of satisfaction, or at least have a strong desire and drawing to minister in this gift? (Y) (N)

f. Discernment Question: Have you prayerfully discerned if this is from God? (Y) (N)

Total number checked (Y) _____

19. The Arts: Music, Design, Crafts, and Others

Definition: Supernatural gifts to worship, perform, build, or create for the glory of God and the work of the ministry. God can take a natural gift and sanctify it for his use as well.

Scripture: Exod 35:35; Col 3:16

Example: In Exodus 25–30 God set apart and anointed several artisans to craft the tabernacle furnishings to exact specifications. We see the gift of music ministered by King David in the writing and performing of the Psalms which were not merely natural songs but were inspired by the Spirit and became Scripture which even included prophecy. Every court in Israel contained singers who would minister in the Spirit to God and the people, singing hymns and spiritual songs. The church is called to worship in psalms, hymns, and spiritual songs.

Use: This gift can be used in the composing and performing of songs, in singing and/or playing. Music is a powerful weapon against the enemy and a habitation for the glory of God. Persons with this gift can paint, sculpt, design, and/or build works of art or works of functional designs and structures for the glory of God and the service of the Gospel. Dance, liturgy, banners, psalms, communion tables, worship facilities, etc. are such examples.

Answer the following six questions:

    a. Maturity Question: Have you been apprenticed and trained in a one-on-one or small group setting with accountability in ministering this gift? Do you operate in this gift with the fruit of the Spirit, specifically love, gentleness, and self-control? (Y) (N)

    b. Church Question: Has God used you corporately in such a way, and has the body of Christ recognized and benefited from your gift? (Y) (N)

    c. Resistance Question: Have you been open, available, and willing when God has tried to use you in this area and have not resisted? (Y) (N)

    d. Leadership Question: Has authorized church leadership recognized this gift in you and told you so? (Y) (N)

    e. Proficiency Question: Do you feel confident operating in this gift, along with a feeling of satisfaction, or at least have a strong desire and drawing to minister in this gift? (Y) (N)

    f. Discernment Question: Have you prayerfully discerned if this is from God? (Y) (N)

Total number checked (Y) _____

20. Intercession

Definition: The gift of interceding and praying through burdens for individuals, groups, churches, cities, nations or situations which usually involve extended seasons of prayer and at times fasting for the loosening of bands and the tearing down of demonic strongholds. This gift is extremely valuable in deliverance. This person, at times, has the gift of prophecy, word of knowledge and wisdom and especially the discerning of spirits that enables them to identify strongholds and to have the knowledge and wisdom to pray against them. Transcends the common intercession that is required of believers. Intercession can also transcend prayer and involve lifestyle, such as acts of compassion on behalf of others that may function as a sign or a conduit for salvation. Often works as prophetic informed intercession.

Scripture: Rom 8:26

Example: In Daniel 9, Daniel intercedes for his people. Ezra 9 also depicts travailing intercession for the post-exilic people of God. In John 17, Jesus intercedes for the unity of the believers. Of course, Christ, as the Lamb of God, atonement, and our High Priest, serves as eternal our intercessor and mediator.

Use: A person with this gift is given burdens, understanding and anointings to pray through strongholds and demonic powers on behalf of others. The prayer may be in identification with sins of an individual, a church, a people group, or a geographic area, seeking repentance on their behalf. Intercession may be used to tear down demonic strongholds in a city or a church for revival. The gift may enable one to decree and make prophetic declarations in the Spirit that will manifest in the natural world. These declarations may tear down the kingdom of darkness or build the kingdom of God. Intercession can be given to one for any person in any number of situations and needs. An intercessor is usually in a team of other intercessors that they may operate in the compounded power of agreement and number. Intercessors, as are all person in the church, under the authority, covering, and care of the pastor so that the pastor is informed of all intercession and its direction.

Answer the following six questions:

    a. Maturity Question: Have you been apprenticed and trained in a one-on-one or small group setting with accountability in ministering this gift? Do you operate in this gift with the fruit of the Spirit, specifically love, gentleness, and self-control? (Y) (N)

    b. Church Question: Has God used you corporately in such a way, and has the body of Christ recognized and benefited from your gift? (Y) (N)

    c. Resistance Question: Have you been open, available, and willing when God has tried to use you in this area and have not resisted? (Y) (N)

    d. Leadership Question: Has authorized church leadership recognized this gift in you and told you so? (Y) (N)

    e. Proficiency Question: Do you feel confident operating in this gift, along with a feeling of satisfaction, or at least have a strong desire and drawing to minister in this gift? (Y) (N)

    f. Discernment Question: Have you prayerfully discerned if this is from God? (Y) (N)

Total number checked (Y) _____

21. Apostle

Definition: A five-fold ministry gift (Eph 4). One who is set apart for the planning, planting, building, organizing, and overseeing a work of God, usually a church(es), a mission(s), or a network of ministries, or a networking ministry. An apostle often operates in all 5-fold ministries and gifts (1 Cor 12; Eph 4) and even equips the other ministry offices.

Scripture: Eph 4:11

Example: Paul was called an apostle set apart by God for the ministry of the Gospel. He planted, built, nurtured, and oversaw many churches and instructed them in righteousness.

Use: An apostle can function as a missionary, an overseer, a bishop, church planter, citywide network leader, superintending elder, or a pioneer or engineer of any expansive work of God.

Answer the following six questions:

    a. Maturity Question: Have you been apprenticed and trained in a one-on-one or small group setting with accountability in ministering this gift? Do you operate in this gift with the fruit of the Spirit, specifically love, gentleness, and self-control? (Y) (N)

    b. Church Question: Has God used you corporately in such a way, and has the body of Christ recognized and benefited from your gift? (Y) (N)

    c. Resistance Question: Have you been open, available, and willing when God has tried to use you in this area and have not resisted? (Y) (N)

    d. Leadership Question: Has authorized church leadership recognized this gift in you and told you so? (Y) (N)

    e. Proficiency Question: Do you feel confident operating in this gift, along with a feeling of satisfaction, or at least have a strong desire and drawing to minister in this gift? (Y) (N)

f. Discernment Question: Have you prayerfully discerned if this is from God? (Y) (N)

Total number checked (Y) _____

22. Prophet

Definition: Prophet is an office ordained by God to speak God's Word to the people of God and to the nations. A prophet is set apart by God to edify, exhort, comfort, foresee, guide, rebuke, tear down, and build again for the kingdom through the inspiration of prophecy and other gifts. Note, one who has the gift of prophecy is not necessarily a prophet, but one who holds the office of a prophecy will have the gift of prophecy. Saul at times had the gift of prophecy come over him, but he was not a prophet, though he enjoyed the praises of those who said he was among the prophets. Prophet is an office established by God to bring order and direction to the people of God. The prophet is an office that demands boldness, compassion, a heart sancti-fied unto God (Isa 6), wisdom, and maturity and depth in the things of God. The office of prophet is not an office for a novice, a carnal believer, or one who falls short of the New Testament standards for leadership. A prophet is given divine vision to see things as God sees them (John in Revelation.) and at times feels as God feels (Jeremiah). A prophet becomes a mouthpiece for the very words of God to his people or to a people group/nation.

Scripture: Eph 4:11

Example: The Bible is filled with examples of God's prophets; Noah, Moses, Elijah, Isaiah, Ezekiel, etc. For the nature of New Testament prophecy see Rev 2–3, where all three elements: edification, exhortation and comfort are employed in the prophetic words to the churches. The Revelation of Jesus Christ is the spirit of prophecy, according to the book of Revelation, and it is what the Spirit says to the churches. Deut 18:21–22 and Isa 8:20 tells us that a false prophecy is one that does not come to pass or does not line up with the Word of God.

Use: The prophet can minister in a variety of settings, such as the local congregation, the larger church, the nations, the marketplace, social me-dia, one on one, the printed page, or to any other context that the Word of God needs to be heard. Prophets prophesy with frequency, accuracy, and specificity in matters of an individual, government, institution, church(s) or nations. True prophets are seasoned ministers who live holy lives unto the

Lord and can be entrusted with God's Word and assignment. They prophesy not to the itching ear or for the flesh of people. Prophets speaks as the Spirit of Truth and does not fear opposition. Prophecy is not always "positive" and filled with good news. The prophets of the Old Testament were given messages that spoke of sin, judgment, and repentance. In Revelation 2–3, the messages to the churches contain both the affirmative and corrective elements of prophecy. Although prophets speak on behalf of God, they are still to be held accountable to pastors, other prophets and apostles, and ecclesial organizations.

Answer the following six questions:

a. Maturity Question: Have you been apprenticed and trained in a one-on-one or small group setting with accountability in ministering this gift? Do you operate in this gift with the fruit of the Spirit, specifically love, gentleness, and self-control? (Y) (N)

b. Church Question: Has God used you corporately in such a way, and has the body of Christ recognized and benefited from your gift? (Y) (N)

c. Resistance Question: Have you been open, available, and willing when God has tried to use you in this area and have not resisted? (Y) (N)

d. Leadership Question: Has authorized church leadership recognized this gift in you and told you so? (Y) (N)

e. Proficiency Question: Do you feel confident operating in this gift, along with a feeling of satisfaction, or at least have a strong desire and drawing to minister in this gift? (Y) (N)

f. Discernment Question: Have you prayerfully discerned if this is from God? (Y) (N)

Total number checked (Y) _____

HOW DO I KNOW WHICH GIFTS I HAVE?

Answering "yes" to all six of the discernment questions for a particular gift is a strong indicator that you may have that gift.

1. Maturity Question: Have you been apprenticed and trained in a one on one or small group setting with accountability in ministering this gift? Do you operate in this gift with the fruit of the Spirit, specifically love, gentleness, and self-control?

2. Church Question: Has God used you corporately in such a way, and has the body of Christ recognized and benefited from your gift?

3. Resistance Question: Have you been open, available, and willing when God has tried to use you in this area and have not resisted? Answering "Yes" to the other four questions and a "no" on the resistance question can still be a strong indicator that you have the gift in question. What is needed is a prayerful openness to being taught and used in this area.

4. Leadership Question: Has authorized church leadership recognized this gift in you and told you so?

5. Proficiency Question: Do you feel confident operating in this gift, along with a feeling of satisfaction, or at least have a strong desire and drawing to minister in this gift?

6. Discernment Question: Have you prayerfully discerned if this is from God?

EVALUATION OF MY GIFTS

How many discernment questions were affirmed for each gift? Score your gifts based on the following scale:

6—Very Strong Indicator
5—Strong indicator
4—Possible indicator
3—Uncertain indicator
2—Unlikely indicator
1—Highly unlikely indicator

A "yes" on all six questions is a strong indicator that you have that gift.

Mark which gifts still need development. I checked "yes" on five of the six questions for each of the following gifts:

1. Maturity Question: The following are gifts that I need to grow in under supervision and with the fruit of the Spirit.

2. Church Question: The following are gifts that need congregational/church confirmation.

3. Resistance Question: The following are gifts that I need to be open to and not resist.

4. Leadership Question: The following are gifts that need leadership confirmation.

5. Proficiency Question: The following are gifts that I need to pray for greater desire and use.

6. Discernment Question: The following are gifts that I need to pray to discern if God's has given them to me.

TESTING THE SPIRITS

When we attempt to hear God, there are several ways to verify if what we hear is from God. First, the word must align with Scripture. Second, the word must align with the character, fruit, and nature of God. Jesus said, "You will know them by their fruit." A good tree cannot produce bad fruit, and a bad tree cannot produce good fruit. Third, our own hearts and lives must align with the character, fruit, and nature of God. Blessed are the pure in heart for they will see God. A pure and sanctified heart will filter the static of self and the flesh that can prevent us from hearing God. Our own self-directed will can often get in the way when trying to discern between self and God. When we come to the end of ourselves on a matter and have decided not 'my will, but your will be done,' then we are free to receive God's will and hear his voice. When we put the matter in his hands without taking it back and die to our own will, then our hearts are clear to hear God.

GIFT MODE AND LANGUAGE

We know that when God speaks, it will line up with the Word of God and the fruit of the Holy Spirit (the Spirit of Truth). When God speaks, he speaks to us specifically and uniquely using various charismatic or gift "languages" or "modes." These gift languages often match our personality types, learning styles, and preferred modes of perceiving. There are many ways to categorize them. Here is one way:

1. **Seeing (Seer):** Your primary mode of perceiving God and the gifts is by inner sight, such as vision, dreams, word pictures, symbols, images, situations, events, etc.

2. **Hearing (Hearer):** Your primary mode of perceiving God and the gifts is by inner hearing, such as God speaking to your spirit or a person speaking to your spirit. You can hear sounds in the Spirit, like rushing wind or water or thunder and lighting.

3. **Feeling (Feeler):** Your primary mode of perceiving God and the gifts is by feeling, such as empathic feeling, feeling burdens and releases, feeling pain on behalf of others, feeling demonic presences, feeling angelic presences, a gut feeling, feeling various types of anointings or manifestations, often electricity, fire, or oil, etc.

4. **Knowing (Knower):** Your primary mode of perceiving God and the gifts is by an inner knowing or intuition, a gut knowing, an immediate, self-evident understanding of what God is communicating.

5. **Scenting (Scenter):** Your primary mode of perceiving God and the gifts is by scent or taste. This is a rare mode, but it exists. Some persons primarily discern through smell and/or taste.

Go back and examine the gifts that this instrument has confirmed in you. Reflect on how God has manifested each gift in you. In which learning language do you best communicate? In which do you best receive gifts? In which do you best give gifts?

CHARISMA AND CHARACTER

After completing and scoring the gifts assessment, you should be aware of the gifts that you have. It is important to submit yourself and your gifts to the Lord and to trustworthy leadership that can train, guide, and hold you accountable for their proper use. 1 Corinthians 12 identifies some of the gifts of the Spirit. 1 Corinthians 14 gives some practical wisdom on the use of the gifts in the church, and chapter 13 shares the more "excellent way" to pursue the gifts and to walk in the fruit of the Spirit as one operates in the gifts. The more excellent way is the way of love.

Paul recognized that the Corinthian church did not have a problem manifesting the gifts. The general problem with the Corinthian church was that its members were "carnal," as Paul called it. They were self-seeking, rather than God-seeking. Their specific problems were many. They were in competition with each other. They had competing loyalties to their teachers. They were living in various types of blatant, outward sin. There was disorder in their worship services. Simply put, they ministered in the charismatic gifts but not in Christ-like character. The Corinthians had charisma without character, ministry without maturity, power without holiness, and gifts without fruit. I call this phenomenon "charismania."

They did not recognize that the nine fruit of the Spirit (Gal 5) were more important than the nine gifts of the Spirit (1 Cor 12). Without maturity undergirding the operation of the gifts, there is chaos in the church. Today, we often face the same problem. We put an emphasis on power over holiness, charisma over character, and ministry over maturity. Much of this is a product of our culture that values stardom, personality cults, and successful ministries over quiet, humble service. We need to remember that Christ is our model on how to conduct ministry.

Jesus did not draw attention to himself, but his purpose was to bear witness to the Father. In Christ, we see power united with meekness modeled for us. Servant leadership should be our primary modality for ministry. The way of the cross (*via crucis*) is the way that disciples are called to service. Luke 9:23 states that in order to be a disciple (a disciplined, learner and follower of Jesus Christ), we must deny ourselves; say "no" to our will when it is against the will of God; take up our cross; die to self-centered living and follow him.

It is vital that in spiritual formation we train our leaders to nurture and embody the fruit of the Spirit in ministry. I like to think of persons who operate in the gifts of the Holy Spirit as messengers, specifically delivery persons. We deliver gifts to people. As a delivery person, we are not the gift, the giver, or the recipient. We are merely the messengers, the delivery persons who bring the gift. It is not about us. Our call is to be faithful and humble in delivering the God's gifts to those in need.

I am reminded of the UPS delivery person. They are so unassuming. They drive a bland brown truck. They are suited in a bland brown uniform, and they tirelessly, quietly, and anonymously do their work, delivering packages to whomever and wherever they are called. They are not the message but the messenger. Humility is integral to gift operation!

Similarly, we are called to deliver God's message unassumingly and faithfully to God's people, not drawing attention to ourselves or building up our own ministries or personas. Such proper prophetic etiquette does not occur automatically. We need to be trained in it. Even though the Spirit is perfect, we are not. Like any skill or practice, operating in the gifts of the Spirit must be learned and developed.

Virtually everything we know and do comes by learning, and learning comes through gradual development and training under the right conditions. We learn under an instructor and in a safe, social setting where we can ask question, make mistakes, experience trial and error, grow, and be in an environment of encouragement. Development of the gifts of the

Spirit occurs best under leadership supervision (an apprenticeship) and in a small, nontoxic environment for learning proper usage. Why is it that in life every bit of knowledge and every skill that we possess was acquired through a *learning process*, but we are supposed to minister in the gifts *perfectly* as novices, never making a mistake, no room for failure and growth? Again, God is perfect (Ps 18:30). His gift is perfect (Jas 1:17). The minister is not perfect just learning (Luke 2:52; Rom 3:23; 1 Cor 13:9).

In summary, we need to be trained in ministering the gifts of the Spirit. And we need to train persons under our leadership in the ministering the gifts of the Spirit. Yet, more so, we need to be trained and train in godliness. Training in the gifts of the Spirit needs to include training in the fruit of the Spirit. Intentional discipleship and the development of Christ-like character are vital to undergirding all training in the charismatic gifts.

Appendix A: Exorcism Prayers

ST. BASIL AND ST. JOHN CHRYSOSTOM

First Prayer of Exorcism and Healing, St. Basil the Great (AD 330–379)

Let us pray to the Lord. Lord, have mercy.

O God of gods and Lord of lords, Creator of the fiery spirits and Artificer of the invisible powers, of all things heavenly and earthly: Thou Whom no man has seen—nor is able to see; Thou Whom all creation fears and before Whom it trembles; Thou Who didst cast into the darkness of the abyss of Tartars the angels who did fall away with him who once was commander of the angelic host, who disobeyed Thee and haughtily refused to serve Thee, do Thou expel by the terror of Thy name the evil one and his legions loose upon the earth, Lucifer and those with him who fell from above. Set him to flight and command him and his demons to depart completely. Let no harm come to them who are sealed in Thy image and let those who are sealed receive dominion, "to tread on serpents and scorpions and all the power of the enemy." For Thee do we hymn and magnify and with every breath do we glorify Thy all-holy name of the Father and of the Son and of the Holy Spirit now and ever and unto ages of ages. Amen.[1]

Second Prayer of Exorcism, St. Basil the Great

Let us pray to the Lord. Lord, have mercy.

I expel you, primal source of blasphemy, prince of the rebel host, originator of evil. I expel you, Lucifer, who was cast from the brilliance on high into the darkness of the abyss on account of your arrogance: I expel you and all the fallen hosts which

1. *Exorcism: Orthodox and Roman Rituals* (New Orleans: Society of Clerks Secular of St. Basil), 44–51, with permission.

followed your will: I expel you, spirit of uncleanness,who revolted against Adonai, Elohim, the omnipotent God of Sabaoth and
the army of His angels. Be gone and depart from the servant/
handmaid ofGod _____.

I expel you in the name of Him Who created all things by
His Word, His Only-Begotten Son, our Lord Jesus Christ, Who
was ineffably and dispassionately born before all the ages; by
Whom was formed all things visible and invisible, Who made
man after His Image: Who guarded him by the angels, Who
trained him in the Law, Who drowned sin in the flood of waters
from above and Who shut up the abysses under the heaven,
Who demolished the impious race of giants, Who shook down
the tower of Babel,Who reduced Sodom and Gomorrah to ashes
by sulfur and fire, a fact to which the unceasing vapors testify;
and Who by the staff of Moses separatedthe waters of the Red
Sea, opening a waterless path for the people whilethe tyranni-
cal Pharaoh and his God-fighting army were drowned forever
in its waves for his wicked persecution of them; and Who in
these last dayswas inexplicably incarnate of a pure Virgin who
preserved the seal of her chastity intact; and Who was pleased to
purge our ancient defilement in thebaptismal cleansing.

I expel you, Satan, by virtue of Christ's baptism in the Jordan,
which for us is a type of our inheritance of incorruption through
grace and sanctified waters: the same One Who astounded the
angels and all the heavenly powers when they beheld God incarnate in the flesh and also revealed at theJordan His beginningless Father and the Holy Spirit with Whom He shares the unity
of the Trinity.

I expel you, evil one, in the name of Him Who rebuked the
winds andstilled the turbulent sea; Who banished the legion
of demons and openedthe eyes of him who was born blind
from his mother's womb; and Who from clay fashioned sight
for him, whereby He re-enacted the ancient refashioning of
our face; Who restored the speech of the speechless, purged
the stigma of leprosy, raised the dead from the grave and Who
Himself de-spoiled Hades by His death and Resurrection
thereby rendering mankindimpervious to death.

I expel you, in the name of Almighty God Who filled
men with theinbreathing of a divinely inspired voice and Who
wrought together with theApostles the piety, which has filled
the universe. Fear and flee, run, leave, unclean and accursed
spirit, deceitful and unseemly creature of the infernal depths,
visible through deceit, hidden by pretense.

Depart wherever you may appear, Beelzebub, vanish as smoke and heat, bestial and serpentine thing, whether disguised as male or female, whether beast or crawling thing or flying, whether garrulous, mute orspeechless, whether bringing fear of being trampled, or rending apart, conniving, whether oppressing him/her in sleep, by some display of weakness, by distracting laughter, or taking pleasure in false tears whether by lechery or stench of carnal lust, pleasure, addiction to drugs, divination or astrology, whether dwelling in a house, whether possessed by audacity, or contentiousness or instability, whether striking him with lunacy, or returningto him after the passage of time, whether you be of the morning, noonday, midnight or night, indefinite time or daybreak, whether spontaneously or sent to someone or coming upon him/her unawares, whether from the sea, a river, from beneath the earth, from a well, a ravine, a hollow, a lake, a thicket of reeds, from matter, land, refuse, whether from a grove, a tree, a thicket, from a fowl, or thunder, whether from the precincts of a bath, a poolof water or from a pagan sepulcher or from any place where you may lurk; whether by knowledge or ignorance or any place not mentioned.

Depart, separate yourself from him/her, be ashamed before him who was made in the image of God and shaped by His hand. Fear the likeness of theincarnate God and no longer hide in His servant/handmaid _____ ;rather await the rod of iron, the fiery furnace of Tartars, the gnashing ofteeth as reprisal for disobedience. Be afraid, be still, flee, neither return norhide in him some other kind of evil, unclean spirits.

Depart into the uncultivated, waterless waste of the desert where no man dwells, where God alone vigilantly watches, Who shall bind you that dares with envy to plot against His image and Who, with chains of darkness shall hold you in Tartars, Who by day and night and for a great length of time has devised all manner of evils, O devil; for great is your fear of God and great is the glory of the Father, of the Son and of the Holy Spirit. Amen.

Third Prayer of Exorcism, St. Basil the Great

Let us pray to the Lord. Lord, have mercy.

O God of the heavens, God of Light, God of the Angels and Archangels obedient to Thine Authority and Power; O God Who art glorified in Thy Saints, Father of our Lord Jesus Christ, Thine Only-begotten Son, Who delivered the souls which were bound to death and Who enlightened them that dwelt in darkness; He Who released us from all our misery

and pain and Who has protected us from the assaults of the
enemy. And Thou, O Son and Word of God, has purposed us
for immortality by Thy death and glorified us with Thy glory;
Thou Who loosed us from the fetters of our sins through
Thy Cross, rendering us pleasing to Thyself and uniting us
with God; Thou Who didst rescue us from destruction and
cured all our diseases; Thou Who set us on the path to
heaven and changed our corruption to incorruption.

Hear Thou me who cry unto Thee with longing and fear,
Thou before Whom the mountains and the firmament under the
heavens do shrink; Thou Who makest the physical elements to
tremble, keeping them within their own limits; and because of
Whom the fires of retribution dare not overstep the boundary
set for them but must await the decision of Thy Will; and for
Whom all creation sighs with great sighs awaiting deliverance;
by Whom all adverse natures have been put to flight and the
legion of the enemy has been subdued, the devil is affrighted,
the serpent trampled underfoot and the dragon slain; Thou
Who has enlightened the nations which confess and welcome
Thy rule, O Lord; Thou through Whom life hath appeared, hope
hath prevailed, through Whom the man of the earth was rec-
reated by belief in Thee. For Whom is like unto Thee, Almighty
God? Wherefore we beseech Thee, O Father, Lord of mercies,
Who existed before the ages and surpasses all good, calling upon
Thy holy name, through the love of Thy Child, Jesus Christ, the
Holy One, and Thine All-powerful Spirit.

Cast away from his/her soul every malady, all disbelief,
spare him/ her from the furious attacks of unclean, infernal,
fiery, evil-serving, lustful spirits, the love of gold and silver, con-
ceit, fornication, every shameless, unseemly, dark, and profane
demon. Indeed, O God, expel from Thy servant/ handmaiden
_____ every energy of the devil, every enchantment and delu-
sion, all idolatry, lunacy, astrology, necromancy, every bird of
omen, the love of luxury and the flesh, all greed, drunkenness,
carnality, adultery, licentiousness, shamelessness, anger, contentiousness, confusion, and all evil suspicion.

Yea, O Lord our God, breathe upon him/her the Spirit of
Thy Peace, watch over him/her and produce thereby the fruits
of faith, virtue, wisdom, chastity, self-control, love, uprightness,
hope, meekness, longsuffering, patience, prudence and understanding in Thy servant/handmaiden that he/she may be
welcomed by Thee in the name of Jesus Christ, believing in the
coessential Trinity, giving witness and glorifying Thy dominion,
along with the Angels and Archangels and all the heavenly host,

guarding our hearts by them; for all things are possible to Thee, O Lord. Therefore, we ascribe glory to the Father, and to the Son and to the Holy Spirit, now and ever and unto the ages of ages. Amen.

PRAYERS OF DELIVERANCE AND EXORCISM, ST. JOHN CHRYSOSTOM (AD 334–407)

First Prayer of St. John Chrysostom

> O Eternal God, Who has redeemed the race of men from the captivity of the devil, deliver Thy servant/handmaid from all the workings of unclean spirits. Command the evil and impure spirits and demons to depart from the soul and body of your servant/handmaid and not to remain nor hide in him/her. Let them be banished from this the creation of Thy hands in Thine own holy name and that of Thine only begotten Son and of Thy life-creating Spirit, so that, after being cleansed from all demonic influence, he/she may live godly, justly and righteously and may be counted worthy to receive the Holy Mysteries of Thine only-begotten Son and our God with Whom Thou art blessed and glorified together with the all holy and good and life-creating Spirit now and ever and unto the ages of ages. Amen.

Second Prayer of St. John Chrysostom

> O Thou Who hast rebuked all unclean spirits and by the power of Thy Word has banished the legion, come now, through Thine only begotten Son upon this creature, which Thou hast fashioned in Thine own image and deliver him/her from the adversary that holds him/her in bondage, so that, receiving Thy mercy and becoming purified, he/she might join the ranks of Thy holy flock and be preserved as a living temple of the Holy Spirit and might receive the divine and holy Mysteries through the grace and compassion and loving kindness of Thine only-begotten Son with Whom Thou art blessed together with Thine all-holy and good and life-creating Spirit now and ever and unto the ages of ages. Amen.

Third Prayer of St. John Chrysostom

> We beseech Thee, O Lord, Almighty God, Most High, un-tempted, peaceful King. We beseech Thee Who has created the heaven and the earth, for out of Thee has issued the Alpha and

the Omega, the beginning and the end, Thou Who has ordained that the fourfooted and irrational beasts be under subjection to man, for Thou hast subjected them. Lord, stretch out Thy mighty hand and Thy sublime and holy arm and in Thy watchful care look down upon this Thy creature and send down upon him/her a peaceful angel, a mighty angel, a guardian of soul and body, that will rebuke and drive away every evil and unclean demon from him/her, for Thou alone are Lord, Most High, almighty, and blessed unto ages of ages. Amen.

Fourth Prayer of St. John Chrysostom

We make this great, divine, holy, and awesome invocation and plea, O devil, for thine expulsion, as well as this rebuke for your utter annihilation, O apostate! God Who is holy, beginningless, frightful, invisible in essence, infinite in power and incomprehensible in divinity, the King of glory and Lord Almighty, He shall rebuke thee, devil!—He Who composed all things well by his Word from nothingness into being; He Who walks upon the wings of the air. The Lord rebukes thee, devil!—He Who calls forth the water of the sea and pours it upon the face of all the earth. Lord of Hosts is His name. Devil: the Lord rebukes thee!

He Who is ministered to and praised by numberless heavenly orders and adored and glorified in fear by multitudes of angelic and archangelic hosts. Satan: the Lord rebukes thee! He Who is honored by the encircling Powers, the awesome six-winged and many-eyed Cherubim and Seraphim that cover their faces with two wings because of His inscrutable and unseen divinity and with two wings cover their feet, lest they be seared by His unutterable glory and incomprehensible majesty, and with two wings do fly and fill the heavens with their shouts of "Holy, holy, holy, Lord Sabaoth, heaven and earth are full of Thy glory!" Devil: The Lord rebukes thee!

He Who came down from the Father's bosom and, through the holy, inexpressible, immaculate and adorable Incarnation from the Virgin, appeared ineffably in the world to save it and cast thee down from heaven in His authoritative power and showed thee to be an outcast to every man. Satan: The Lord rebukes thee! He Who said to the sea, be silent, be still, and instantly it was calmed at His command. Devil: The Lord rebukes thee! He Who made clay with His immaculate spittle and refashioned the wanting member of the man blind from birth and gave him his sight. Devil: The Lord rebukes thee!

He Who by His word restored to life the daughter of the ruler of the synagogue and snatched the son of the widow out from the mouth of death and gave him whole and sound to his own mother. Devil: The Lord rebukes thee! The Lord Who raised Lazarus the four-days dead from the dead, undecayed, as if not having died, and unblemished to the astonishment of many. Satan: The Lord rebukes thee! He Who destroyed the curse by the blow on His face and by the lance in His immaculate side lifted the flaming sword that guarded Paradise. Devil: The Lord rebukes thee!

He Who dried all tears from every face by the spitting upon His precious expressed image. Devil: The Lord rebukes thee! He Who set His Cross as a support, the salvation of the world, to thy fall and the fall of all the angels under thee. Devil: The Lord rebukes thee! He Who spoke from His Cross and the curtain of the temple was torn in two, and the rocks were split, and the tombs were opened and those who were dead from the ages were raised up. Devil: The Lord rebukes thee!

He Who by death put death to death and by His rising granted life to all men. May the Lord rebuke thee, Satan!—that is, He Who descended into Hades and opened its tombs and set free those held prisoner in it, calling them to Himself; before Whom the gatekeepers of Hades shuddered when they saw Him and, hiding themselves, vanished in the anguish of Hades. May the Lord rebuke thee, devil!—That is, Christ our God Who arose from the dead and granted His Resurrection to all men.

May the Lord rebuke thee, Satan!—He Who in glory ascended into heaven to His Father, sitting on the right of majesty upon the throne of glory. Devil: May the Lord rebuke thee! He Who shall come again with glory upon the clouds of heaven with His holy angels to judge the living and the dead. Devil: May the Lord rebuke thee! He Who has prepared for thee unquenchable fire, the unsleeping worm and the outer darkness unto eternal punishment. Devil: May the Lord rebuke thee! For before Him all things shudder and tremble from the face of His power and the wrath of His warning upon thee is uncontainable. Satan: The Lord rebukes thee by His frightful name!

Shudder, tremble, be afraid, depart, be utterly destroyed, be banished! Thee who fell from heaven and together with thee all evil spirits: every evil spirit of lust, the spirit of evil, a day and nocturnal spirit, a noonday and evening spirit, a midnight spirit, an imaginative spirit, an encountering spirit, either of the dry land or of the water, or one in a forest, or among the reeds, or in trenches, or in a road or a crossroad, in lakes, or streams, in houses, or one sprinkling in the baths and chambers, or one altering the mind of man. Depart swiftly from this creature of the Creator Christ our God! And be gone from the servant/handmaid of God _____, from his/her mind, from his/her soul, from his/her heart, from his/her reins, from his/her senses, from all his/her members, that he/she might become whole and sound and free, knowing God, his/her own Master and Creator of all things, He Who gathers together those who have gone astray and Who gives them the seal of salvation through the rebirth and restoration of divine Baptism, so that he may be counted worthy of His immaculate, heavenly and awesome Mysteries and be united to His true fold, dwelling in a place of pasture and nourished on the waters of repose, guided pastorally and safely by the staff of the Cross unto the forgiveness of sins and life everlasting. For unto Him belong all glory, honor, adoration and majesty together with Thy beginningless Father and His all-holy, good and life-giving Spirit, now and ever, and unto ages of ages. Amen.

Fifth Prayer of St. John Chrysostom

Let us pray to the Lord. Lord, have mercy.

Everlasting God, who delivered humankind from bondage to the Evil One, free this Your servant [N] from every action of unclean spirits. Command these evil and impure spirits and demons to withdraw from the soul and body of Your servant [N] and not to hide and indwell in him (her).

In Your Holy Name, and that of Your only-begotten Son and of Your Holy Spirit, let them be driven out of the work of Your hands, so that free of every satanic assault, he (she) may live a holy, righteous, and devout life, deserving of the sacred Mysteries of Your only-begotten Son and our God, with Whom You are blessed and glorified, together with Your all-Holy, Good and Life-Giving Spirit, now and always and forever and ever. Amen.

A BASIC PRAYER FOR DELIVERANCE, PETER BELLINI

In the name of the Lord Jesus Christ, I bind you, Satan, and all the forces of darkness that have come against _Person's name. I take authority over the spirit of (name the spirits)_ and all curses, generational or otherwise, witchcraft, spells, incantations, caging, hexes, demonic activity, and words directed against Person's name and everything that relates to the covenant, including but not limited to their family, friends, possessions, home, finances and their digital identity.

I break these demons and their strongholds by the power and authority of our Lord Jesus Christ. I cancel all demonic communications, strategies and tactics devised against Person's name and everything that pertains to the covenant in the name of Jesus Christ. Person's name repents of every sin known and unknown and resigns them to the cross where Christ condemns them in his body. He/she has made a decision to forever turn from their sins and turn to Christ. He/she renounces every demonic spirit attached to those sins and commands them to leave his/her spirit, soul, and body and be broken from his/her family and everything that pertains to the covenant. He/she renounce every unholy vow or alliance and bondage in the name of Jesus. May the power of your blood free him/her from sin, guilt, shame, and condemnation.

Satan, your legal power has been broken at the cross and is made ineffective with their repentance. I declare that each of these demons and their works have been judged by Jesus on the cross and can no longer legally stay. Every demon, evil spirit, and device of darkness has been denounced, deactivated, dismantled, destroyed, and judged and must come out now in the name of Jesus. He/She asks for forgiveness for their sins and opening the door to these spirits. Grant forgiveness O Lord according to your work on the cross. Seal their soul and every shut door with the blood of Jesus. Protect Person's name and all of us who pray with your blood and your holy angels. Fill Person's name with your Holy Spirit and power to overcome sin and evil. Cause them to grow in Christ and never look back from this moment. I pray all these things in the precious name of our Lord and Savior, Jesus Christ. Amen.

Appendix B: "The Whole Armour of God" by Charles Wesley[1]

"THE WHOLE ARMOUR OF GOD" EPHESIANS VI.

1 Soldiers of Christ, arise,
And put your armour on,
Strong in the strength which God supplies
Thro' his eternal Son;
Strong in the Lord of hosts,
And in his mighty power,
Who in the strength of Jesus trusts
Is more than conqueror.

2 Stand then in his great might,
With all his strength endu'd,
And take, to arm you for the fight,
The panoply of God;
That having all things done,
And all your conflicts past,
Ye may o'ercome thro' Christ alone,
And stand entire at last.

3 Stand then against your foes,
In close and firm array,
Legions of wily fiends oppose
Throughout the evil day;
But meet the sons of night,
But mock their vain design,

1. C. Wesley, "Whole Armour of God," 18–20.

Arm'd in the arms of heavenly light
In righteousness divine.

4 Leave no unguarded place,
No weakness of the soul,
Take every virtue, every grace,
And fortify the whole;
Indissolubly join'd,
To battle all proceed,
But arm yourselves with all the mind
That was in Christ your head.

5 Let truth the girdle be
That binds your armour on,
In faithful firm sincerity
To Jesus cleave alone;
Let faith and love combine
To guard your valiant breast,
The plate be righteousness divine,
Imputed and imprest.

6 Still let your feet be shod,
Ready his will to do,
Ready in all the ways of God
His glory to pursue:
Ruin is spread beneath,
The gospel greaves put on,
And safe thro' all the snares of death
To life eternal run.

7 But above all, lay hold
On FAITH'S victorious shield,
Arm'd with that adamant and gold
Be sure to win the field;
If faith surround your heart,
Satan shall be subdu'd,
Repell'd his ev'ry fiery dart,
And quench'd with Jesu's blood.

8 Jesus hath died for you!
What can his love withstand?
Believe; hold fast your shield; and who
Shall pluck you from his hand?
Believe that Jesus reigns,
All power to him is giv'n,
Believe, 'till freed from sin's remains,
Believe yourselves to heaven.

9 Your Rock can never shake:
Hither, he saith, come up!
The helmet of salvation take,
The confidence of hope:
Hope for his perfect love,
Hope for his people's rest,
Hope to sit down with Christ above
And share the marriage feast.

10 Brandish in faith 'till then
The Spirit's two-edg'd sword,
Hew all the snares of fiends and men
In pieces with the word;
'TIS WRITTEN; this applied
Baffles their strength and art;
Spirit and soul with this divide,
And joints and marrow part.

11 To keep your armour bright
Attend with constant care,
Still walking in your Captain's sight,
And watching unto prayer;
Ready for all alarms
Stedfastly set your face,
And always exercise your arms,
And use your every grace.

12 Pray, without ceasing pray,
(Your Captain gives the word)
His summons chearfully obey,
And call upon the Lord;
To God your every want

In instant prayer display,
Pray always; pray, and never faint,
Pray, without ceasing pray.

13 In fellowship; alone
To God with faith draw near,
Approach his courts, besiege his throne
With all the power of prayer:
Go to his temple, go,
Nor from his altar move;
Let every house his worship know,
And every heart his love.

14 To God your spirits dart,
Your souls in words declare,
Or groan, to him who reads the heart,
Th' unutterable prayer.
His mercy now implore,
And now shew forth his praise,
In shouts, or silent awe adore
His miracles of grace.

15 Pour out your souls to God,
And bow them with your knees,
And spread your hearts and hands abroad,
And pray for Sion's peace;
Your guides and brethren, bear
Forever on your mind;
Extend the arms of mighty prayer
Ingrasping all mankind.

16 From strength to strength go on,
Wrestle, and fight, and pray,
Tread all the powers of darkness down,
And win the well-fought day;
Still let the Spirit cry
In all his soldiers, "Come,"
'Till Christ the Lord descends from high,
And takes the conqu'rors home.

Bibliography

Abraham, William J. "The Epistemological Significance of the Inner Witness of the Holy Spirit." *Faith and Philosophy: Journal of the Society of Christian Philosophers* 7 (1990) art. 4. https://place.asburyseminary.edu/faithandphilosophy/vol7/iss4/4.

Anderson, Allan. *An Introduction to Pentecostalism: Global Charismatic Christianity.* 2nd ed. Cambridge: Cambridge University Press, 2013.

Arnold, Clinton E. *Three Crucial Questions about Spiritual Warfare.* Grand Rapids: Baker, 1997.

Aulen, Gustav. *Christus Victor.* Eugene, OR: Wipf and Stock, 2003.

Bainbridge, William Sims. *The Sociology of Religious Movements.* Oxfordshire, UK: Routledge, 1996.

Barbour, Ian G. *Religion and Science: Historical and Contemporary Issues.* San Francisco: HarperCollins, 1997.

Baudelaire, Charles. "The Generous Gambler." In *Devil Stories: An Anthology*, edited by Maximillian J. Rudwin, 164. Ingersoll, Can.: Devoted, 2018.

Bellini, Peter J. *The Cerulean Soul.* Waco, TX: Baylor University Press, 2021.

———. *Participation: Epistemology and Mission Theology.* Lexington: Emeth, 2010.

———. *Truth Therapy.* Eugene, OR: Wipf and Stock, 2014.

———. *Unleashed!* Eugene, OR: Wipf and Stock, 2018.

———. *The X-Manual: Exousia—A Comprehensive Handbook on Deliverance and Exorcism.* Eugene, OR: Wipf and Stock, 2022.

Billman, Frank. *The Supernatural Thread in Methodism: Signs and Wonders among Methodists Then and Now: Revised and Updated.* Independently published, 2021.

Anglican Church in North America. *Book of Common Prayer, 2019.* https://bcp2019.anglicanchurch.net/.

Brantley, Richard. *Locke, Wesley, and the Method of English Romanticism.* Gainesville, FL: University Press of Florida, 1984.

Browne, Peter. *Things Divine and Supernatural Conceived by Analogy with Things Nature and Divine (1733).* Ithaca, NY: Cornell University Library, 2009.

———. *The Procedure Extent: And Limits of Human Understanding (1729).* Miami: HardPress, 2017.

Burns, R. M. *The Great Debate on Miracles.* London: Bucknell University Press, 1981.

Burtt, E. A. *The Metaphysical Foundations of Modern Science.* New York: Doubleday, 1954.

Clark, Randy. *The Biblical Guidebook to Deliverance.* Lake Mary, FL: Charisma 2019.

CNS. "Catholic Church recruits more exorcists after spike in demand." https://www.thetablet.co.uk/news/2789/catholic-church-recruits-more-exorcists-after-spike-in-demand.

Collins, Kenneth J. *John Wesley: A Theological Journey.* Nashville: Abingdon, 2003.

———. *The Theology of John Wesley: Holy Love and the Shape of Grace.* Nashville: Abingdon, 2007.

Coulter, Dale. "Defining Pentecostal-Charismatic Christianity." https://firebrandmag.com/articles/firebrand-big-read-defining-pentecostal-charismatic-christianity.

"Course on the Exorcism Minister and the Liberation Prayer." Sacerdos, n.d. https://sacerdos.org/en/training-offer/course-on-the-exorcism-minister-and-the-liberation-prayer/.

Davies, Owen. "Methodism, the Clergy, and the Popular Belief in Witchcraft and Magic." In *History* 82 (1997) 264.

Dayton, Donald. *The Theological Roots of Pentecostalism.* Peabody, MA: Hendrickson, 1987.

Edwards, Jonathan. "Love More Excellent than Extraordinary Gifts of the Spirit." In *The Works of Jonathan Edwards*, 8:157. Peabody, MA: Hendrickson, 1993.

"Exorcism: Vatican Course Opens Doors to 250 Priests." *BBC.* https://www.bbc.com/news/world-europe-43697573.

Felton, Gayle. *This Gift of Water: The Practice and Theology of Baptism Among Methodists in America.* Nashville: Abingdon, 1993.

Finke, Roger, and Rodney Stark. *The Churching of America, 1776–2005: Winners and Losers in Our Religious Economy.* New Brunswick, NJ: Rutgers University Press, 2005.

Gallagher, Richard. *Demonic Foes: My Twenty-five Years as a Psychiatrist Investigating Possessions, Diabolic Attacks, and the Paranormal.* New York: HarperCollins, 2020.

"Gift of Tongues." https://www.discipline.wesleyan.org/wiki/Gift_of_tongues.

Green, Joel B., and David F. Watson. *Wesley, Wesleyans, and Reading the Bible as Scripture.* Nashville: Abingdon, 2012.

Gunter, Stephen W. "Personal and Spiritual Knowledge: Kindred Spirits in Polanyian and Wesleyan Epistemology." *WTJ* 35 (Spring 2000) 135–37.

Hiebert, Paul G. *Transforming Worldviews: An Anthropological Understanding of How People Change.* Grand Rapids: Baker, 2008.

Hume, David. "Of Miracles." In *An Enquiry Concerning Human Understanding.* 2nd ed. Indianapolis: Hackett, 1993.

Hummel, Charles E. "The Faith behind the Famous: Isaac Newton." *Christian History* 30 (1991). https://christianhistoryinstitute.org/magazine/article/faith-behind-the-famous-isaac-newton.

Jefferson, Thomas. *The Jefferson Bible.* New York: Penguin, 2012.

Jenkins, Philip. *The New Faces of Christianity: Believing the Bible in the Global South.* Oxford: Oxford University Press, 2008.

Jennings, Daniel. *The Supernatural Occurrences of John Wesley.* Independently published, 2012.

Kraft, Charles. *Christianity Power: Your Worldview and Your Experience of the Supernatural.* Eugene, OR: Wipf and Stock, 2005.

———. *Confronting Powerless Christianity.* Grand Rapids, MI; Baker, 2002.

Kraft, Marguerite. *Understanding Spiritual Power: A Forgotten Dimension of Cross-Cultural Mission and Ministry.* Eugene, OR: Wipf and Stock, 2003.

Long, D. Stephen. *John Wesley's Moral Theology: The Quest for God and Goodness.* Nashville: Kingswood, 2005.

Lovejoy, Arthur. *Great Chain of Being.* Cambridge, MA: Harvard University Press, 1976.

Maddox, Randy L. *Responsible Grace: John Wesley's Practical Theology.* Nashville: Abingdon, 1994.

Middleton, Conyers. *A Free Inquiry into the Miraculous Powers Which Are Supposed to Have Subsisted in the Christian Church from the Earliest Ages through Several Successive Centuries. By Which It Is Shown That We Have No Sufficient Reason to Believe, upon the Authority of the Primitive Fathers, That Any Such Powers Were Continued to the Church after the Days of the Apostles.* London: Manby and Cox, 1748.

Miles, Rebekah L. "The Instrumental Role of Reason." In *Wesley and the Quadrilateral: Renewing the Conversation,* 86, 91–93. Nashville: Abingdon, 1997.

Natale, Simone. *Supernatural Entertainments: Victorian Spiritualism and the Rise of Modern Media Culture.* University Park: Penn State University Press, 2017.

Newport, Kenneth, and Gareth Lloyd. "George Bell and Early Methodist Enthusiasm: A New Manuscript Source from the Manchester Archives." https://www.escholar.manchester.ac.uk/api/datastream?publicationPid=uk-ac-man-scw:1m4038&datastreamId=POST-PEER-REVIEW-PUBLISHERS-DOCUMENT.PDF.

Oden, Thomas C. *John Wesley's Scriptural Christianity: A Plain Exposition of His Teaching on Christian Doctrine.* Grand Rapids: Zondervan, 1994.

Oord, Thomas J. "Types of Wesleyan Philosophy: The General Landscape and My Own Research Agenda." In *WTJ* 39 (Spring 2004) 154–62.

Owen, John. *Pneumatologia.* Cedar Lake, MI: Waymark, 2012.

Peck, Scott. *Glimpses of the Devil: A Psychiatrist's Personal Accounts of Possession.* New York: Free, 2009.

Rack, Henry. *Reasonable Enthusiast: John Wesley and the Rise of Methodism.* London: Epworth, 1989.

Reid, Leia. "Interest in 'The Occult' Booms during Lockdown." https://www.brandwatch.com/blog/react-covid-19-occult/.

"Renewal of Baptismal Vows." https://bcp2019.anglicanchurch.net/wp-content/uploads/2019/08/25-Renewal-of-Baptismal-Vows.pdf.

Roman Catholic Church. *Catechism of the Catholic Church.* 2nd ed. New York: Doubleday, 1995.

Russell, Robert J. NIODA. (Source?)

Ruthven, Jon. *On the Cessation of the Charismata: The Protestant Polemic on Post-biblical Miracles.* Tulsa, OK: Word and Spirit, 2011.

Sell, Allan P.F. *Philosophy, History, and Theology: Selected Reviews 1975–2011.* Eugene, OR: Wipf and Stock, 2012.

Sheehan, Jonathan. *The Enlightenment Bible: Translation, Scholarship, Culture.* Princeton, NJ: Princeton University Press, 2007.

Snyder, Howard. "The Church as Holy and Charismatic." In *WTJ* 15 (Fall 1980) 14, 28.

———. *The Divided Flame: Wesleyans and Charismatic Renewal.* Grand Rapids: Zondervan, 1986.

Starkey, Lycurgus M. *The Work of the Holy Spirit: A Study in Wesleyan Theology.* Nashville: Abingdon, 1962.

Tillyard, E. M. W. *The Elizabethan World Picture.* New York: Random House, 1959.

Toland, John. *Christianity Not Mysterious, or, A Treatise Shewing That There Is Nothing in The Gospel Contrary to Reason, Nor above It and That No Christian Doctrine Can Be Properly Call'd a Mystery.* London: Buckley, 1696.

"Tongues Speaking." Study Commission on Doctrine, Free Methodist Church USA. https://scod.fmcusa.org/tongues-speaking/#:~:text=All%20Free%20Methodists%20affirm%20the,%2C%20tradition%2C%20reason%20and%20experience.

"The Transitional Book of Doctrines and Discipline: The Global Methodist Church" https://globalmethodist.org/wp-content/uploads/2022/04/Transitional-Discipline.2022041257.pdf. 26.

Twelftree, Graham. *In the Name of Jesus: Exorcism among Early Christians.* Grand Rapids: Baker, 2007.

———. *Jesus the Exorcist: A Contribution to the Study of the Historical Jesus.* Eugene, OR: Wipf and Stock, 2011.

Waring, E. Graham. *Deism and Natural Religion.* New York: Frederick Ungar, 1967.

Webster, Robert. *Methodism and the Miraculous: How John Wesley's Idea of the Supernatural and the Identification of Methodists in the Eighteenth Century.* Lexington: Emeth, 2013.

Wesley, Charles. "The Whole Armour of God." Supplement to John Wesley's *The Character of a Methodist* (Bristol: Farley, 1742) 18–20. Produced by the Duke Center for Studies in the Wesleyan Tradition under the editorial direction of Randy L. Maddox, with the assistance of Aileen F. Maddox.

Wesley, John. "Acts 8:15." In *Explanatory Notes upon the New Testament,* 1:425. London: William Bowyer, 1755. Reprinted, Kansas City: Beacon Hill, 1983.

———. "Acts 1:5." In *Explanatory Notes upon the New Testament,* 1:393. London: William Bowyer, 1755. Reprinted, Kansas City: Beacon Hill, 1983.

———. "The Appeals to Men of Reason and Religion." In *Bicentennial Edition of the Works of John Wesley,* edited by Gerald R. Cragg, 11:108. Nashville: Abingdon Press, 1976.

———. "Awake, Thou That Sleepest." In *Works of John Wesley,* edited by Thomas Jackson, 5:34. London: Wesleyan Conference Office, 1872.

———. "Caution against Bigotry." In *Works of John Wesley,* edited by Thomas Jackson, 5:483. London: Wesleyan Conference Office, 1872.

———. "An Earnest Appeal to Men of Reason and Religion." In *Works of John Wesley,* edited by Thomas Jackson, 8:4, 13–27. London: Wesleyan Conference Office, 1872.

———. "Ephesians 6:17." In *Explanatory Notes upon the New Testament, Vol. 2.* London: William Bowyer, 1755. Reprinted, Kansas City: Beacon Hill, 1983.

———. "A Farther Appeal to Men of Reason and Religion." In *Works of John Wesley,* edited by Thomas Jackson, 8:107–97. London: Wesleyan Conference Office, 1872.

———. "1 Corinthians 12:9." In *Explanatory Notes upon the New Testament, Vol. 2.* London: William Bowyer, 1755. Reprinted, Kansas City: Beacon Hill, 1983.

———. "The First Fruits of the Spirit." In *Works of John Wesley,* edited by Thomas Jackson, 5:87. London: Wesleyan Conference Office, 1872.

———. "1 Thessalonians 1:5." In *Explanatory Notes upon the New Testament, Vol. 2,* 754. London: William Bowyer, 1755. Reprinted, Kansas City: Beacon Hill, 1983.

———. "The General Deliverance." In *Works of John Wesley,* edited by Thomas Jackson, 6:248–49. London: Wesleyan Conference Office, 1872.

———. "General Spread of the Gospel." In *Works of John Wesley,* edited by Thomas Jackson, 6:280. London: Wesleyan Conference Office, 1872.

———. "The Great Privilege of those Born of God." In *Works of John Wesley,* edited by Thomas Jackson, 5:224–26. London: Wesleyan Conference Office, 1872.

———. "The Imperfection of Human Knowledge." In *Works of John Wesley*, edited by Thomas Jackson, 6:339–44. London: Wesleyan Conference Office, 1872.

———. "Journal Entries from December 15, 1742." In *Works of John Wesley*, edited by Thomas Jackson, 1:405. London: Wesleyan Conference Office, 1872.

———. "Journal Entries from December 4–26, 1762." In *Works of John Wesley*, edited by Thomas Jackson, 3:123–24. London: Wesleyan Conference Office, 1872.

———. "Journal Entries from November 22–26." In *Works of John Wesley*, edited by Thomas Jackson, 3:122–23. London: Wesleyan Conference Office, 1872.

———. "Journal Entry from April 11, 1763." In *Works of John Wesley*, edited by Thomas Jackson, 3:131–32. London: Wesleyan Conference Office, 1872.

———. "Journal Entry for April 17, 1739." In *Works of John Wesley*, edited by Thomas Jackson, 1:187–89. London: Wesleyan Conference Office, 1872.

———. "Journal Entry for April 16, 1773." In *Works of John Wesley*, edited by Thomas Jackson, 3:490. London: Wesleyan Conference Office, 1872.

———. "Journal Entry for August 4, 1759." In *Works of John Wesley*, edited by Thomas Jackson, 2:509. London: Wesleyan Conference Office, 1872.

———. "Journal Entry for August 28, 1759." In *Works of John Wesley*, edited by Thomas Jackson, 2:511–12. London: Wesleyan Conference Office, 1872.

———. "Journal Entry for July 30, 1739." In *Works of John Wesley*, edited by Thomas Jackson, 1:213. London: Wesleyan Conference Office, 1872.

———. "Journal Entry for July 19, 1759." In *Works of John Wesley*, edited by Thomas Jackson, 2:502. London: Wesleyan Conference Office, 1872.

———. "Journal Entry for July 24, 1776." In *Works of John Wesley*, edited by Thomas Jackson, 4:82. London: Wesleyan Conference Office, 1872.

———. "Journal Entry for July 22, 1759." In *Works of John Wesley*, edited by Thomas Jackson, 2:506. London: Wesleyan Conference Office, 1872.

———. "Journal Entry for June 4, 1772." In *Works of John Wesley*, edited by Thomas Jackson, 3:471. London: Wesleyan Conference Office, 1872.

———. "Journal Entry for March 12, 1743." In *Works of John Wesley*, edited by Thomas Jackson, 1:415. London: Wesleyan Conference Office, 1872.

———. "Journal Entry for May 24, 1738." In *Works of John Wesley*, edited by Thomas Jackson, 1:98. London: Wesleyan Conference Office, 1872.

———. "Journal Entry for October 1, 1763." In *Works of John Wesley*, edited by Thomas Jackson, 3:148–51. London: Wesleyan Conference Office, 1872.

———. "Journal Entry for October 16, 1756." In *Works of John Wesley*, edited by Thomas Jackson, 2:387. London: Wesleyan Conference Office, 1872.

———. "Justification by Faith." In *Works of John Wesley*, edited by Thomas Jackson, 5:57–63. London: Wesleyan Conference Office, 1872.

———. "Letter from John Wesley to John Mason, November 21, 1776." In *Works of John Wesley*, edited by Thomas Jackson, 12:453. London: Wesleyan Conference Office, 1872.

———. "Letter to a Roman Catholic." In *Works of John Wesley*, edited by Thomas Jackson, 10:82. London: Wesleyan Conference Office, 1872.

———. "Letter to Mary Bishop." In *The Letters of the Rev. John Wesley*, edited by John Telford, 6:297–98. London: Epworth, 1931.

———. "A Letter to Mr. Downes." In *Works of John Wesley*, edited by Thomas Jackson, 9:98–102. London: Wesleyan Conference Office, 1872.

———. "Letter to Mr. John Smith." In *Works of John Wesley*, edited by Thomas Jackson, 12:77–78, 84–85. London: Wesleyan Conference Office, 1872.

———. "Letter to Robert Carr Brackenbury, September 15, 1790." In *The Letters of the Rev. John* Wesley, edited by John Telford, 8:238. London: Epworth, 1931.

———. "A Letter to the Lord Bishop of Gloucester." In *Works of John* Wesley, edited by Thomas Jackson, 9:118–65. London: Wesleyan Conference Office, 1872.

———. "A Letter to the Reverend Dr. Conyers Middleton." In *Works of John Wesley*, edited by Thomas Jackson, 10:16. London: Wesleyan Conference Office, 1872.

———. "A Letter to the Reverend Dr. Rutherforth." In *Works of John Wesley*, edited by Thomas Jackson, 14:357–58. London: Wesleyan Conference Office, 1872.

———. "Marks of the New Birth." In *Works of John Wesley*, edited by Albert Outler, 1:428–30. Nashville: Abingdon, 1984.

———. "Matthew 7:22." In *Explanatory Notes upon the New Testament, Vol. 1*. London: William Bowyer, 1755. Reprinted, Kansas City: Beacon Hill, 1983.

———. "Matthew 10:8." In *Explanatory Notes upon the New Testament, Vol. 1*. London: William Bowyer, 1755. Reprinted, Kansas City: Beacon Hill, 1983.

———. "Minutes of Several Conversations." In *Works of John Wesley*, edited by Thomas Jackson, 8:315. London: Wesleyan Conference Office, 1872.

———. "The More Excellent Way." In *Works of John Wesley*, edited by Thomas Jackson, 7:26–27. London: Wesleyan Conference Office, 1872.

———. "The New Birth." In *Works of John Wesley*, edited by Albert Outler, 6:200. Nashville: Abingdon, 1984.

———. "Of Evil Angels." In *Works of John Wesley*, edited by Thomas Jackson, 6:373–80. London: Wesleyan Conference Office, 1872.

———. "Of the Church." In *Bicentennial Edition of the Works of John Wesley*, edited by Gerald R. Cragg, 11:3, 50. Nashville: Abingdon Press, 1984.

———. "Of Hell." In *Works of John Wesley*, edited by Thomas Jackson, 6:381–91. London: Wesleyan Conference Office, 1872.

———. "On Divine Providence." In *Works of John Wesley*, edited by Thomas Jackson, 6:313–25. London: Wesleyan Conference Office, 1872.

———. "On Good Angels." In *Works of John Wesley*, edited by Thomas Jackson, 6:362. London: Wesleyan Conference Office, 1872.

———. "On the Deceitfulness of the Human Heart." In *Works of John Wesley*, edited by Thomas Jackson, 7:335. London: Wesleyan Conference Office, 1872.

———. "On the Resurrection of the Dead." In *Works of John Wesley*, edited by Thomas Jackson, 7: 476. London: Wesleyan Conference Office, 1872.

———. "On Working Out Your Own Salvation." In *Works of John Wesley*, edited by Thomas Jackson, 2:509–12. London: Wesleyan Conference Office, 1872.

———. "Peter 4:10." In *Explanatory Notes upon the New Testament*. 884. London: William Bowyer, 1755. Reprinted, Kansas City: Beacon Hill, *Vol. 2*. 1983.

———. "Preface to the Standard Sermons." In *Works of John Wesley*, edited by Thomas Jackson, 5:3. London: Wesleyan Conference Office, 1872.

———. *Primitive Physick*. 17th ed. Farmington Hills, MI: Gale ECCO Print Editions, 2018.

———. "Repentance of Believers." In *Works of John Wesley*, edited by Thomas Jackson, 5:157–66. London: Wesleyan Conference Office, 1872.

———. "The Righteousness of Faith." In *Works of John Wesley*, edited by Thomas Jackson, 5:65–76. London: Wesleyan Conference Office, 1872.

———. "Salvation by Faith." In *Works of John Wesley*, edited by Thomas Jackson, 5:7–16. London: Wesleyan Conference Office, 1872.

———. "Satan's Devices." In *Works of John Wesley*, edited by Thomas Jackson, 6:32. London: Wesleyan Conference Office, 1872.

———. "Scriptural Christianity." In *Works of John Wesley*, edited by Thomas Jackson, 5:37–38. London: Wesleyan Conference Office, 1872.

———. "The Scripture Way of Salvation." In *Works of John Wesley*, edited by Thomas Jackson, 6:43–50. London: Wesleyan Conference Office, 1872.

———. "On Sin in Believers." In *Works of John Wesley*, edited by Thomas Jackson, 5:146–47. London: Wesleyan Conference Office, 1872.

———. "The Spirit of Bondage and of Adoption." In *Works of John Wesley*, edited by Thomas Jackson, 5:98–106. London: Wesleyan Conference Office, 1872.

———. "Thoughts upon Methodism." In *Works of John Wesley*, edited by Thomas Jackson, 13:258. London: Wesleyan Conference Office, 1872.

———. "Treatise on Baptism." In *Works of John Wesley*, edited by Thomas Jackson, 10:188–92. London: Wesleyan Conference Office, 1872.

———. "The Witness of our own Spirit." In *Works of John Wesley*, edited by Thomas Jackson, 5:135–41. London: Wesleyan Conference Office, 1872.

———. "Wandering Thoughts." In *Works of John Wesley*, edited by Thomas Jackson, 6:27. London: Wesleyan Conference Office, 1872.

———. "The Witness of the Spirit." In *Works of John Wesley*, edited by Thomas Jackson, 5:113, 122, 133. London: Wesleyan Conference Office, 1872.

Whitehead, John. *The Life of John Wesley, vol. 2.* London: Stephen Couchman, 1793.

Wigglesworth, Smith. *Ever Increasing Faith.* Springfield, MO: Gospel, 1971.

William Burt Pope, *Peculiarities of Methodist Doctrine* (London: Wesleyan Conference Office, 1873), quoted in Lycurgus M. Starkey, *The Work of the Holy Spirit: A Study in Wesleyan Theology* (Nashville: Abingdon, 1962), 63.

Williams, Colin. *John Wesley's Theology Today: A Study of the Wesleyan Tradition in the Light of Current Theological Dialogue.* Nashville: Abingdon, 1960.

Xhemajli, Rimi. *The Supernatural and the Circuit Riders: The Rise of Early American Methodism.* Eugene, OR: Wipf and Stock, 2021.

Yong, Amos. *The Spirit Poured Out on All Flesh: Pentecostalism and the Possibility of Global Theology.* Grand Rapids: Baker Academic, 2005.

Index

Made in United States
North Haven, CT
24 April 2023